Mel Bay's First Lessons

Djembe

It doesn't get any easier.....

by Paulo Mattioli

GW00597183

CD Contents

Track	Content	Length	Track	Lessons	Length
#1	Opener	2:44	#9	Djole Kenkeni Play Along	2:26
#2	Bass Tone Slap	5:04	#10	Djole Dunun Play Along	2:15
#3	Signals/Breaks	3:54	#11	Djole Ensemble Play Along	2:17
#4	Djole DJ 1 Instruction	1:46	#12	One Rhythm DJ 1 Instruction	2:08
#5	Djole Djembe 1 Play Along	2:15	#13	One Rhythm DJ 2 Instruction	1:12
#6	Djole Djembe 2	1:02	#14	One Rhythm Mix	4:02
#7	Djole Djembe 2 Play Along	2:16	#15	Finale	2:00
#8	Djole Sangban Play Along	2:19			

1 2 3 4 5 6 7 8 9 0

Visit us on the Web at www.melbay.com — E-mail us at email@melbay.com

About the Author

Paulo Mattioli is a world-renowned percussionist, author, educato
and facilitator whose mission is to uplift the hearts of others, create com
munity, health and harmony through music.

"Paulo Mattioli is a walking illustration of his passion for West Afr
can drumming!"   • The Los Angeles Times

"By sharing the power of rhythm through hands on experience, throug
teaching, performances and recordings, I intend to open the door for oth
ers to experience the positive power of rhythm."

"For me music is all about heart! It is the heart one puts into the musi
that gives it substance and meaning. When I play or compose, I becom
a vehicle for the expression of Spirit within. It is this heartfelt expressio
that strikes a chord within the hearts of others. Rhythm is a universal lan
guage, understood and appreciated by all. In rhythm we find a commo
ground. It moves us, it connects us, it uplifts us, it heals us, in ways w
are only beginning to fully comprehend."

"I love your spark! This is the best band I have ever had!"
• Kenny Loggins in a letter to Paulo, following their performance
together.

Paulo has brought his rhythmical passion to performances with superstars Kenny Loggins, Mickey Hart, Lenn
Kravitz and Babatunde Olatunji. Paulo's drumming has provided the driving force of feature films: "The Air U
There" with Kevin Bacon and "George of the Jungle" with Brendan Fraser. Paulo is the founder and musical directo
of *Drums of Fire West African Drumming & Dance Ensemble*. Paulo performed live in international showcases an
for ESPN II Television's: *The Method Show* and Network TV's *The Other Half*.

Paulo is a gifted artist educator and producer, bent on sharing the joy of drumming with others. He has recorde
and produced three drumming CD's and ten highly acclaimed DVD'S on Djembe drumming. Here is what the critic
are saying about his instructional videos:

"The best video we've seen this year..." - DRUM Magazine

"4.5 drums out of 5" - MODERN DRUMMER Magazine.

Building community through drumming is a major part of Paulo's work. He uses the drum as a tool to suppo
health, build interpersonal relationships and bridge cultural diversity across the globe. He has presented his *"Rhyth*
Journey" community building programs for youth at risk in Los Angeles, Venice and Compton, California. The may
or of Los Angeles has honored him for his work with the city. He has implemented drumming programs for Toyota
The Men's Center of Los Angeles, The LA Unified School District and Universities nationwide. His FitRhythms™
programs are accredited by the American Council on Exercise and help fight the current epidemic of childhood obe
sity. He has trained over 100 facilitators across the US, Canada, Mexico and Japan. Paulo has dedicated his life t
building health, wellness and community through rhythm.

Contact: paulomattioli@mac.com

Website: www.paulomattioli.com

Special Thanks to Remo World Percussion for providing:
Paulo Mattioli Signature Series Djembes and Dununs used in this program.

For supporting drum programs including Health Rhythms™ Music Therapy Programs, FitRhythms™ rhythm based fitne
programs, and World Music Drumming education programs. Remo supports drumming programs for the Los Angeles com
munity at the Remo Recreational Music Center in North Hollywood, (where this program was filmed) and in a variety of oth
programs worldwide. Remo: 50 Years of Passion, 50 Years of Play!

For more information visit: www.Remo.com

Welcome to the First Lessons-Djembe!

Paulo Mattioli Signature Series
Kenkeni, Sanban, Dununbs and Djembe drums

Table of Contents   Page

World Music Drumming CD's By Paulo Mattioli:
FIRE CD: World Beat Dance Music by Paulo Mattioli and Ken Givens
Master of the Forest CD: Traditional West African Djembe Rhythms and Songs
Around the World in Rhythm CD: World Music Compilation of African, Afro-Brazilian, Afro-Latin & Contemporary Jazz

Introduction

First Lessons Djembe provides a fun and easy way to learn to play the Djembe. It was conceived for the beginning Djembe player, yet contains information and reference material that is valuable for players at all levels.

Playing the Djembe is a lifelong journey of self-expression, as well as self-discovery. While the material presented herein may at first glance seem elementary, the value and importance of it in terms of moving forward on the drumming path with the Djembe is truly invaluable. The fundamentals of playing dynamics and tonality are the benchmarks of mastering musicality on the Djembe and worthy of a lifetime of continued practice and refinement. I encourage you to enjoy this journey every step of the way.

What Makes <u>First Lessons Djembe</u> Unique?

It is the first comprehensive multi-media program to offer instruction not only on traditional Djembe rhythms, but also original rhythms and how to apply them in contemporary music. The program was created using audiophile quality recording (24 bit, 48khz sound recording) and was shot in "High Definition Anamorphic Widescreen" video. It was then formatted, and optimized for the best possible quality audio/video output on standard DVD players in windscreen format (i.e.: anamorphic widescreen standard definition video with 44.1 khz audiophile quality CD sound). <u>First Lessons-Djembe</u> will give you a solid foundation to begin playing immediately.

What's Included?

The DVD:

- *"Play Along & Learn"* Player's eye view teaching of strokes & tones
- Djembe communication skills: Learning the Signals/Breaks
- 10 traditional and original rhythm parts, in two arrangements
- In depth instructional breakdown of all Djembe parts and grooves
- *"Play along and learn"* sections for all traditional rhythm patterns
- Ensemble play along practice sessions with solo examples
- Interactive Menus: allow you to customize each session to suit your learning needs and pace

Book:

- Transcriptions of traditional Djembe rhythms in both standard and phonetic notation
- Transcriptions of grooves for contemporary rhythms
- Professional photo illustrations provide visual support
- Exercises to develop tonality, co-ordination, balanced left and right-hand development
- Cultural and historical information on the Djembe and the traditional rhythms presented
- Resources for further Djembe learning and music
- Drum tuning information, drum care and web links

Audio CD:

The Audio CD is a valuable tool intended to allow you to practice by playing along, using a high quality sound source such as a portable CD player, home stereo system, iPod, amplifier, p. a. system, computer or boom box. The CD contains all material from the DVD, edited and indexed so you can select or repeat sections to best support your study.

If drumming is an issue at home, you can use an MP3 player, iPod or portable CD player and go to a park, a beach or any place where you can practice without disturbing your neighbors. I suggest you view the DVD in full before practicing with the CD, to get a grasp of the material and hand positions.

The Goals of <u>First Lessons-Djembe</u>:

The goal of <u>First Lessons-Djembe</u> is to impart to the new player essential fundamentals of playing the Djembe musically, gracefully and safely including:

- The physical dynamics of hand positions, playing postures, strokes and gesture.
- The fundamentals of how to tune your drum with links to online information about tuning.
- Learning the tones and strokes for the Djembe.
- The key to caring for your hands.
- Learning the method of communication between lead and supporting Djembe ensemble drummers and some common "Signals/Breaks".
- Gaining an understanding of the fundamentals of rhythm and some of the various means of rhythm notation employed in representing rhythms.
- A fundamental background of the historical and cultural significance of the Djembe.
- Learning traditional Djembe rhythm parts and their polyrhythmic relationships.
- The historical and cultural background of the traditional rhythm *"Djole"*.
- Learning original Djembe Rhythms and how to apply them to contemporary music, utilizing the World Beat Song *"One Rhythm"* from the *FIRE* CD.
- Offering resources for further Djembe instruction and Djembe music.

Chapter I
Getting Started

Using the Book and DVD

The multi-media format of *First Lessons-Djembe* is designed to support your learning process through a combination of text, photos, standard music notation, phonetic music notation and audio/visual means. All of us learn differently. Whether you prefer auditory, visual, or written material, you have the option. I encourage you to begin using the medium that works best for you, then reference the other media for further support and detail.

The phonetic system of notation is offered on the traditional rhythms in addition to standard musical notation. With the contemporary grooves you can play with either hand, there are no prescribed customs or limitations.

Practice Sessions

I suggest you utilize the book and DVD in combination together in the manner that best supports your learning style. It is best to move through the lesson in the order of the sequence presented below. Take your time and do not try to learn everything from cover to cover in one setting, as there is a lot of material. Take ample time to practice your tones and warm up at the beginning of each practice session.

Daily practice will speed you along on the drumming path! I suggest you practice for at least 45 minutes a day, making your way through the lesson sequence below. Make it focused time, your sacred "Drum time!" Whenever you can, carve out a longer chunk of time for yourself. Get together with friends who drum and play the rhythm parts together. You are sure to enjoy these times! Study with a live teacher is also important so that you can gain personal feedback and guidance on your drumming. If you miss a day or two of practice from time to time, it's okay, just get back to regular practice as soon as possible. Regular practice is key to learning!

Suggested Lesson Sequence:
DVD Menu: MAIN MENU SELECTIONS > Rhythm Menu Selections

1. BASS/TONE/SLAP

I suggest you begin each practice session by working on individual tones, (Bass/Tone/Slap), combinations and warm ups (exercises 1, 2, 3 in book). DVD: Choose Bass/Tone/Slap from Main Menu.

2. BREAKS

Then learn the Breaks, which are used to signal the beginning, end and tempo for each rhythm part.

3. RHYTHMS > Djole > Instruction > DJ-1

This brings you to instruction on the "Djembe 1" part for Djole. You may also refer to the written part for "Djembe 1" in the book.

4. RHYTHMS > Djole > 1st Djembe

Now you're ready to move on to the DVD *Play Along and Learn* section for "Djembe 1" of Djole! Follow along on the written music as well, to reinforce your understanding of the rhythm.

5. RHYTHMS > Djole > Ensemble

Now you are ready to play the "Djembe 1" part along with the Ensemble! Focus on holding your part steady. As you get more proficient on your part, listen to how all the parts fit together.

6. RHYTHMS > Djole > Instruction > DJ-2

Now you will receive instruction on the second Djembe part for Djole. You may also refer to the written part for "Djembe 2" in the book. Follow along as you play to support the learning process.

7. RHYTHMS > Djole > 2nd Djembe

Now you are in the *Play Along and Learn* section for the 2nd Djembe part for Djole.

8. RHYTHMS > Djole > Ensemble

Now practice playing your part along with the ensemble. Hold your part steady by focusing on it. Then as you g proficient on it, listen to how your part relates to the others.

9. RHYTHMS > Djole > Sangban

Now you are in the *Play Along and Learn* section on the section for the Sangban. You may also reference the wri ten part for the Sangban. Pay attention to how the hand and arm control the stick to create the different tones: ope tone (rebound) and muff (press). Practice the drum only, then bell only, then play together.

10. RHYTHMS > Djole > Ensemble

Now you can play the Sangban along with the ensemble. Again, strive for solidarity on your part by focusing o it. Then bring your awareness to the relationships of the part.

11. RHYTHMS > Djole > Kenkeni

Now you are in the *Play Along and Learn* section for the Kenkeni. Refer to the notation of the Kenkeni part in th book for Djole. Once you have learned a part, practice playing it from memory.

12. RHYTHMS > Djole > Ensemble

Now you are ready to play Kenkeni along with the Ensemble. Focus on holding your part steady. Then listen a you play to the relationships of all parts.

13. RHYTHMS > Djole > Dununba

Great! You have made it to the Dununba *Play Along and Learn* section! Refer to the Dununba part in the bool Remember to relax as you play. One can learn the bell separately then add the drum.

14. RHYTHMS > Djole > Ensemble

Fantastic! You have now learned all the parts for Djole, have fun playing along with the Ensemble! You may als try some call and response with solo djembe, or improvise your own solo patterns to the rhythm. Listen to ho your drum rhythm relates to all the rhythms of the ensemble.

15. RHYTHMS > One Rhythm > Instruction DJ-1

Here you will learn the fundamental groove for the song: "One Rhythm".
You may also refer to the written notation in the book.

16. RHYTHMS > One Rhythm > Ensemble

Now jam along, have fun with it and experiment with your own variations on the introduction and fundament groove patterns as well. Refer to notation as needed for additional support and ideas. Listen to how your part re lates to the ensemble, and get a feel for the "phrasing" and structure of the song (4, 8, 16 bar phrases).

17. RHYTHMS > One Rhythm > DJ-2

Now you can learn a second rhythm part, for jamming along with "One Rhythm".
You may refer to the notation as needed, for additional support and rhythmical ideas.

18. RHYTHMS > One Rhythm > Ensemble

Try jamming along using this second rhythm part with the ensemble! Experiment going back and forth between th two patterns or create your own! Have FUN with it! There is no "wrong" way, concentrate on feeling the beat an playing from the heart, not the head. Suspend self-judgement as you allow your creativity to flow on the drum.

Getting Comfortable with your Drum: Proper Playing Positions

You are about to embark on a long and happy relationship with your drum, so the first step is to get comfortable with it!

Playing the Djembe is all about finesse, not force! The first step is relaxing your body as you play. Having good playing position helps your body mechanics and ability to play relaxed.

The Djembe can be played in many positions:

The positions in which you play your drum can have important ramifications on your body comfort level, safety, playing ease and sound quality.

Seated:

Use a drum throne or armless stool that is slightly higher than your average chair. This will put the drum at the proper level in relationship to your body and allow you to play in a relaxed manner that will help prevent unnecessary tension in your shoulders, arms and back. The drum should be resting on the ground and tilted slightly away from you. One can cradle the drum with crossed legs at the ankles or use a waist strap to stabilize the drum.

Standing position:

I actually prefer the standing position. I like the body dynamics and freedom to move or dance to the beat. I can project the sound of my drum in any direction, and change the way it sounds to the listener. The Djembe has more potential for sonic projection when you play it standing up as well. Standing offers more possibilities for expression using "Body Language", an important aspect of Djembe expression.

Standing with Drum Between Legs

Various Standing Positions

Between the legs:

Use a strap which comes up over your shoulders, crosses at mid-back and reconnects to the drum at the base of its bowl. Knees slightly bent, shoulders back, hips tucked slightly forward for good support and core stabilization. The drum should hang between your legs and you should easily be able to play all three tones without feeling like you need to reach.

(**Note:** Do not attempt any standing positions with drum strapped on if you have any kind of known or suspected neck or back aliments. Check with a doctor if there is any question whatsoever. Drumming is healthy exercise, good for body, mind and spirit! Like any form of exercise one should check in with a doctor before embarking on a new physical activity.)

Mid-position:

This position projects the sound of your drum more directly toward the listener, enhancing and strengthening the sonic projection of your drum. Use the same body dynamics as if you were in a medium "squat" at the gym. Feet shoulder width apart, back straight, shoulders relaxed.

Between the Legs, Mid-Position.

Low-position:

This position has the drum resting on the ground with you squatting low over it. This maximizes the projection of the drum to the listener. You are also neutralizing any gravitational pull on your arms, allowing for more speed with less arm/shoulder effort. Like the mid-position, this position also requires a strong, healthy back and legs.

10

Aside the legs:

Standing with knees bent, shoulders back, hips tucked, the Djembe outside the right or left leg, this position is especially useful for walking or marching with your drum. Utilize this position when performing processionals, parades for ease of mobility.

"The Secret!":

Play with ease, sound better, play faster, play longer and injury-free with "The Secret!"

The secret is "UP!" Pull up out of your drum with each stroke. Remember, it is all about finesse and not force, which goes for strokes as well as posture. Snap back upwards off of the drum as if you were "pulling a punch". This gives you a better sound because you get up off the drum faster and the head resonates more. It also means you are ready to strike again sooner, meaning you can play faster and with more ease. It gives your playing a light clean tonality instead of a heavy clangorous quality. Last, but not least, it will be helpful in protecting your hands from impact and potential injury.

Various Playing Positions for Dunun and Djembe

Hand Positions for the Three Fundamental Tones of the Djembe: Bass/Tone/Slap

The hand positions on the drum are critical in producing the three basic tones of the Djembe: Bass, Tone and Slap. All of the traditional rhythms for the Djembe are created using these three fundamental tones. In addition to the position of the hand on the drum, the manner in which the hand contacts and rebounds off the head will affect the clarity of ones' drum tones and hence the musicality of ones' playing. The clearer and more distinct one can make these tones, the more musical your drumming will sound. This is how you make your drum "Speak".

If you refer to the photos below and DVD segment: **BASS/TONE/SLAP** on the main menu of the DVD, you will be playing all three tones very quickly and easily. I cannot emphasize enough the importance of taking time to practice your hand positions and tones, especially as you embark on the drumming path.

Use your listening skills to listen for:

    – a deep, resonant bass

    – a warm, rich, open tone

    – crisp, sharp, slap tone.

Use your eyes to check your hand position and attitude as it strikes and rebounds off the drum, as well as the gesture involved in that process. Use your sense of feel, to feel into the sensation in your hand and body when you produce a clear tone. Doing so will insure that you develop good playing habits, "neuro-muscular memory" and will help prevent you from bruising or injuring your hands. The Djembe drum is very user friendly in that you can get started making music quickly as compared to many other instruments. The process of refining your tones is a life-long journey that one can enjoy every step of the way. Great tonality on the drum draws in the listener and is part of mastering the instrument.

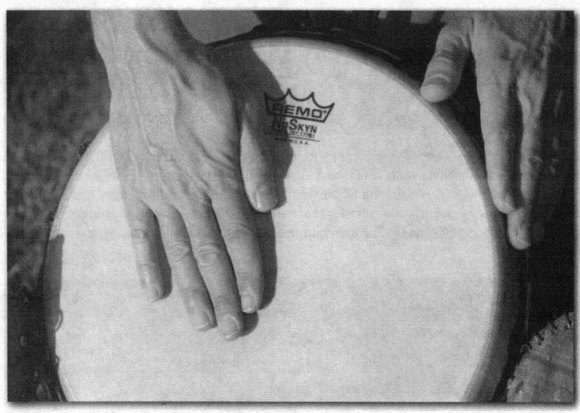

Bass Tone hand position

Bass Tone:

The bass is created using the entire palm surface of the hand, striking between the center and edge of the drum. Do not make your bass tones in the center of the drum. The center point of the drums head is a point of no vibration; scientists call a "Node". It turns out the drum head resonates all around this point, but not at this point. Imagine the drum heads surface as a pie, divided into four pieces. Play your bass tone in the two slices closest to you, which I will refer to as the right and left quadrant. The entire hand works like a unit, sort of like a paddle. It comes down into the drum, inside the edge of the drum, strikes using the entire surface of the palm and immediately rebounds off the head. The goal is a rich, pure, resounding deep bass tone.

Open Tone with right hand. Note position on drum head and flat hand.

Open Tone:

The hand again functions like a paddle, fingers together, but not too tightly. The wrist is relaxed and complements the movement of the forearm fluidly. The hand will cross the edge of the drum just beneath the knuckles, on the palm surface. On contact your hand should be roughly parallel to the surface of the drum, wrists in line with forearms. The entire surface of the hand from just beneath the knuckles to the tip of the fingers contacts the drum head simultaneously and then immediately rebounds, arcing back upwards, allowing the skin maximum resonance. Note that the thumbs are pulled back and up, so that they do not contact the edge of the drum. The goal is for a warm, rich woody tone with a strong component of bass overtones. It should have the same volume as your slap, sounding warm and tom-tom like, without the high harmonics of the slap.

Slap Tone hand position, same position, fingers spread and arched.

Slap Tone:

The slap tone is created with the exact same position, gesture and dynamics as the open tone, the only difference is your fingers are slightly spread and completely relaxed. Thus, the natural arch of the hand allows the fingertips to contact the skin, rather than the entire surface of the hand. The instant they do, you snap your hand back with a quick upward movement, which creates a whipping action. The whipping of the fingertips upward generates a high harmonic out of the Djembe head, producing a crisp "Crack" sound. You will feel a slight tingle in your finger tips when you get it right, and hear a crisp clear slap. It's a very bright sound, with very little mid-range and having slight bass overtones. Keep your hand in the position shown throughout the arc of your gesture. Don't open and close your hand. Keep your wrists relaxed, their movement complements that of the forearm. Use your bicep muscles (upper arm), to snap up quickly following contact with the head. Remember it's about finesse, not force.

Left hand deadens head vibration, while right hand slaps.

Slap variation-The Dead Slap:

A dead slap is a variation on the slap, used for a distinctly different sounding, very staccato, "accented" slap. The dead slap is achieved by deadening the skin surface by applying pressure with one hand, while slapping with the other. This creates an even dryer, brighter sounding slap tone, great for variation and punctuating a rhythmic phrase. You can deaden the skin with the entire palm, or just a finger for variation, at the center (node) of the drum. You can also execute a dead slap without using the other hand to deaden; simply execute the slap, but don't rebound off the head. This produces its own distinct variation of the slap, much brighter and more staccato than a standard slap. The dead slap is a great way to punctuate the end of a rhythmic solo phrase.

Protecting your hands from injury:

If you follow the guidelines for Bass, Tone and Slap I have offered above and on the DVD, you will produce a clean, resonant, musical sounding tonality that is at once powerful, yet pure. You will be able to play with ease, without hurting your hands and your tonality will draw in the listener with a pleasing timbre. I view drumming as giving your spirit a voice, through tone and timing, so take time to work on your tones, it's so important!

Paulo Mattioli and Lemine "Dibo" Camara performing together

14

Chapter II
About the Djembe

Cultural Origins

The Djembe originates in West Africa, from the great Mali empire founded by the Malinke ethnic group of the Manding (or Mande) people. While its exact year of origin is difficult to pinpoint, it dates back at least to the 15th century and likely as far back in history as 1200 AD, when the Mali Empire was established. The Mali Empire encompassed the present day countries of Mali, Guinea, Burkina Faso, Ivory Coast, Sierra Leone, Liberia, Gambia and Senegal.

According to Kemoko Sano and Mamady Keita the Djembe was likely born out of the mortar, which was carved by the blacksmiths and used to pulverize grain. Mamady has taught that it was the women in the village who first created the rhythms and in turn inspired the creation of the Djembe. The women would gather around a mother who had given birth, celebrating with song and three distinct tones created by clapping hands. The men of the village felt they would like to support and contribute to the celebration, and by stretching a skin (originally antelope was used) over the top of the mortar, the Djembe was born. In the region of southern Senegal and the Gambia, the villagers play drums that retain the shape of the mortar, called boogaraboo.

The Djembe evolved over generations, under the skilled hands of blacksmiths who had the tools and expertise to shape it. Over time, the bottom was opened up, the bowl enlarged and resonator lengthened to become what Kemoko Sano called "The Magic Drum!" Magic he said, because nobody could resist dancing when they heard its song!

The Djembe plays an integral role, in the music, ceremonies and traditions of the Manding. Every traditional rhythm has a purpose and cultural context, in which it played a key role. Birth, coming of age, planting of crops, marriage, and prayer are marked by ritual ceremonies, all of which include specific rhythms, music, dances and songs. The traditional rhythms, music and dances weave together to create the very fabric of life. Music is key in providing communication, connection to family, to village, to ancestors and to the spiritual realm. The role of music for the Manding is integral to life itself.

Music is provided not just by the Djembe, but also the other instruments in its immediate family; the Sangban, Dununba and Kenkeni. These cylindrical, double headed drums are used to accompany the Djembe and provide the rhythmical and melodic foundation for its song. Of these three accompaniments, the Sangban identifies the rhythm.

The Manding instrument family is vast and includes the ancestors of most instrument types we have today. It includes the baliphone (marimba/keyboard), the kora (harp/guitar), bolon (bass), flutes, rattles, bells, talking drums, and dji dunun (water drums), to name a few.

Djembe comes from the words "Dje Ni Be" which means "come together in peace", according to Malian master drummer, Abdul Dumbia. This is the essence of the djembe. It has been bringing people together in harmony for generations and generations. It will no doubt continue to do so for all time. In fact, I believe the Djembe will continue to grow in its popularity and influence in the future. From its origins in West Africa, it has already transcended all boundaries of diverse geography, languages, cultures, ages, and gender. The Djembe brings a diverse array of people from across the entire planet, the joy, healing and heartfelt connection that arises from drumming together in harmony. The Djembe has traditionally always had social, as well as sacred applications. It is important to know and honor its Manding cultural origins and to learn its language of rhythms. This can only enhance ones' expression, ability and experience in playing Djembe.

The Djembe in Contemporary Music Making

The Djembe is a living instrument that continues to evolve and expand. Traditional African masters like Mamady Keita, Kemoko Sano and many others have composed original rhythms for it. Les Ballets Africains, tours internationally sharing the folkloric drum, dance and history of the Manding with Djembe orchestras executing magnificent musical arrangements. It can be heard in community drum circles around the globe. It is used in music therapy sessions in hospitals and medical centers, in Remo Health Rhythms™ programs. It is played in schools, churches and gatherings internationally. It can be heard in the Afro-pop music of artists such as Youssou N'dour, and Baaba Maal. It is heard in the contemporary music of African American, American and European artists including Ben Harper, Leon Mobley, Brandon Boyd (Incubus) and Peter Gabriel. Its voice brings a dynamic rhythmic foundation to modern music that touches your innermost essence. My passion is not to only share its traditional rhythms, but also to share how one can integrate the rich voice of the djembe into contemporary music, to create a fresh new sound!

Chapter III
Drum Tuning

General Guidelines

It is important to tune your drum properly before playing. Tensioning the head properly is crucial in order to be able to produce the proper tonality on the drum. The drum should be tensioned tight enough to facilitate the production of a crisp clean slap tone (see: **Bass/Tone/Slap** on your DVD). There are many types of Djembe tensioning systems, including traditional "Mali weave" rope tuning, key tuning, lug tuning and inline tuning. Follow the specific directions that came with your drum to tension it evenly around its circumference. Additionally, you may

visit the online guide to Djembe drum tuning at:
http://www.paulomattioli.com/djembetuning

Be aware that if your drum has an animal skin (goatskin) on it, it will change tension as the humidity changes. High humidity will make it go flat (loose tension), while low humidity will make it go sharp (tighten up). Know that an animal skin can easily tear if it is over tensioned. So be aware that if you tighten your drum and humidity drops due to weather, travel, exposure to sun or other heat sources, it will be important to loosen it in advance or it may tear. Don't despair too much if your drumhead tears, as it will sooner or later. You can fix it yourself using simple hand tools and your drum will be as good as new! It can be a very satisfying process; you will need to allow 2-3 days to complete the job.

For a complete guide to reheading your traditional rope tuned drum I refer you to: **"Skin It, Tune It, Play It"** DVD from Mel Bay. It is a step-by-step guide to reheading, tuning and caring for your traditional Djembe, or other rope tuned/animal skin drum.

A Fiberskin™, Nuskin™ or Skyn Deep™ djembe head by Remo will not change with the weather! It will keep its tune regardless of any humidity changes. Therefore it is not necessary to loosen it or try to anticipate changes in your drums exposure to humidity. The heads are extremely durable as well. The head can last for several years. Anyone can easily change the head in 5-10 minutes on the key tuned and inline tuned Remo Djembes. It takes only about 1-2 hours on the rope tuned models, and once tuned they will not go out of tune due to humidity changes, a real asset for any player!

Paulo Mattioli Signature Series Rope Tuned, Inline Tuned Djembes by Remo

Key Tuned Djembes: Earth, Leon Mobley and Nickel Silver by Remo

Chapter IV
Key to Notation of Rhythms
Time Signature

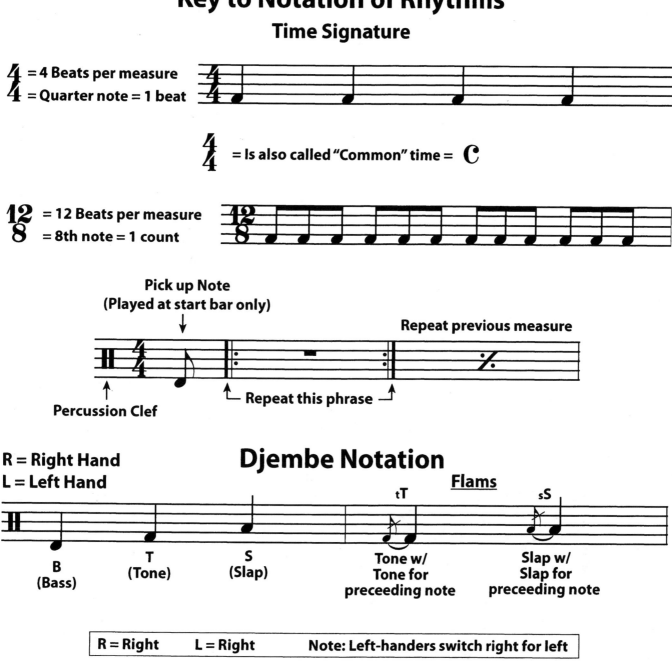

$\frac{4}{4}$ = 4 Beats per measure
$\frac{4}{4}$ = Quarter note = 1 beat

$\frac{4}{4}$ = Is also called "Common" time = **C**

$\frac{12}{8}$ = 12 Beats per measure
$\frac{12}{8}$ = 8th note = 1 count

Pick up Note
(Played at start bar only)

Repeat previous measure

Percussion Clef

← **Repeat this phrase** →

R = Right Hand
L = Left Hand

Djembe Notation

Flams

tT

sS

B
(Bass)

T
(Tone)

S
(Slap)

Tone w/
Tone for
preceeding note

Slap w/
Slap for
preceeding note

R = Right   L = Right   Note: Left-handers switch right for left

Phonetic Notation:

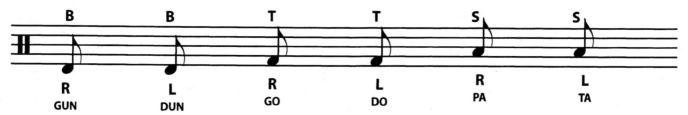

B   B   T   T   S   S

R   L   R   L   R   L
GUN   DUN   GO   DO   PA   TA

Kenkeni; Sangban; Dununba and Bell Rhythms

Rebounding Stroke
(O = Open)

Press Stroke
(P = Press)

Bell

Phonetic Notation Key

	Right Hand	Left Hand
Bass:	GUN	DUN
Tone:	GO	DO
Slap:	PA	TA

Note: Left-Handed Drummers switch Left for Right in Key above

Key to Notation–Note Values:
4/4 or Common Time

Whole Note = 4 Beats **Half Note = 2 Beats**

Beats: 1   2   3   4   1   2   3   4

𝄴 = **Common Time**

Quarter Note = 1 Beat **Eighth Note = 1/2 Beat**

1   2   3   4   1   +   2   +   3   +   4   +

Sixteenth Note = 1/4 Beat | **Repeat Previous Measure** |

1 e + ah 2 e + ah 3 e + ah 4 e + ah

Whole Rest = 4 Beats **Half Rest = 2 Beats**

Beats: 1   2   3   4   1   2   3   4

Quarter Rest = 1 Beat **Eighth Rest = 1/2 Beat**

1   2   3   4   1   +   2   +   3   +   4   +

Sixteenth Rest = 1/4 Beat

1 e + ah 2 e + ah 3 e + ah 4 e + ah

Key to Notation–Note Values

Dotted Notes and Rests

A dot placed after a note or rest increases its duration by one half. Eg.:

Quarter Note = 2 Eighth Notes   Dotted Quarter = 3 Eighth Notes   Dotted Quarter Rest = 3 Eighth Rests

Eighth Note = 2 Sixteenth Notes   Dotted Eighth = 3 Sixteenth Notes   Dotted Eighth Rest = 3 Sixteenth Rests

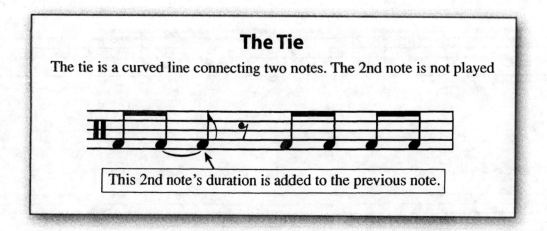

The Tie

The tie is a curved line connecting two notes. The 2nd note is not played

This 2nd note's duration is added to the previous note.

Repeat Signs

A pair of double dotted bars means: repeat the music between them

End of a Section   **End of a Piece**

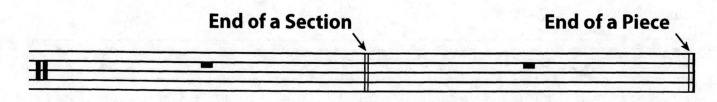

Chapter V
Djembe Playing Exercises

Djembe Exercise 1: Bass, Tone, Slap

Slowly

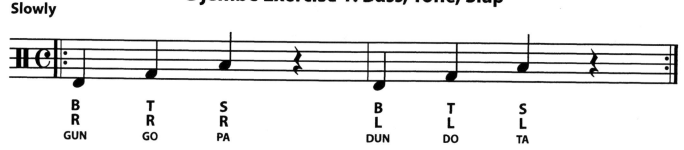

Djembe Exercise 2: Bass/Bass, Tone/Tone

Slowly, then gradually speed up keeping each tone distinct. Also practice with Left Hand lead.

Djembe Exercise 3: Warm Up

Slowly, then gradually speed up keeping each tone distinct. Also practice with Left Hand lead.

Chapter VI
Traditional Rhythm: Djole

The Manding (or Mande) rhythm Djole (or Jole) has its origins in a traditional mask dance of the Temine ethnic group of Forecaria, located in Guinea, West Africa, near its southerly border with Sierra Leone. The mask was customarily worn by a man and represented a woman. The rhythm was originally played on a family of drums called the "Sikko", four square shaped drums of varied sizes played together. The rhythm gained great popularity as a result of it being brought to the current day capital of Guinea, Conakry. It is customarily played at village and regional festivals including celebrations of the harvest, the end of Ramadan and weddings. Today the Djole rhythm is also commonly played on the Djembe and Dunun family of drums.

The rhythm is binary, each beat subdivided by factors of two, with the pattern based principally on 16th notes (each beat subdivided into a group of four. Four 16th notes = 1 beat). The feel is upbeat and celebratory.

Rhythm-Djole (or Jole)

Djembe: Lead signal to begin and end and gives tempo

Djembe I

Djembe 2

Rhythm-Djole (cont.)

Sangban

Bell

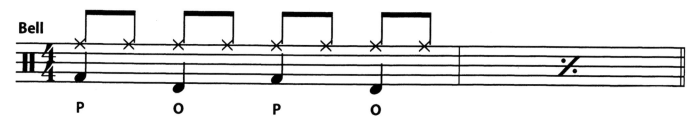

Kenkeni

Dununba

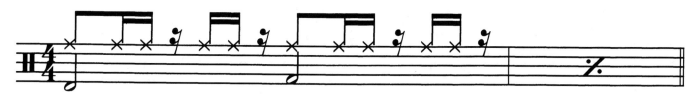

Dununba: Alternate bell pattern (Basic)

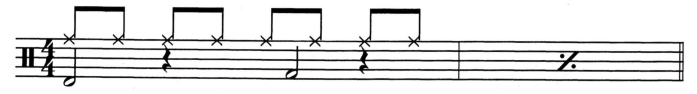

Chapter VII
One Rhythm

Instruction: Basis of "Groove" Pattern

B DS B DS B DS B DS
R R R R

Groove Pattern – Example 1

Groove Pattern – Example 2

Instruction

Ensemble – Introduction groove

Main groove – Example 3

One Rhythm

Building together in Unity,
Growing together in Unity,

The Music fills my Soul,
The Music fills my Soul,

Building together and growing stronger,
Building together and growing stronger,

One Rhythm, One People,
One Planet, One Tribe,

One Purpose, One Vision,
One Heartbeat, One Life,

Feel the Heartbeat,
Feel the Heartbeat...

Fire CD: Composed and produced by Paulo Mattioli and Ken Givens

Continuing on the Drumming Path:

Resources for further learning from Paulo Mattioli and Mel Bay Publications

Hands on Drumming: Session #1 of 4: DVD (60 Min.) (99327DVD)
Universal Keys to Hand Drumming:

- ❖ Quick & Easy Learning for All Levels
- ❖ Djembe Hand Techniques & Tones
- ❖ Djembe Communication & Signals
- ❖ Rhythm / Dexterity Builders
- ❖ 19 Rhythm Parts with In Depth Instruction
- ❖ On Screen Phonetic Notation
- ❖ Two PolyRhythmic Ensemble Arrangements:
- ❖ Yankadi and Macrou
- ❖ Djembe, Dununba, Sangban, Kenkeni, Bell

$24.95

Skin It, Tune It, Play It! : DVD (99332DVD)
The Easy "Do it Yourself" Guide to Drum Care
For all Rope Tuned Drums!

Step By Step Directions for:
- ❖ Drum Head Replacement
- ❖ Drum Tuning
- ❖ Drum Shell Maintenance
- ❖ Step-By-Step, real time guidance
- ❖ Anyone can "Do it yourself"
- ❖ Using Only Simple Hand Tools
- ❖ Veteran Drum Making Tips & Tricks
- ❖ Giving your drum a voice
- ❖ Saving Big Money on Maintenance

$19.95

Hands on Drumming: Session #2 of 4: DVD (60 Min.) (99328DVD)
Universal Keys to Hand Drumming

- ❖ Quick & Easy Learning for All Levels
- ❖ Djembe Hand Techniques & Tones
- ❖ Djembe Communication & Signals
- ❖ Rhythm/Dexterity Exercises
- ❖ 15 Rhythm Parts with In Depth Instruction
- ❖ On Screen Phonetic Notation
- ❖ Two Polyrhythmic Ensemble Arrangements:
- ❖ Kassagbe and Kassa
- ❖ Djembe, Dununba, Sangban, Kenkeni, Bell

$24.95

Anyone Can Play – Djembe: DVD (21374DVD)

- ❖ "Play Along & Learn" Quickly & Easily
- ❖ 26 Rhythms Parts, Technique, Signals
- ❖ 4 Polyrhythmic Arrangements including:
- ❖ Traditional Djembe Rhythms
- ❖ Kuku, Djaa, and Moribayassa
- ❖ Contemporary World Music Rhythm:
- ❖ "Straight Ahead"
- ❖ Downloadable Rhythm Notation Scores
- ❖ Web Links for Tuning Djembe Drums

$19.95

Hands on Drumming: Session #3 of 4: DVD (60 Min.) (99329DVD)
Universal Keys to Hand Drumming

- ❖ Quick & Easy Learning for All Levels
- ❖ Djembe Hand Techniques & Tones
- ❖ Djembe Communication & Signals
- ❖ Rhythm/Dexterity Builders
- ❖ 18 Rhythm Parts
- ❖ On Screen Phonetic Notation
- ❖ Two Polyrhythmic Ensemble Arrangements:
- ❖ Kassagbe and Kassa
- ❖ Djembe, Dununba, Sangban, Kenkeni, Bell

$24.95

Beyond the Basics – Djembe: DVD and Book (21375DP)

- ❖ "Play Along & Learn" Quickly & Easily
- ❖ 26 Rhythms Parts, Technique, Signals
- ❖ 4 Arrangements including:
- ❖ Traditional Djembe Rhythms
- ❖ Djansa, Garangedon, Sofa
- ❖ Contemporary World Music Rhythm:
- ❖ "Straight Ahead"
- ❖ Notation of All Rhythm Parts
- ❖ Professional Photo Illustrations Provide Visual Support
- ❖ Drum Tuning Information and Web Links

$29.95

Hands on Drumming: Session #4 of 4: DVD (60 Min.) (99330DVD)
Universal Keys to Hand Drumming

- ❖ Quick & Easy Learning for All Levels
- ❖ Djembe Hand Techniques & Tones
- ❖ Djembe Communication & Signals
- ❖ Rhythm/Dexterity Builders
- ❖ 16 Rhythm Parts
- ❖ On Screen Phonetic Notation
- ❖ Two Polyrhythmic Ensemble Arrangements
- ❖ Tiriba and Mindiani
- ❖ Djembe, Dununba, Sangban, Kenkeni, Bell

$24.95

The Art of Djembe: DVD and Book (21376DP)

- ❖ "Play Along & Learn" Quickly & Easily
- ❖ 32 Rhythms Parts, Technique, Signals
- ❖ 5 Polyrhythmic Arrangements including:
- ❖ Traditional Djembe Rhythms
- ❖ Soliwoulen, Kakilambe, Soko and Sunun
- ❖ Contemporary World Music Rhythm:
- ❖ "Let it Move Ya!"
- ❖ Notation of All Rhythm Parts
- ❖ Drum Tuning Information and Web Links

$29.95

Drumming and World Music CD'S

FIRE! : World Beat Dance Remix

An upbeat and exciting collection of African, Latin and Brazilian Percussion powered dance tracks: Guaranteed to get you on your feet and Dancing to the beat!

By Paulo Mattioli & Ken Givens
PLUS: Special guest Artists on
Guitar, Sax, Flute, Keyboards & Vocals
10 Dance Tracks: Total 60 Minutes

$14.95 CD $9.95 Download

Around The World in Rhythm: World Music Sampler

A collection of African, Afro-Latin and Afro-Caribbean music.

By Paulo Mattioli & Ken Givens
Enjoy rhythms from around the world
with tasty guitar, flute, sax, keyboards
and vocals by top world music artists!

$14.95 CD $9.95 Download

Master of the Forest: Traditional West African Rhythms

Featuring Kemoko Sano and artists from Les Ballets Africans Red Hot Djembe drumming with incredible West African vocal harmonies.

An inspiring recording of traditional
West African drumming and chants!

$14.95 CD $9.95 Download

31

World Percussion Instruments
Durable. Portable. Tunable. Playable.

Designer Series Djembes

Camouflage

Festival Djembe

Adinkra

Black Earth

Paulo Mattioli Signature Series

In-Line Djembe

Rope-tuned Djembe

Dunun

my revisi⏻n notes

AQA (A) A2
PSYCHOLOGY

Jean-Marc Lawton

With thanks to all the students whose valuable feedback helped develop this book.

Hodder Education, an Hachette UK company, 338 Euston Road, London NW1 3BH

Orders

Bookpoint Ltd, 130 Milton Park, Abingdon, Oxfordshire OX14 4SB

tel: 01235 827827

fax: 01235 400401

e-mail: education@bookpoint.co.uk

Lines are open 9.00 a.m.–5.00 p.m., Monday to Saturday, with a 24-hour message answering service. You can also order through the Hodder Education website: www.hoddereducation.co.uk

© Jean-Marc Lawton 2012

ISBN 978-1-4441-6305-6

First printed 2012

Impression number 5 4 3 2 1

Year 2017 2016 2015 2014 2013 2012

Cover photo reproduced by permission of rolffimages/Fotolia

Typeset by Datapage, India

Printed in India

Hachette UK's policy is to use papers that are natural, renewable and recyclable products and made from wood grown in sustainable forests. The logging and manufacturing processes are expected to conform to the environmental regulations of the country of origin.

P02039

Get the most from this book

Everyone has to decide his or her own revision strategy, but it is essential to review your work, learn it and test your understanding. These Revision Notes will help you to do that in a planned way, topic by topic. Use this book as the cornerstone of your revision and don't hesitate to write in it — personalise your notes and check your progress by ticking off each section as you revise.

☑ Tick to track your progress

Use the revision planner on pages 4 and 5 to plan your revision, topic by topic. Tick each box when you have:

● revised and understood a topic

● tested yourself

● practised the exam questions and gone online to check your answers and complete the quick quizzes

You can also keep track of your revision by ticking off each topic heading in the book. You may find it helpful to add your own notes as you work through each topic.

Features to help you succeed

Examiner's tips and summaries

Throughout the book there are tips from the examiner to help you boost your final grade.

Summaries provide advice on how to approach each topic in the exams, and suggest other things you might want to mention to gain those valuable extra marks.

Definitions and key words

Clear, concise definitions of essential key terms are provided on the page where they appear.

Key words from the specification are highlighted in bold for you throughout the book.

Typical mistakes

The examiner identifies the typical mistakes candidates make and explains how you can avoid them.

Now test yourself

These short, knowledge-based questions provide the first step in testing your learning. Answers are at the back of the book.

Exam practice

Practice exam questions are provided for each topic. Use them to consolidate your revision and practise your exam skills.

Online

Go online to check your answers to the exam questions and try out the extra quick quizzes at **www.therevisionbutton.co.uk/myrevisionnotes**

My revision planner

Unit 4 Psychopathology, psychology in action and research methods

Exam practice answers and quick quizzes at **www.therevisionbutton.co.uk/myrevisionnotes**

Countdown to my exams

6–8 weeks to go

- Start by looking at the specification — make sure you know exactly what material you need to revise and the style of the examination. Use the revision planner on pages 4 and 5 to familiarise yourself with the topics.
- Organise your notes, making sure you have covered everything on the specification. The revision planner will help you to group your notes into topics.
- Work out a realistic revision plan that will allow you time for relaxation. Set aside days and times for all the subjects that you need to study, and stick to your timetable.
- Set yourself sensible targets. Break your revision down into focused sessions of around 40 minutes, divided by breaks. These Revision Notes organise the basic facts into short, memorable sections to make revising easier.

Revised ☐

4–6 weeks to go

- Read through the relevant sections of this book and refer to the examiner's tips, examiner's summaries, typical mistakes and key terms. Tick off the topics as you feel confident about them. Highlight those topics you find difficult and look at them again in detail.
- Test your understanding of each topic by working through the 'Now test yourself' questions in the book. Look up the answers at the back of the book.
- Make a note of any problem areas as you revise, and ask your teacher to go over these in class.
- Look at past papers. They are one of the best ways to revise and practise your exam skills. Write or prepare planned answers to the exam practice questions provided in this book. Check your answers online and try out the extra quick quizzes at **www.therevisionbutton.co.uk/ myrevisionnotes**
- Try different revision methods. For example, you can make notes using mind maps, spider diagrams or flash cards.
- Track your progress using the revision planner and give yourself a reward when you have achieved your target.

Revised ☐

One week to go

- Try to fit in at least one more timed practice of an entire past paper and seek feedback from your teacher, comparing your work closely with the mark scheme.
- Check the revision planner to make sure you haven't missed out any topics. Brush up on any areas of difficulty by talking them over with a friend or getting help from your teacher.
- Attend any revision classes put on by your teacher. Remember, he or she is an expert at preparing people for examinations.

Revised ☐

The day before the examination

- Flick through these Revision Notes for useful reminders, for example the examiner's tips, examiner's summaries, typical mistakes and key terms.
- Check the time and place of your examination.
- Make sure you have everything you need — extra pens and pencils, tissues, a watch, bottled water, sweets.
- Allow some time to relax and have an early night to ensure you are fresh and alert for the examinations.

Revised ☐

My exams

A2 Psychology Unit 3

Date: ....

Time: ....

Location: ....

A2 Psychology Unit 4

Date: ....

Time: ....

Location: ....

1 Biological rhythms and sleep

Biological rhythms

Circadian, infradian and ultradian rhythms

Revised

Circadian rhythms are biological cycles lasting around 24 hours (an example is the sleep–wake cycle) facilitated by time checks and regular events such as meal times, and controlled by an endogenous pacemaker working as a 'body clock'.

> **Siffre (1972)** spent 6 months in a cave with no time cues, settling into a sleep–wake cycle of 25–30 hours.
>
> **Aschoff and Weber (1965)** found that participants in a bunker with no natural light settled into a sleep–wake cycle of 25–27 hours, implying that endogenous pacemakers exert a strong influence on circadian rhythms.

- Isolation studies have few participants, making generalisation problematic.
- It seems unlikely that humans have evolved a 25-hour biological clock. Animals display a 24-hour cycle, and therefore humans should follow this pattern.

Infradian rhythms are biological cycles lasting more than 24 hours (for example, the menstrual cycle) controlled by the hypothalamus acting as an endogenous pacemaker, with exogenous zeitgebers also playing a role. Infradian rhythms include **circannual rhythms** occurring once a year, such as hibernation.

> **Russell et al. (1980)** applied donors' underarm sweat to the upper lips of female participants, finding that menstrual cycles became synchronised. This suggests that pheromones act as exogenous zeitgebers.
>
> **McClintock and Stern (1998)** found that pheromones in donors' sweat affected recipients' menstrual cycles, suggesting that exogenous zeitgebers have a regulating effect.

- Synchronised periods have evolutionary significance in allowing women who live together to coincide pregnancies and share child-caring duties.
- Women working in proximity to men have shorter cycles, bestowing an evolutionary advantage in giving more opportunities to get pregnant.

Ultradian rhythms are biological cycles lasting less than 24 hours (such as the cycle of brain activity during sleep).

> **Rechtschaffen and Kales (1968)** measured the electrical activity of the brain, finding different patterns of activity at different times of sleep, supporting the idea of sleep being an ultradian cycle.

---

biological rhythms — regular patterns of physiological, cognitive and behavioural activity that occur as circadian, infradian and ultradian rhythms.

circadian rhythms — bodily cycles that occur once a day.

infradian rhythms — bodily cycles that occur less than once a day.

ultradian rhythms — bodily cycles that occur more than once a day.

Typical mistakes

Unit 3 questions require the inclusion of material concerning *issues*, *debates* and *approaches* (IDA). Many students use the poor tactic of tagging such material onto the end of their answers in a general and uninformative way (e.g. 'this is reductionist'). It is much better to build relevant IDA material into answers at appropriate points, explaining how such material is applicable to the point being commented on.

Dement and Kleitman (1957) found that 90% of participants awakened during REM sleep reported dreaming, compared with only 7% of those awoken during NREM sleep, suggesting that this is the part of the ultradian cycle where dreams occur.

- Lesions to brain areas controlling circadian rhythms have no effect on behaviours with ultradian rhythms, suggesting that circadian and ultradian rhythms have different controlling mechanisms.
- The artificial surroundings of sleep laboratories, with electrodes having to be worn, suggest that sleep findings may lack ecological validity.

Control of circadian rhythms   Revised

Role of endogenous pacemakers and exogenous zeitgebers

The main pacemaker is the superchiasmatic nucleus (SCN), a small group of cells in the hypothalamus generating a circadian rhythm reset by light entering the eyes. A rhythm is produced from the interaction of proteins, producing a biological clock.

Morgan (1995) found that removing SCN cells from hamsters made circadian rhythms disappear, but that they returned when cells were transplanted in, illustrating the role of the SCN as an endogenous pacemaker.

Hawkins and Armstrong-Esther (1978) found that shift work altered nurses' sleep–wake cycles but not their temperature cycles, suggesting that different body clocks regulate different circadian rhythms.

endogenous pacemakers — internal body clocks that regulate biological rhythms.

exogenous zeitgebers — external stimuli involved in the control of biological rhythms.

- There is an adaptive advantage in animals having endogenous pacemakers reset by exogenous zeitgebers, keeping them in tune with day/night changes etc.

Zeitgebers such as light help reset circadian rhythms and **endogenous pacemakers** respond to **exogenous zeitgebers**, coordinating behaviours regulated with external environments.

Klein et al. (1993) found that a blind man with a circadian rhythm of 24.5 hours got out of synchronisation with the 24-hour day. He took medication to regulate his sleep–wake cycle. This suggests that light acts as an exogenous time cue.

- Relying on exogenous zeitgebers could threaten survival; therefore internal cues are important too.

Disruption of biological rhythms   Revised

Usually exogenous zeitgebers change gradually, giving time to adjust. However, rapid change disrupts coordination between internally regulated rhythms and external exogenous zeitgebers, creating consequences for the ability to function properly.

Jet lag is caused by travelling across time zones so quickly that biological rhythms cannot match external cues, causing sleepiness during daytime and restlessness at night. These symptoms last until resynchronisation

jet lag — temporary disruption of biological rhythms caused by high-speed travel across time zones.

occurs. The effects of jet lag are worse when travelling from west to east, because it is easier to adjust biological clocks if they are ahead of local time (**phase delay**) than behind (**phase advance**). Jet lag also occurs when the biological clock regulating temperature needs time to reset, causing desynchronised rhythms in the meantime.

Klein et al. (1972) found that adjustment to jet lag occurred more easily on westbound flights, whether outbound or homebound, implying that phase advance has more severe consequences than phase delay.

Schwartz et al. (1995) found that eastern-based US baseball teams did better against teams in the west than vice versa, suggesting the same conclusion.

- Concentration levels are affected by jet lag (and shift work), implying disruption to cognitive processes.
- Much research utilises naturalistic field studies. These are high in ecological validity but incur many confounding variables, making the establishment of causality problematic.

Shift work involves working during the hours that are normally spent asleep and sleeping during normal waking hours, which disrupts the coordination between internal biological clocks and external cues. This can result in an almost permanent state of desynchronisation that impairs concentration and physical performance and increases stress levels, incurring long-term health risks.

shift work — periods of work performed outside regular employment hours.

Shift-work patterns involving phase delay (changing shifts forward in time) cause less disruption, as does an adjustment time before changing shifts.

Czeisler et al. (1982) found that shift workers had high illness rates, sleep disorders and elevated stress levels, suggesting that internal body clocks were out of synchronisation with exogenous zeitgebers. Moving to a phase delay system of rotating shifts forward in time reduced negative effects.

Sharkey (2001) found that melatonin reduced the time required to adjust to shift-work patterns and rotations, demonstrating the effects of practical applications based on psychological knowledge.

Examiner's tip

An IDA point relevant to the disruption of biological rhythms is that much research on shift work involves only males and is therefore gender biased with the findings not necessarily generalisable to females. Practical applications of such research are also relevant, including the phase-delay system of rotating shifts forward to reduce negative effects and improve output, and melatonin supplements and strategies to combat jet lag, such as regular meal times.

- Some accidents (such as the Chernobyl meltdown) occur due to early-morning concentration and decision failures, suggesting that the desynchronisation effects of working irregular hours impair performance.
- Research suggests that disrupting biological rhythms affects cognitive, emotional and physical functioning, demonstrating the severity of consequences.

Now test yourself

Tested

1   Explain what is meant by the following terms:
    (a) biological rhythms (b) circadian rhythms (c) infradian rhythms (d) ultradian rhythms.
2   Outline and evaluate one research study each of circadian, infradian and ultradian rhythms.
3   Outline what research has revealed about the role of endogenous pacemakers and exogenous zeitgebers in the control of circadian rhythms.
4   Outline the effects of disruption to biological rhythms through (i) shift work, and (ii) jet lag.
5   Compile a list of evaluative points relating to disruption of biological rhythms.
6   Explain two IDA points that relate to biological rhythms.

Answers on p. 122

Sleep

The nature of sleep

Sleep occurs as a circadian rhythm and an ultradian cycle of four separate stages (see Table 1.1).

sleep — a natural and periodic state of rest during which responsiveness to the external environment and its stimuli is diminished.

Table 1.1 The stages of sleep

Stage 1	A light sleep where heart rate declines and muscles relax
Stage 2	A deeper sleep with noticeable bursts of sleep spindles
Stage 3	Increasingly deep Sleep spindles decline, replaced by long, slow delta waves
Stage 4	Deep sleep Metabolic rate is low and growth hormones are released
REM	Eye movements are noticeable and dreaming occurs

Stages 1 to 4 take about 1 hour, and then stage 3 is re-entered, followed by stage 2 and rapid eye movement (REM) sleep. After 15 minutes, stages 2, 3 and 4 re-occur in order, and then another cycle begins. There are about five ultradian cycles per night, with increasingly more time spent in REM sleep. This pattern is shown fairly universally, although there are developmental differences.

The physiology of sleep

The brain stem has a role in key functions such as alertness but it also controls sleep. Several hormones are also involved.

The suprachiasmatic nucleus (SCN) reacts to light, stimulating melatonin production from the pineal gland, causing the release of serotonin and allowing reticular activating system activity to lessen, bringing the onset of sleep.

The release of **noradrenaline** causes the onset of REM sleep and the hormone **acetylcholine** is involved both with brain activation during wakefulness and REM sleep.

Dement and Kleitman (1957) found that sleep consists of a sequential series of five stages, each with different characteristics, occurring in a set pattern.

- The development of electroencephalograph (EEG) readings allowed an objective means of studying sleep.
- As sleep has five stages, it is likely that each stage has a different function. Since REM sleep is identifiable in warm-blooded but not cold-blooded creatures, it might be that REM sleep keeps brain temperature at a safe level by increasing brain metabolism.

Lifespan changes in sleep

Alterations in sleep patterns developing over the course of a lifetime are termed 'lifespan changes in sleep' (see Table 1.2).

Table 1.2 Lifespan changes in sleep

Age	Sleep description
Neonates	16 hours sleep daily over several periods Active sleep (REM) gradually decreases, while quiet sleep (non-rapid eye movement — NREM) increases
1 year olds	11 hours sleep daily Increasingly adult-like sleep patterns REM declines to 50% of duration, with longer and fewer sleep periods
5 year olds	10 hours daily, a third being REM
Adolescents	9 hours daily, with less REM than children
Middle age	Normal adult sleep patterns Increased levels of sleep disorders
Senescence	Total sleep duration unchanged REM decreases to 20% of duration, with stage 2 increasing to 60% Sleep disturbance is common

Van Cauter et al. (2000) examined male sleep patterns, finding that sleep decreased between 16 and 25, and 35 and 50 years.

Floyd et al. (2007) found that REM decreases by 0.6 % per decade, with its proportion increasing from age 70, although this may be due to overall sleep duration declining.

- The fact that neonates sleep for long periods may be an adaptive response, freeing up essential time for their parents.
- Males over 45 years old often have little stages 1–4 sleep, affecting hormone production; this may explain why their physical injuries take longer to heal.

Functions of sleep

Revised ☐

Evolutionary explanations

- **Sleep has a survival value** — different species evolved different types and patterns of sleep for different environmental needs (e.g. predator avoidance). Sleep keeps animals dormant when activities vital for survival are not required.
- **Predator–prey sleep — Meddis (1979)** believes that sleep evolved to keep animals hidden when usual activities, such as foraging, are not required. Therefore prey animals should sleep less because they are more at risk and need to be alert and vigilant.
- **Body size** — smaller animals evolved a greater need to sleep, their metabolic rates being high and energy consumption rapid. Long periods of sleep help conserve energy stores.

> **evolutionary explanations of sleep** — perceive sleep as serving an adaptive purpose related to survival.

Stear (2005) found that sleep saves energy and is an adaptation to ecological factors differing across species (supporting the evolutionary explanation).

Siegel (2008) found less risk of injury when asleep than awake, sleep being a safety device when essential activities are not necessary.

- Predators sleep longer than prey, supporting the evolutionary prediction. However prey animals are usually herbivores that require a lot of time to graze; this leaves them less time to sleep.

> **Typical mistakes**
>
> Students often find it difficult to evaluate explanations for the functions of sleep and may resort to a list of unconnected, unexplained points. A better strategy is to compare theories (e.g. the evolutionary and restoration explanations), drawing out differences and similarities as a form of elaborated commentary that shows real insight. This will earn high-level credit.

Restoration theory

People sleep when tired, suggesting that sleep provides a period for rejuvenation. Growth hormone is released during sleep, stimulating tissue growth and aiding protein synthesis to repair damaged tissues. Waste products are also removed.

> restoration theory — an explanation of sleep that sees it as a period of rejuvenation and repair.

Oswald (1980) developed restoration theory — accelerated brain activity during REM sleep indicates brain restoration, while growth hormone production during stages 1 to 4 sleep indicates bodily restoration.

Horne (1988) developed the core sleep model — during stage 4 and REM sleep the brain refreshes itself for the next day.

Stern and Morgane (1974) believe that during REM sleep neurotransmitter levels are replenished, supporting the restoration theory. This is backed up by the fact that antidepressants increase neurotransmitter levels, reducing REM activity.

- Endurance athletes use naps after training to promote protein synthesis, which repairs tissues, supporting the restoration theory.
- Infants sleep for a great deal of time, possibly because of rapid brain and body growth, again supporting restoration theory.
- Sufferers of the condition fatal familial insomnia cannot sleep and usually die within 2 years, implying support for the restoration theory. However such cases are few and sufferers also have brain damage that may be responsible.

Examiner's tip

Relevant IDA points to include in answers to questions about the nature and functions of sleep concern (1) how much research into the nature of sleep can be regarded as reductionist (e.g. the dividing of sleep into separate stages on the basis of EEG readings) and (2) how descriptions of the nature of sleep can be perceived as deterministic, sleep being regarded as a behaviour that humans have little, if any, control over.

Now test yourself

Tested

7 Outline as bullet points the stages of sleep.
8 Outline the physiology of sleep.
9 Outline the changes in sleep patterns that occur throughout an individual's life.
10 Compile a list of evaluative points regarding the stages of sleep and lifespan changes in sleep.
11 Outline the main points of (i) evolutionary (ii) restoration explanations of sleep.
12 What research support is there for these two explanations?
13 What other evaluative points can be made about these two explanations?
14 Explain two IDA points that relate to the nature and functions of sleep.

Answers on p. 122

Sleep disorders

Insomnia

Revised

Primary insomnia has clear underlying causes, such as brain abnormalities and environmental stress. Behaviour before sleep, sleep patterns and the sleeping environment (being too hot, too cold or noisy) are other causes of primary insomnia.

Secondary insomnia is secondary to other medical conditions, such as psychological problems (e.g. depression, grief, dementia), physical disorders (e.g. arthritis, pain) and medicines/recreational drugs.

> **insomnia** — a long-term problem initiating and/or maintaining sleep.
>
> **primary insomnia** — insomnia attributable to a clear underlying cause.
>
> **secondary insomnia** — insomnia not attributable to an underlying cause.

Factors influencing insomnia

Apnoea is a medical condition. Sufferers experience persistent pauses in their breathing lasting for minutes and give occasional loud snorts as breathing recommences.

> **Chest (2001)** found a positive correlation between insomnia and obstructive sleep apnoea, suggesting a relationship between the two.

● Sleep apnoea can lead to insomnia being prevalent in older adults. As the population ages, there is an assumption that the disorder will grow, increasing the need for treatments.

Personality factors sometimes influence sleep patterns. Psychasthenia, a personality disorder similar to OCD, is especially implicated. Other factors include over-sensitivity, low self-esteem, lack of autonomy and heightened emotional arousal.

> **Kales et al. (1976)** found that 85% of insomniacs had abnormal personalities characterised by psychasthenia, elevated levels of depression and conversion hysteria.

● Rather than personality traits leading to insomnia, insomnia may create changes in personality. However, research indicates that treating abnormal personality traits and disorders is more successful in reducing insomnia than treating insomnia to address personality defects, implying that abnormal personality traits are the causal factor.

apnoea — a medical condition affecting breathing patterns during sleep.

personality factors — individual dispositional traits affecting behaviour/experiences (e.g. traits associated with or affecting normal sleep patterns).

Typical mistakes

As the specification focuses on 'explanations for sleep disorders', this will be reflected in the wording of exam questions. Care should therefore be taken in the answers to such questions to outline *explanations* of, not just *describe*, the features of various sleep disorders.

Sleepwalking
Revised

Sleepwalking is when normally conscious activities are performed unconsciously during sleep (e.g. eating). It is more prevalent in childhood, declining sharply in adulthood. Sleepwalking (also known as somnambulism) is associated with personality disorders relating to anxiety.

sleepwalking — performing unconscious activities when asleep.

> **Hublin et al. (1997)** found sleepwalking to be more common among children, indicating that the condition is linked to development and maturation.
>
> **Broughton (1968)** found sleepwalking to be heritable, with sufferers ten times more likely than the general population to have close relatives with the disorder, suggesting a genetic factor.

● Children may have higher incidences of somnambulism because they spend long amounts of time in slow wave sleep, where the condition tends to occur. Children are also observed more while asleep, so episodes are more likely to be detected.

● The current focus of research is that a group of sleep disorders known as parasomnias, such as somnambulism and sleep terrors, share a common genetic cause.

Narcolepsy
Revised

Sufferers from **narcolepsy** fall asleep at unexpected times and feel sleepy during the day, appearing drunk. Another symptom of narcolepsy is **cataplexy**, where muscular control is lost through over-excitement.

Sleep paralysis can occur when the brain awakes from an REM state, leaving the sufferer's body paralysed but their mind fully conscious.

narcolepsy — a sleep disorder characterised by falling asleep at unexpected times.

sleep paralysis — a sleep disorder involving an inability to move at the onset of sleep or on wakening.

Sufferers can also experience terrifying hallucinations and a sense of danger. The condition usually appears in adolescence and may originate from a genetic abnormality or a shortage of the neurotransmitter hypocretin, or an autoimmune disease.

Mignot et al. (1999) found a defective gene (hypocretin receptor 2) in dogs, one of the few species suffering from narcolepsy. The defective form of the gene inhibits wakefulness, suggesting a genetic basis to the disorder.

Hufford (1982) reports on an ancient sleep paralysis myth, 'hag riding'. This suggests that narcolepsy is long lasting and thus hereditary, and is backed up by the fact that such legends are cross-cultural.

● The identification of genes associated with the disorder does not imply a definite genetic cause. Researchers stress the need to identify environmental triggers.

Examiner's tip

An IDA point relevant to insomnia is that research is holistic in its approach, considering a wide range of physiological and psychological influences (e.g. hormonal fluctuations, personality factors, maladaptive learning experiences and cognitive functioning). Conversely an IDA point relevant to narcolepsy is that research concentrates on genetic influences, so can be perceived as determinist because it fails to acknowledge the influence of environmental triggers (e.g. heightened stress levels).

Now test yourself

Tested ☐

15 (a) Outline explanations of (i) insomnia (ii) sleepwalking (iii) narcolepsy.
    (b) To what extent does research support these explanations?
    (c) Apart from research evidence, what other evaluative points can be made concerning these explanations?

16 Explain two IDA points relating to disorders of sleep.

Answers on p. 122

Exam practice

1 (a) Outline one example of an infradian rhythm.   [4]
   (b) Outline the role of endogenous pacemakers in the control of circadian rhythms.   [4]
   (c) Evaluate explanations for sleep disorders.   [16]

2 Outline and evaluate lifespan changes in sleep.   [24]

3 Discuss evolutionary and restoration explanations of sleep.   [24]

4 (a) Outline and evaluate the role of ultradian rhythms.   [4 + 8]
   (b) Outline and evaluate the disruption of biological rhythms.   [4 + 8]

Answers and quick quiz 1 online

Online ☐

Examiner's summary

✔ Biological rhythms are behaviours that are repeated periodically: circadian rhythms over 24 hours, infradian longer than 24 hours and ultradian less than 24 hours.

✔ Endogenous pacemakers are rhythms from within an organism, while exogenous zeitgebers are external time cues that help regulate circadian rhythms.

✔ Shift work and jet lag can negatively disrupt biological rhythms.

✔ Sleep is a circadian rhythm comprised of an ultradian rhythm of separate stages.

✔ Sleep varies with age in terms of the stages of sleep and amount of sleep.

✔ Evolutionary theory sees sleep as having an adaptive advantage, while restoration theory perceives sleep as for restoration and repair.

✔ Insomnia results from stress, abnormalities in brain mechanisms, misperception of sleep, psychiatric and medical disorders.

✔ Sleepwalking is associated with personality disorders relating to anxiety.

✔ Narcolepsy is associated with faulty brain mechanisms, genetic abnormality, abnormal neurotransmitter levels and autoimmune disease.

2 Perception

Theories of perceptual organisation

Gregory's indirect theory — Revised

Perception is seen as the best interpretation of sensory data based on previous experience and is learnt through environmental interactions. Information from sensory data (**direct processing**) is incomplete without the perceptions gained using higher level cognitive processing, i.e. **indirect processing**.

Perceptual set is a readiness to perceive certain features of sensory data based on **expectation**, motivational and emotional factors, and cultural influences.

Aarts and Dijksterhuis (2002) asked participants to think about 'fast' or 'slow' animals. This influenced the participants' estimates of walking speed by creating an expectation of what it should be, demonstrating how experience biases perception.

Motivational and emotional factors affect perception by creating a bias to perceive certain features of sensory data. **Perceptual defence** occurs where emotionally threatening stimuli take longer to perceive.

Solley and Haigh (1948) found that children drew a bigger Santa as Christmas approached but after Christmas the size of their drawings of Santa shrank, illustrating how motivational factors influence perception.

McGinnies (1949) found that people took longer to recognise emotionally threatening words, suggesting that perceptual defence and emotional factors influence perception.

People from different cultural backgrounds sometimes perceive sensory data differently, because their perceptual set predisposes them to perceive it in certain ways.

Segall (1963) found that Africans living in open country were susceptible to the horizontal–vertical illusion, while dense jungle dwellers were not, implying that physical environment shapes cultural influences, which in turn affects perception.

- Gregory conducted experiments on incomplete/isolated stimuli. Real-world sensory data is richer than this and thus Gregory underestimated human ability to perceive directly.
- There is a logical sense to the theory that we make inferences based on previous experience when viewing conditions are incomplete or ambiguous.

> **perception** — the interpretation of sensory data.
>
> **direct processing** — perception arising directly from sensory input without further cognitive processing.
>
> **indirect processing** — perception involving cognitive processing beyond mere sensory input.
>
> **perceptual set** — a readiness to interpret sensory information in a preordained manner.
>
> **expectation** — perceiving what is expected based on previous experience.

Gibson's direct theory — Revised

Gibson believes that the **optic array** contains sufficient information to permit direct perception. Our movements and those of objects in an environment assist the process. Perception occurs through direct perception of invariants — constant features of the optical array. No inferences from previous experience are necessary nor is any higher information processing.

Features of the optical array:

- **Optic flow patterns** — unambiguous sources of information concerning height, distance and speed.

> **Johansson (1973)** found that a black-clad actor wearing lights, walking in a darkened room, was perceivable as a moving person, demonstrating how movement determines optic flow patterns.

- **Texture gradient** — surface patterns provide information about depth, shape etc. as well as the 'flow' of texture gradients with movement.

> **Frichtel (2006)** found that 4-month-old infants could perceive information from texture gradients, implying that the ability is innate.

- **Horizon ratios** — concern the position of objects in relation to the horizon; objects of different sizes at equal distances from an observer have different horizon ratios.

> **Creem-Regehr (2003)** found that restricting viewing conditions did not affect the ability to judge distances using horizon ratios, suggesting that these are powerful means of direct perception.

- **Affordances** — involve attaching meaning to sensory information. They concern the quality of objects to permit actions (e.g. a brush 'affords' sweeping). Affordances are directly perceivable and do not rely on experience.

> **Warren (1984)** found that the 'climbability' of stairs was deduced from the invariant properties of light reflected from staircases, supporting the idea of affordances not being reliant on experience.

- Gibson's theory explains how perception occurs so quickly, which Gregory's theory cannot.

---

optic array — the structure of patterned light received by the eyes, providing a data source rich enough for direct perception.

Typical mistakes

An independent assessment of Gregory's theory and Gibson's theory is an ineffective method of comparison. It is much more useful to compare the theories with each other, drawing out the strengths and weaknesses of each, for example in terms of research support and practical applications and even how the theories can be combined to offer a fuller understanding of perceptual organisation.

Examiner's tip

IDA material must be explained fully and related directly to the material being discussed. For instance, a practical application of Gibson's theory is the painting of parallel lines increasingly closer together on a road surface as the road approaches a junction. This gives a false impression of speed to make drivers slow down. Gaver (1996) applied the idea of affordances to designing computer displays.

Now test yourself

Tested ☐

1. Outline the role of perceptual set in Gregory's theory in terms of expectation, motivational/emotional factors and cultural influences.
2. To what extent does research support the role of perceptual set in determining perception?
3. Compile a list of evaluative points concerning Gregory's theory.
4. Outline Gibson's theory, including references to optic flow patterns, texture gradients, horizon ratios and affordances.
5. What research support is there for Gibson's theory?
6. Compile a list of evaluative points for Gibson's theory.
7. Explain two IDA points that relate to theories of perceptual organisation.

Answers on p. 122

Development of perception

Perceptual abilities

Revised

The concepts of depth and distance are involved in the perception of the environment as three-dimensional and in judging distances of objects from each other and ourselves. **Monocular** cues are apparent to one eye and **binocular** cues are apparent to both eyes. These cues are divided into primary (innate and not dependent on learning) and secondary (dependent on learning). Infants use primary cues.

Gibson and Walk (1960) found that babies would not cross an apparent vertical drop, suggesting that depth perception is innate, while Bower et al. (1970) found that new-born babies shielded their eyes at approaching objects, also suggesting that depth perception is innate.

Campos (1970) found that the heart rate of 2-month-old babies decreased when they moved across an apparent vertical drop, suggesting that depth perception is innate. Nine-month-old babies showed an increased heart rate, indicating anxiety. This suggests that depth perception is innate, but that recognition of the dangers associated with depth is learned through experience.

- It is not certain that depth perception is innate in humans because babies need to be able to crawl to be tested, by which time they have had learning experiences.

- The development of depth perception in animals appears to be related to the role of vision in the survival of their species. Depth perception is not as important for turtles, for example, because they have less to fear from falling since they are aquatic, suggesting an inherited, evolutionary component in fear of depth.

The idea of **visual constancies** concerns how objects appear to remain unchanging regardless of viewing conditions. Visual constancy has a survival value since a predictable world is safer to interact with.

The main visual constancies are size constancy, shape constancy, brightness constancy and colour constancy, with familiar objects appearing to have unchanging size, shape, brightness and colour regardless of retinal images produced and the viewing conditions.

Examiner's tip

When evaluating/commenting on the development of perception, it is good practice to include content on the nature versus nurture debate as long as the debate is explained in terms of the material being used (e.g. that the earlier perceptual abilities occur, the more they can be regarded as innate — nature). The nature versus nurture debate can also be applied to theories of perception, with Gregory's being more a theory of nurture and Gibson's more one of nature.

Imura (2008) found that sensitivity to shading and line junctions as a means of determining shape constancy appears between 6 and 7 months of age.

Bower (1966) trained infants to respond to a certain cube at a certain distance. Other cubes of differing sizes and at various distances were presented, but infants mainly responded to the cube of the same size, regardless of retinal image, suggesting that size constancy develops early on.

Dannemiller and Hanko (1987) found that infants could recognise familiar colours under some conditions but not all, indicating that colour constancy appears early in life but needs time to develop.

- A newborn baby's visual system is not well developed at birth, making it difficult to determine the presence of innate skills.

- Innate abilities may not be apparent at birth but emerge later as a result of biological maturation rather than learning.

Neonate studies

Revised

Perceptual abilities present at birth are assumed to be innate, since learning experiences have not occurred. **Neonate** studies present ethical and

neonates — newborn babies with no previous learning experiences.

practical challenges, and various methodologies have been developed, such as preference studies (demonstrating preferred stimuli), monitoring sucking, heart and breathing rates (indicating interest), reinforcement (showing recognition) and brain scans (showing neural activity).

> **Sann and Steri (2007)** found that neonates visually recognised objects they had held, but could not recognise by touch alone objects they had previously seen, indicating that sensory modes used to perceive shape constancy differ in how much they are learned or innate.
>
> **Chien (2003)** found that 4-month-old infants could judge the relative brightness of objects and their surroundings, indicating support for brightness constancy being innate.

- Neonate studies can be criticised: older infants are often used, and they may have learned perceptual abilities from experience.

- Inferences made about a neonate's perceptual world may be neither reliable nor accurate and could be vulnerable to researcher bias.

- Neonate research tends to be short term because neonates lose interest easily, making findings difficult to validate.

- Many innate perceptual abilities may emerge some time after birth, as a result of biological maturation, meaning that neonate studies may not detect them.

Typical mistakes

One common failing in examination answers is to provide evaluation as a series of unconnected points. This approach probably reflects how the material was learned. It is much more effective to build a well argued, elaborated commentary by linking evaluative points together. This is a skill that takes time to develop and you should practise it regularly throughout your studies and revision.

Cross-cultural studies ───────────────────────────── Revised ☐

If people from different cultures have similar perceptual abilities, it is assumed that those abilities are innate. Conversely, if abilities are different, it is assumed they are learned.

cross-cultural studies — research that compares people of different cultures to assess biological and environmental influences.

> **Allport and Pettigrew (1957)** found that people from Western cultures perceive the rotating trapezoid illusion, interpreting it as a window. Rural Zulus, with no experience of windows, do not perceive the illusion, supporting the idea that perceptual abilities are learned.
>
> **Turnbull (1961)** reported that a forest pygmy with no experience of long-distance cues thought distant buffalo on savannah grassland were insects, suggesting that depth cues necessary for size constancy are learned.
>
> **Montello (2006)** performed a meta-analysis of cross-cultural studies of depth/distance, finding cultural differences to be small. This suggests that these perceptual abilities are innate.

- Cross-cultural research has focused mainly on visual illusions, which may not relate to more everyday perceptual abilities.

- The use of depth cues in pictures as a research tool has been criticised, because they do not relate to the actual world.

- Cross-cultural studies are susceptible to biased interpretation, especially in terms of the culture of the researcher.

- It is difficult with cross-cultural studies to obtain similar samples and replicate methodologies exactly, decreasing the validity of findings.

Typical mistakes

Students sometimes understand a topic but apply the material wrongly when answering questions. Make sure that you know what command words such as 'outline' and 'evaluate' mean. Be aware that if a question asks only for an outline, then offering evaluative material would accrue no credit and waste valuable time. Similarly, a question asking only for evaluation requires no descriptive material, while 'discuss' means that both descriptive and evaluative material is required.

Now test yourself

8 Outline the development of (i) depth/distance perception (ii) visual constancies.

9 What evaluative points can be made concerning the development of the perceptual abilities outlined in question 8?

10 Outline what both infant and cross-cultural research have revealed about the development of perception.

11 Compile a list of evaluative points relating to research into perceptual development, including methodological and ethical points.

12 Explain two IDA points that relate to the development of perception.

Answers on p. 122

Face recognition and visual agnosias

Bruce and Young's theory of face recognition
Revised

This is a stage theory, with **face recognition** involving two different mechanisms:

- **Familiar faces** — structural encoding followed by face recognition nodes, person identity nodes and name generation.
- **Unfamiliar faces** — structural encoding followed by expression analysis, facial speech analysis and directed visual processing.

Face recognition is a holistic process involving eight independent sub-processes (components) working together, in which facial features are processed collectively (see Table 2.1). Different processing modules process different types of information (e.g. the analysis of facial characteristics to infer emotional state).

> **face recognition** — the means by which the appearances of human faces are processed and made sense of in the brain.

Table 2.1 The eight sub-components of face recognition

Type of component	Description of component
Structural encoding	Creation of descriptions and representations of faces
Expression analysis	Analysis of facial characteristics to infer emotional state
Facial speech analysis	Analysis of facial movements to comprehend speech
Directed visual processing	Selective processing of specific facial data
Facial recognition nodes	Stored structural descriptions of familiar faces
Person identity nodes	Stored information about familiar people
Name generation	Separate store for names
Cognitive storage	Extra information that aids the recognition process

Recognition of familiar faces involves matching the results of structural encoding and stored structural codes that describe familiar faces — located in the face recognition nodes — and then obtaining identity-specific semantic codes from the person identity nodes so that name codes can be retrieved. Both facial features and the configuration of features are used to recognise faces as being familiar.

Bruce and Valentine (1988) found that expressive movements, such as smiling, convey little variant information to aid identification, suggesting that invariant information is used more to perform face recognition.

Ellis et al. (1979) found that external facial features, such as hairstyles, are used to recognise unknown faces, while internal features, such as noses, are used with familiar faces. Only static pictures of faces were used, so the results may not reflect how face recognition occurs in real life.

● The theory's central idea (that face recognition is a holistic process consisting of a series of independent stages) is generally accepted, lending support to the theory.

● The theory cannot explain how unfamiliar face recognition occurs or how familiarity is achieved, weakening support for the theory.

● It is not clear how some sub-components, such as cognitive storage, work in helping to determine face recognition.

Examiner's tip

A good means of building high-level IDA evaluation into answers concerning Bruce and Young's theory is to comment on the development of practical applications, such as computer security systems that use face recognition software. The theory also illustrates how science works: since it was first proposed the theory has gone through several developments, as other psychologists comment and perform research based on it. In this way, psychology is seen as a search for verisimilitude, or closeness to the truth.

Prosopagnosia   Revised

Visual agnosias often result from stroke damage to the posterior occipital area and/or the temporal lobes of the brain, although visual systems remain undamaged. Sufferers can usually describe objects or faces in terms of features and colours etc. but cannot name them, even if they were previously familiar.

It was believed that the perception of objects and faces involved processing by the same neural mechanisms. However, case studies have indicated that there might be a specific processor for faces.

Prosopagnosia is associated with damage to the fusiform gyrus brain area, and sufferers can generally recognise objects but not faces.

There are different types and levels of prosopagnosia, indicating that each stage of face recognition can be affected, giving strength to Bruce and Young's notion that face recognition consists of sequential stages. There is no long-term effective treatment for the condition, but a fuller understanding may lead to one.

visual agnosia — a condition involving an inability to make sense of or use familiar visual stimuli.

prosopagnosia — a visual agnosia where faces can be described but not recognised.

Bauer (1984) found a patient whose galvanic skin response went up when looking at a familiar face and the correct name was read out, suggesting that although face recognition may not appear to be present at a conscious level, unconsciously it is there.

Brunsdon et al. (2006) reported on a boy who could not recognise familiar or unfamiliar faces, suggesting that his damage was at the level of structural encoding, right at the beginning of the face recognition process.

Kurucz et al. (1979) reported on prosopagnosics who could name familiar faces but could not identify their facial expression.

Bruyer et al. (1983) had a patient unable to name familiar faces but who could understand their facial expressions, suggesting that facial expression analysis and name generation are separate components of face recognition.

Campbell et al. (1986) found a prosopagnosic who was unable to name familiar faces, or identify their facial expressions, but who could perform speech analysis, suggesting that facial speech analysis, in line with the theory, is a separate component of face recognition.

Kanwisher et al. (1997) found fMRI scans suggested that face recognition involves a separate processing mechanism with the fusiform gyrus more active in face recognition than in object recognition, implying that this brain area is associated specifically with face recognition processing.

● Humphreys and Riddoch (1987) suggest that face recognition is simply a more complex form of object recognition. If so, slight damage to a general-purpose recognition system would affect object recognition less than face recognition. Supporting this is the fact that prosopagnosics tend to have slight damage to object recognition and severe damage to face recognition.

- Prosopagnosia affects face recognition in different ways, suggesting that face recognition is a holistic process of sequential, independent sub-components.
- There is a concern as to how representative case studies are of the general population, especially as they involve people with abnormal brain conditions.

Examiner's tip

If you are called on to evaluate case studies of prosopagnosia, it is a useful strategy to include material focused directly on the research method itself (e.g. that case studies are not generalisable). Such material is more effective here than in questions about explanations/theories (where it is more useful to evaluate the explanation/theory, rather than concentrating on the methodologies of related research studies).

Now test yourself

Tested ☐

13 Outline the main features of Bruce and Young's face recognition theory.

14 To what extent does research support the theory?

15 Evaluate the theory in terms of its strengths and weaknesses.

16 Outline explanations of prosopagnosia.

17 What has research revealed about prosopagnosia in terms of Bruce and Young's theory?

18 Compile a list of evaluative points relating to case studies of prosopagnosia, including methodological and ethical points.

19 Explain two IDA points that relate to face recognition/prosopagnosia.

Answers on p. 122

Exam practice

1 (a) Outline and evaluate Gregory's indirect theory of perception.   [4 + 8]

   (b) Outline and evaluate Gibson's direct theory of perception.   [4 + 8]

2 Critically compare Gregory and Gibson's theories of perceptual organisation.   [24]

3 Outline and evaluate infant and cross-cultural research into perceptual development.   [24]

4 (a) Outline Bruce and Young's theory of face recognition.   [8]

   (b) Evaluate case studies of prosopagnosia.   [16]

5 (a) Outline either the development of depth/distance perception or visual constancies.   [4]

   (b) Outline and evaluate explanations of prosopagnosia.   [4 + 8]

6 Discuss Bruce and Young's theory of face recognition.   [24]

Answers and quick quiz 2 online

Online ☐

Examiner's summary

✔ Gregory sees perception as involving cognitive processing that goes beyond sensory input, while Gibson believed perception arose directly from sensory input.

✔ Perceptual abilities vary in the degree to which they are innate and environmentally determined.

✔ Infant and cross-cultural research is conducted to assess the degree to which perception is innate or environmentally determined.

✔ Bruce and Young see face recognition as an independent, holistic process of eight sequential processing modules.

✔ Prosopagnosia is a visual agnosia where objects but not faces are recognisable. It involves damage to the fusiform gyrus brain area.

✔ Case studies of prosopagnosia give insight into face recognition.

3 Relationships

Formation, maintenance and breakdown of romantic relationships

Formation ——————————————————————————————————— Revised ☐

The sociobiological explanation

The **sociobiological explanation** of romantic relationships is an evolutionary theory with differing focus between genders. Males cannot be certain of paternity and produce lots of sperm, so their best strategy is to have multiple partners. Males value signs of fertility (such as smooth skin) and faithfulness, because they do not want to waste resources raising another man's child. Females produce few eggs but are certain of maternity. They seek genetically strong children by being selective in their choice of partner and encouraging their partner to invest resources. Females look for kindness, indicating a willingness to share resources.

> **Dunbar (1995)** analysed personal advertisements, finding that males sought youthfulness and attractiveness more than females. This supports the sociobiological idea that males and females have different reasons for forming relationships.
>
> **Davis (1990)** analysed personal advertisements, finding that men look for health and attractiveness, while offering resources. Females look for resources and status, while offering beauty and youth, supporting the evolutionary theory of gender differences in relationship formation.

- The theory is oversimplified because it presumes heterosexuality, that children are wanted and that all relationships are sexual.
- The explanation supports gender stereotypes of housebound women and sexually promiscuous males.

Reinforcement and need satisfaction

The **reinforcement and need satisfaction** theory sees conditioning as an explanation for relationship formation. Someone may reward us, directly (e.g. by meeting psychological needs for love and sex) or indirectly (e.g. because they are associated with pleasant circumstances), making us more likely to form a relationship. If we associate someone with being in a good mood, or removing a negative mood, we find them attractive, increasing the chances of relationship formation.

> **Cunningham (1988)** studied males who watched a happy or sad film, then interacted with a female. More positive interactions came from those watching the happy film, supporting the explanation.
>
> **May and Hamilton (1980)** asked females to rate photos of males, while pleasant or unpleasant music was played. Those making their choices to pleasant music rated the males as more attractive, supporting the theory.

---

sociobiological explanation of romantic relationships — perceives them to be based on evolutionary determinants.

reinforcement and need satisfaction — a behaviourist theory of relationship formation based on conditioning.

Typical mistakes

When constructing IDA (*issues, debates* and *approaches*) material in Unit 3 answers many candidates merely 'tag on' general, uninformative and poorly linked points (e.g. 'this is reductionist'). Such material should instead be specific to the area being discussed and informative (e.g. 'the sociobiological theory is reductionist, seeing relationships purely as a means of reproduction and ignoring important emotional factors, such as love, commitment and companionship').

Exam practice answers and quick quizzes at **www.therevisionbutton.co.uk/myrevisionnotes**

- The theory is best at explaining friendships, where people are generally reciprocal with their feelings, but is less successful at explaining the intricacies of long-term romantic relationships.
- The theory sees people as fundamentally selfish in trying only to satisfy their own needs. Many people have a genuine concern for the needs of others.

Maintenance

Revised ☐

Social exchange theory

The **social exchange theory** explains the maintenance of relationships in terms of maximising benefits and minimising costs. There is a mutual exchange of rewards between partners (e.g. friendship) and the costs of being in the relationship, (e.g. freedoms given up). Rewards are assessed by comparisons:

- **The comparison level (CL)** — rewards are compared to costs in order to judge profits.
- **The comparison level for alternative relationships (Clalt)** — rewards and costs are compared against the perceived rewards and costs of possible alternative relationships.

Relationships are maintained if rewards exceed costs, and if profit levels are not exceeded by possible alternative relationships.

> **Examiner's tip**
>
> Relevant IDA points to make concerning the reinforcement and need satisfaction theory are (1) that many non-Western cultures feature relationships that do not prioritise receiving rewards or fulfilling selfish needs — therefore the theory cannot account for cultural differences, and (2) the explanation does not account for gender differences — women focus more on the needs of others and males and females find different things rewarding, suggesting that the explanation is oversimplified.

> **Rusbult (1983)** found that the costs and rewards of relationships were compared to the costs and rewards of potential alternative relationships to decide if relationships should be maintained, supporting the theory.
>
> **Hatfield (1979)** looked at people who felt over or under-benefited. The under-benefited felt angry and deprived, while the over-benefited felt guilty and uncomfortable, supporting the theory by suggesting that, regardless of whether individuals are benefited, they may not desire to maintain a relationship.

- Argyle (1988) criticised methodologies used to evaluate social exchange theory, declaring them to be contrived and artificial with little relevance to real life.
- The theory applies to people who 'keep score'. Murstein et al. (1977) devised the exchange orientation tool to identify such scorekeepers, who are suspicious and insecure, suggesting that the theory suits relationships lacking confidence and mutual trust.

> **social exchange theory** — an economic explanation of relationship maintenance based on maximising profits and minimising costs.
>
> **equity theory** — an explanation of relationship maintenance based on motivation to achieve fairness and balance.

Equity theory

The **equity theory** perceives individuals as motivated to achieve fairness (equity) in their relationship and to feel dissatisfied with inequity (unfairness). Maintenance of the relationship occurs through balance and stability. Relationships where individuals put in more than they receive, or receive more than they put in, are inequitable, leading to dissatisfaction and possible dissolution.

Relationships may alternate between periods of perceived balance and imbalance, with individuals motivated to return to equity. The greater the perceived imbalance, the greater the efforts to realign relationships.

> **Yum et al. (2009)** looked at various types of heterosexual romantic relationships in different cultures. As predicted by equity theory, maintenance strategies differed, suggesting that equity theory can be applied cross-culturally.
>
> **Canary and Stafford (1992)** assessed the degree of equity in romantic relationships, finding a link between the degree of perceived equity and the prevalence of maintenance strategies, implying that equitable theories are maintained.

- Equity may be more important to females. Hoschchild and Machung (1989) found that women work harder to make relationships equitable, suggesting that the theory is gender biased.
- Mills and Clark (1982) believe that it is not possible to assess equity in loving relationships, because much input is emotional and unquantifiable and doing so diminishes the quality of love.

Dissolution

Revised

Duck's stage theory

Duck (1984) proposed a four-stage theory of **dissolution** (see Table 3.1).

> **dissolution** — the process by which romantic relationships break down.

Table 3.1 The four stages of Duck's theory

Phase of dissolution	Description
Intra-psychic phase	One partner privately perceives dissatisfaction with the relationship
Dyadic phase	The dissatisfaction is discussed If not resolved, there is a move to the next stage
Social phase	The breakdown is made public Negotiation about children, finances etc., with wider families and friends becoming involved
Grave-dressing phase	Establish post-relationship view of the break-up, protecting self-esteem and rebuilding life towards new relationship

Kassin (1996) found women more likely to stress unhappiness and incompatibility as reasons for dissolution, while men blame lack of sex. Women wish to remain friends, while males want clean breaks, implying that the model does not consider gender differences.

- The model has practical applications in counselling. Assessing which phase a couple is in helps in forming strategies to rescue relationships.
- The model is plausible, relating to many people's experiences of relationship dissolution.

Akert (1992) found that instigators of break-ups suffer less negative consequences than non-instigators, suggesting that the model does not explain individual differences in the effects of dissolution.

Lee's five-stage model

Lee (1984) proposed a five-stage model of relationship dissolution, seeing dissolution as a process occurring over time, rather than a single event (see Table 3.2).

Table 3.2 The five stages of Lee's theory

Stage of dissolution	Description
Dissatisfaction	An individual becomes dissatisfied with the relationship
Exposure	Dissatisfaction is revealed to the partner
Negotiation	Discussion occurs over the nature of the dissatisfaction
Resolution	Attempts are made to resolve the dissatisfaction
Termination	If the dissatisfaction is not resolved, the relationship ends

Lee (1984) surveyed non-marital romantic relationship breakdowns, finding that negotiation and exposure were most distressing and emotionally exhausting. Individuals who missed out stages, going straight to termination, had less intimate relationships. Those going through the stages in a lengthy and exhaustive fashion felt attracted to former partners after termination and felt lost and lonely.

Argyle and Henderson (1984) found that rule violations caused breakdowns, with jealousy, lack of tolerance for third-party relationships, disclosing confidences, not volunteering help and public criticism most critical.

- Stage theories describe the process of dissolution but do not provide explanations of why the process occurs.
- Lee only studied students in pre-marital relationships, which may not relate to long-term relationships.

Examiner's tip

A good IDA point to make concerning Duck's and Lee's models of dissolution is that they are perceived to be culturally biased, in that they do not explain cultural differences in relationship dissolution. Many non-Western cultures have arranged marriages, which are regarded as permanent and the concern of the whole family in the event of marital crisis. Another good IDA point that compares the models in terms of implications is that Lee's theory is more positive than Duck's, seeing more opportunities for problematic relationships to be saved.

Now test yourself

Tested ☐

1 Outline the following theories of relationship formation, maintenance and dissolution: (i) sociobiological (ii) reinforcement and needs (iii) social exchange (iv) equity (v) Duck (vi) Lee.
2 Provide positive and negative criticisms (evaluation) of each theory. Research support (or lack of) could be used here, as well as comparisons of theories.

Answers on pp. 122–123

Evolutionary explanations of human reproductive behaviour

Sexual selection ────────────────────────────── Revised ☐

The term **sexual selection** describes the selection of characteristics that tend to increase reproductive success, i.e. producing healthy children who survive to sexual maturity. Male and female sexual behaviours differ, because they are subject to different selective pressures.

sexual selection — the selection of characteristics increasing reproductive success.

Males produce many small, mobile sperm and can fertilise many females at little cost to reproductive potential. Males cannot be sure of paternity, so natural selection favours male behaviours that maximise the number of potential pregnancies for which they are responsible, resulting in intrasexual competition between males and polygamy (where one individual mates with many partners). Males seek signs of fertility, such as wide, childbearing hips.

Females are always sure of maternity and each egg represents a sizeable reproductive investment. Natural selection favours female behaviours that maximise the chances of potential reproductions being successful, such as careful mate selection, monogamy and high parental investment. Females seek signs of genetic fitness in potential mates (e.g. resource richness) and indulge in intersexual competition, choosing males from those available.

> **evolution** — the process of adaptation through natural selection.

Singh (1993) found that males prefer females with a waist to hip ratio of 0.7:1, suggesting choice on the basis of potential fertility.

Penton-Voak et al. (2001) found that females prefer males with greater facial symmetry, indicating developmental stability, to pass onto her sons, increasing reproductive potential.

Boone (1986) found that females prefer older males with resources.

Kenrick and Keefe (1992) found that males prefer younger females, supporting the theory.

Male strategies

> **human reproductive behaviour** — the different mating strategies used by males and females.

- **Courtship rituals** allow males to compete and display genetic potential. Miller (1997) believes that **evolution** shaped cultural aspects of behaviour (e.g. humour) to attract sexual partners.

- **Size** — males evolved to be bigger than females, demonstrating strength, to gain success against other males.

- **Sperm competition** — natural selection favoured males with larger testicles, more copious ejaculations and faster-swimming sperm.

- **Jealousy** — Buss (1993) found that males fear partners being sexually unfaithful, while females fear emotional unfaithfulness, demonstrating the male fear of cuckoldry and the female fear of partners spending resources on other females.

- **Sneak copulation** — males will mate with other females when possible. Women gain, because having different fathers brings wider genetic diversity, increasing children's survival chances.

Typical mistakes

Many candidates will offer an explanation of evolutionary theory without linking the theory to the actual topic being discussed. Ensure that in questions on this topic you link evolutionary theory specifically to the relationship between sexual selection and **human reproductive behaviour**, for example by explaining male and female strategies in terms of evolutionary theory.

Birkhead (1990) found that 8% of Zebra finch offspring came from females' matings with non-partner males, supporting the idea of sneak copulations.

Dewsbury (1984) reported that rats have a mating system where multiple males mate with females, especially at high population densities. Rats have large testicles producing copious sperm, increasing the chances of reproduction and supporting the idea of sperm competition.

- It is difficult to identify and separate the effects of sexual selection from natural selection, making research problematic.

- Evolutionary theory is often retrospective and difficult to test.

Female strategies

- **The sexy sons hypothesis** — females select attractive males to produce sons with similar attractive features, increasing reproductive fitness. Attractive male characteristics have an adaptive advantage and natural selection favours their enhancement (until the enhancement becomes bizarre, like the highly decorated bowers that male Bowerbirds construct to attract females).

- **Handicap hypothesis** — Zahavi (1975) believes that females select males with handicaps because it advertises their ability to thrive despite handicaps, demonstrating superior genetic quality. Therefore females may find males who drink alcohol or take drugs in large amounts attractive, because they are demonstrating their ability to handle toxins, a sign of genetic fitness.

Partridge (1980) allowed female fruit flies to mate freely or have forced random matings. Offspring of free-choice matings had greater competitive ability, suggesting that females improve reproductive success by selection of partners.

Moller (1992) reported that females choose males with symmetrical features, because only good genetic quality males produce them, supporting the handicap hypothesis.

- Female choosiness and male promiscuity can alternatively be explained by gender role socialisation.
- Care should be taken when generalising the findings of animal studies to humans.

Sex differences in parental investment
Revised

The gender differences shown in male and female sexual strategies have created gender differences in **parental investment** in children's chances of survival. These include:

- **Order of gamete release** — internal fertilisation gives males the chance to desert, leaving childcare duties to females. With external fertilisation the situation is reversed.
- **Paternal certainty** — with internal fertilisation, males are more likely to desert than with external fertilisation, because they are unsure of paternity.
- **Parental certainty** — maternal grandparents know that grandchildren are genetically related. Therefore, more care and resource allocation comes from maternal grandparents than paternal grandparents.
- **Monogamy** — in species with offspring born in early development, or with intensive childcare needs, pair bonds are exclusive and enduring, increasing offspring's survival chances.

> **parental investment** — resources provided by parents that increase individual offspring's survival chances at the expense of the parent's ability to invest in other children.

Pollett et al. (2007) found that maternal grandparents had more contact with grandchildren than paternal grandparents, fitting predictions of parental certainty.

Gross and Shine (1981) found that where there is internal fertilisation parental care is performed by females in 86% of species; while for reproduction with external fertilisation, parental care is carried out by males in 70% of species, supporting predictions based on paternal certainty.

- Dawkins and Carlisle (1976) found that in 36 of 46 species with simultaneous gamete release, where both sexes have equal chances of deserting, males provide the monoparental care, refuting the prediction.
- Krebs and Davies (1981) found that external fertilisation does not always lead to increased paternal certainty. In sunfishes, cuckoldry occurs during the female's egg positioning.

Now test yourself
Tested

3 Why do differences occur between males and females in terms of sexual selection?
4 Outline male and female reproduction strategies.
5 To what extent does research support these strategies?
6 Outline sex differences in sexual investment.
7 Compile a list of evaluative points, including research support, concerning sex differences in sexual investment.

Answers on p. 123

Effects of early experience and culture on adult relationships

Influence of childhood experiences Revised

Bowlby (1951) believed that the type and quality of relationships individuals have with primary caregivers provides the foundation for adult relationships by creating an **internal working model**, which acts as a template for the future. This is the **continuity hypothesis**, the belief that similar relationships will occur as an adult.

Several attachment styles are developed in infancy, providing children with a set of beliefs about themselves, others and the nature of relationships. Therefore securely/insecurely attached children will have similar relationships throughout life, even with their own children.

> **internal working model** — a template for adult relationships formed from infant attachment types with primary caregivers.
>
> **continuity hypothesis** — that infant attachment types persist into adulthood, predicting the nature of adult relationships.

Hazan and Shaver (1987) applied Bowlby's theory to adult relationships, finding that early attachment patterns affect three areas of adulthood: romantic relationships, caregiving and sexuality.

McCarthy (1999) found that women with insecure-avoidant attachments in childhood did not have successful later romantic relationships, while those with insecure-resistant attachments had poor friendships. Those with secure early attachments had successful romantic relationships and friendships, in line with the hypothesis.

- Attachment types are not as fixed as first thought. Hamilton (1994) found that securely attached children could become insecure as a result of life events.

> **temperament hypothesis** — an alternative to the continuity hypothesis that sees the quality and type of adult relationships as based on innate personality.

The **temperament hypothesis** sees the quality of adult relationships as determined biologically from innate personality, suggesting that attempts to develop better-quality relationships by changing people's attachment styles to more positive ones is unlikely to work.

The influence of culture Revised

In Western cultures, partners select one another and can enter into a **voluntary marriage**; relationships end when one or both partners wish it. In collectivist cultures, with society more important than individual needs, relationships are more permanent and often arranged by outside parties, creating a union between whole families. In two-thirds of the world, a man or his family must pay a dowry for his bride; in return he gets her labour and childbearing qualities.

> **voluntary marriage** — a relationship entered into by both partners on a free choice basis.
>
> **arranged marriage** — a union of partners organised by others than those entering into the relationship.

In multicultural societies, tensions and conflicts occur, with young people valuing individual choice more and older generations favouring traditional **arranged marriages**.

Mwamwenda and Monyooe (1997) found that 87% of Xhosa students in South Africa supported the dowry system, seeing it as a sign of the groom's appreciation for his bride.

McKenry and Price (1995) reported that in cultures where females are more independent and influential, divorce rates have risen, suggesting that the lower divorce rates seen in non-individualistic cultures are a reflection not of happy marriages but of male dominance.

- Totally arranged marriages, where the partners have no say in their union, are rare. Most partners in arranged marriages have a right to consent and the majority meet each other at social functions or through a third party.

- The dowry system protects women, because husbands are reluctant to abuse wives they have paid for. However, it is also used to justify children remaining with the husband's family in the event of divorce, the children also having been 'paid for'.

Typical mistakes

Candidates often receive lower marks when they do not use the question's command terms and mark allocations as an indicator of what and how much to write. For instance, questions with the command term 'outline' merely require descriptive material, while those with the command term 'evaluate' require evaluative material. 'Discuss' means that both description and evaluation are required. An outline carrying 8 marks will require more detail in the answer than an outline carrying 4 marks.

Examiner's tip

Relevant IDA material to supplement evaluation of the influence of culture on romantic relationships could focus on how research can involve researcher bias (e.g. seeing arranged marriages as being fundamentally inferior to voluntary marriages). You could also focus on the use of an imposed etic, where Western methodologies are applied inappropriately to research involving non-Western cultures.

Now test yourself

Tested ☐

8 Explain (a) the continuity hypothesis (b) the temperament hypothesis.
9 What evaluative points can be made concerning these hypotheses?
10 Outline cultural differences in romantic relationships.
11 What evaluative points can be made concerning cultural differences in romantic relationships?

Answers on p. 123

Exam practice

1 Outline and evaluate theories of relationship formation. [24]
2 (a) Outline one theory of relationship maintenance. [8]
   (b) Evaluate the influence of culture on romantic relationships. [16]
3 (a) Outline one theory of relationship breakdown. [4]
   (b) Discuss the influence of childhood on adult relationships. [20]
4 (a) Outline differences between the sexes in parental investment. [4]
   (b) Discuss the relationship between sexual selection and human reproductive behaviour. [24]

Answers and quick quiz 3 online

Online ☐

Examiner's summary

✔ The sociobiological explanation sees relationship formation as based on evolutionary determinants, while the 'reinforcement and need satisfaction' explanation is a behaviourist theory based on conditioning.

✔ The social exchange theory is an economic explanation of relationship maintenance focused on maximising profits and minimising costs, while equity theory is an economic explanation based on motivation to achieve fairness and balance.

✔ Both Duck and Lee see relationship breakdown as occurring in sequential stages.

✔ Sexual selection involves the evolutionary determined selection of characteristics increasing reproductive

success, leading to different mating strategies between genders.

✔ Evolutionary determined differences exist between male and female parents' investment in individual offspring, which increase the offspring's chances of achieving reproductive success, at the expense of parents' ability to invest in other children.

✔ The continuity hypothesis, supported by research, perceives infant attachment types as related to adult ones.

✔ There are culturally determined differences in adult romantic relationships.

4 Aggression

Social psychological approaches to explaining aggression

Social learning theory
Revised ☐

Social learning theory sees aggression as learned in two ways, both involving operant conditioning:

- **Direct reinforcement** — where behaviours are reinforced, making them likely to be repeated.
- **Indirect reinforcement** — where observed behaviours that are reinforced are imitated (**vicarious learning**).

Through social learning theory, humans learn the value of aggressive behaviour and how and when to imitate specific acts of aggression. Much research has been done on media influences, showing that if observers identify with the perpetrators of aggressive acts and/or the more realistic or believable aggressive acts are, the more likely it is that these acts will be imitated.

> **social learning theory** — the idea that aggression is learned through observation and imitation.
>
> **deindividuation** — the idea that aggression occurs through loss of individual identity and loosening of normal inhibitions.

> **Bandura et al. (1961, 1963)** found that children imitated aggressive acts on a Bobo doll more if the model was reinforced. Aggression was more likely if the child identified with the model or had low self-esteem. This supports social learning theory.
>
> **Williams (1981)** found that aggression increased in children after the introduction of television in Canada, suggesting that the media is an influential source of aggression.

- There are methodological issues with Bandura's research: Bobo dolls are not real, do not retaliate and are designed to be hit. There are also ethical considerations in encouraging children to be aggressive.
- Social learning theory does not account for emotional factors in aggression.
- Social learning theory explains individual and cultural differences in aggression as resulting from different learning experiences.

Deindividuation

Losing a sense of individual identity deindividuates people. Individuals normally refrain from aggression because they are identifiable, but in situations such as crowds, social restraints and personal responsibility are reduced and aggression occurs.

The normative view sees **deindividuation** as causing people unquestioningly to follow group instead of personal norms, and that this sometimes leads to aggression.

Zimbardo sees people in crowds as anonymous, with decreased awareness of individuality and reduced sense of guilt or fear of punishment. The bigger the crowd, the more this is so.

> **Watson (1973)** conducted a cross-cultural study, finding that warriors who disguised their appearance with face paint were more aggressive. This suggests that deindividuation effects are universal.
>
> **Silke (2003)** found that people in disguise perpetrated most assaults in Northern Ireland. The more severe the assault, the more likely the attacker was disguised, suggesting that disguises deindividuate people, reducing guilt and fear of punishment.

- Deindividuation in crowds can also lead to increased pro-social behaviour, as in religious gatherings.
- Deindividuation is used to explain football hooliganism. However, Marsh et al. (1978) found that mainly ritualised behaviour occurred, actual violence being rare.

Examiner's tip

When creating IDA points it is a good idea to use material concerning practical applications and ethics, because such material is generally easier to embed into the topic being discussed. For example, one practical application arising from an understanding of deindividuation is the use of closed-circuit television cameras to film crowds at football matches; they tend to reduce violence levels because the presence of the cameras make people feel they are identifiable.

Institutional aggression

Revised ☐

Institutional aggression occurs through situational and dispositional (personality) factors.

- **Instrumental aggression** — institutional groups sharing a common identity, such as the army, use aggression in non-emotive ways, as a calculated means of achieving goals.
- **Hostile aggression** — people living in institutions (e.g. jails) use aggression emerging from emotional states, such as frustration.

> **institutional aggression** — aggression that occurs as a result of being in an institutionalised setting.

Warfare

Warfare involves instrumental aggression occurring mainly through situational factors. Warfare is not uniquely human. Ant colonies wage war and research into warfare among animals led to evolutionary explanations, which see warfare arising from carnivores' hunter-killer instincts, or from group defence behaviour against predators.

Modern human warfare is particularly destructive, because aggression is not face-to-face, divorcing humans from the consequences of their actions. Opponents are dehumanised, so it is easier to aggress against them, and armies deindividuate soldiers by the use of uniforms.

> **Kruuk (1972)** reported that spotted hyenas wage war over territorial issues and kill other hyenas hunting prey on their territory, suggesting that warfare arises out of group defence mechanisms.
>
> **Goodall (1986)** reported that groups of chimpanzees wage war on others in order to kill and eat them, suggesting that warfare evolved out of group hunting skills.

- Ardrey (1961) argued that human warfare arose out of the evolution of group hunting skills to catch prey.
- Ehrenreich (1997) argued that warfare arose from humans collectively protecting themselves from attackers and the perception of threatened attacks. In the American 'Indian Wars', settlers wiped out indigenous peoples because they were perceived as potential attackers.

Terrorism

Terrorism emanates from cultural and sub-cultural clashes and is a form of minority influence, where minority groups seek to effect social change by altering majority views. Behaviour and beliefs are consistent and persistent, leading to gradual changes in public opinion.

Terrorism justifies aggression through 'collective responsibility' (e.g. the targeting of random civilians by suicide bombers).

> **Ministry of Defence Report (2005)** found that the majority of Iraqis privately, but not publicly, supported the terrorist insurgency, reinforcing the view that terrorism is a form of minority influence.
>
> **Barak (2004)** reported that terrorists are generally exhibiting suppressed anger and have experienced economic and political marginalisation, suggesting that terrorism has its roots in cultural and sub-cultural clashes.

● It is debatable whether terrorism results from economic and political marginalisation. Many terrorists, such as the Baader-Meinhof gang, were university educated and from affluent families.

● The idea that there is a 'typical' terrorist is simplistic. It is more probable that a range of explanations are needed to describe the variety of terrorist groups and actions, including instrumental and hostile acts, encompassing both situational and dispositional factors.

Now test yourself

1 Outline how aggression can be acquired through (i) SLT (ii) deindividuation.
2 Assess the value of SLT and deindividuation through research support, IDA and other evaluative points.
3 Explain what is meant by (i) hostile aggression (ii) instrumental aggression.
4 Outline (i) warfare (ii) terrorism as explanations of institutional aggression.
5 What evaluative points can be made concerning warfare and terrorism?

Answers on p. 123

Tested

Biological explanations of aggression

Biological explanations view aggression as having internal physiological causes. Biological factors in aggression can be perceived as sole causes or as working in conjunction with other factors.

> **biological explanations of aggression** — those referring to physiological causes.

Neural and hormonal influences   Revised

The neurotransmitter **serotonin** and the hormone **testosterone** are associated with aggression.

Serotonin

Low levels of serotonin are associated with increased levels of aggression (and high levels with reduced aggression).

> **serotonin** — a neurotransmitter linked to heightened aggression.
>
> **testosterone** — a hormone often associated with heightened aggression.

> **Delville et al. (1997)** found that drugs increasing serotonin production lead to reduced levels of aggression, suggesting that low levels of serotonin are linked to increased aggression.
>
> **Huber et al. (1997)** argued that reducing serotonin activity in many species, from crustaceans to humans, increases aggression, further supporting the idea that reduced levels of serotonin are linked to increased aggression.
>
> **Popova et al. (1991)** found that animals selected for domesticity because of reduced aggression levels had lower serotonin levels than wild, more aggressive counterparts.

● Evidence linking low levels of serotonin and aggression is correlational and does not indicate causality.

Examiner's tip

A useful means of incorporating IDA material into answers concerning hormonal and neural mechanisms in aggression would be to comment on how such mechanisms perceive aggression as being biologically determined and thus ignore the role of free will (in the form of self-control) that individuals can exercise in behaving (or not behaving) aggressively.

Testosterone

Testosterone is associated with males. Castration lowers testosterone levels and reduces aggression.

If testosterone is given to females, their levels of aggression increase, although these effects are not universal, with some research failing to find links between heightened testosterone levels and aggression.

Testosterone modulates the levels of various neurotransmitters that mediate effects on aggression. There is a critical period early in life when exposure to testosterone is essential to elicit aggression in adulthood. It is believed that testosterone helps to sensitise an androgen responsive system (a system responsive to male hormones).

Higley et al. (1996) reported that individuals with elevated testosterone levels exhibit signs of aggression but rarely commit aggressive acts, suggesting that social and cognitive factors play mediating roles.

Edwards (1968) found that giving testosterone to neonate female mice made them act like males, with increased aggression, when given testosterone as adults. However, control females only given testosterone as adults did not react like this, suggesting that testosterone masculinises androgen-sensitive neural circuits underlying aggression in the brain.

- Castration research indicates reduced aggression. However, castration also disrupts other hormone systems, so these may be playing a part. One problem with studying animals is that certain brain structures are involved with different types of aggression in different species, creating problems in generalising findings to humans.
- Results from human studies are often subjective, relying on questionnaires and observations.

Role of genetic factors

The monoamine oxidase A (MAOA) **gene**, which helps to eliminate excess amounts of neurotransmitters such as serotonin and dopamine, is implicated, as well as the sex chromosome gene Sry.

genes — regions of DNA (deoxyribonucleic acid) seen as controlling hereditary characteristics.

Rissman et al. (2006) investigated Sry, a gene leading to the development of testes and high androgen levels in males. Male and female mice with and without the gene were tested, with the Sry gene being associated with high levels of aggression, suggesting that genes and hormones interact and that sex chromosome genes also play a role.

Brunner et al. (1993) studied a family where all the males had a mutant form of the MAOA gene. All reacted aggressively when angry, fearful or frustrated, suggesting that abnormal MAOA activity is associated with aggression.

- Generalising from animals to humans is problematic, because similar results are not always found. For example, mice lacking the HTR1B gene, associated with serotonin production, have elevated levels of aggression, but humans do not.
- Drug treatments may be possible for people with the low-level activity version of the MAOA gene to help control aggressive urges. However, drug treatments have not proved successful, suggesting that other non-biological factors may be involved.

Typical mistakes

When answering questions about neural and/or hormonal factors in aggression many candidates offer material on genetics. Such material will not earn marks unless it is specifically linked to neural/hormonal factors, such as the link between the MAOA gene and serotonin and dopamine.

6 Outline the role of serotonin and testosterone in aggression.

7 (a) What research support do hormonal and neural mechanisms have as explanations of aggression?

   (b) What other evaluative points can be made about hormonal and neural mechanisms? Try to include IDA material in your answer.

8 To what extent are genetic factors associated with aggression?

Answers on p. 123

Evolution and human aggression

Evolutionary explanations of human aggression — Revised

Aggression is seen as having an adaptive advantage, becoming widespread through natural selection.

Lorenz (1966) saw aggression as an instinct that has evolved into rituals (e.g. males' dominance fights), thus protecting animals from incurring harm, because one animal generally backs down.

Evolutionary theory sees aggression as a means of solving adaptive problems over a wide range of behaviours, between and within species:

- **Between species:** prey animals use aggression to defend themselves and their offspring by evolving the ability to gauge the strength of predators. The 'flight or fight' response is dependent on this calculation. Altruistic alarm calls alerting others to the presence of predators have also evolved as a prey defence mechanism.

- **Within species:** aggression between members of one species serves several purposes, such as establishing dominance hierarchies. Males compete for access to females and so are more aggressive towards one another.

evolutionary explanations of aggression — focus on its role in increasing survival chances and reproductive success.

jealousy — an emotional response to anticipated loss of affection and/or status.

Jealousy

The emotional response of **jealousy** is characterised by feelings of resentfulness, bitterness and envy. Jealousy can motivate aggressive behaviours through:

- **male–male rivalries** — males compete for access to females, often in ritualised ways

- **female–female rivalries** — females compete to be attractive and criticise other females' appearances, because males value attractiveness as a sign of fertility

- **sibling rivalry** — siblings compete for parental resources to maximise adaptive fitness

Daly and Wilson (1988) reported that male–male aggressive rivalries are found among young males in most cultures, suggesting that the behaviour is universal as a result of evolution.

Buss and Dedden (1990) found that females criticise the appearance and sexual promiscuity of other females, to reduce potential rivals' attractiveness and raise their own, in line with evolutionary theory.

- Harris (2004) believes that sibling jealousy evolved to maximise parental resources and that this explains the origins of jealousy better than infidelity.
- The tendency towards aggression over minor territorial disputes between neighbours is explained in evolutionary terms as territorial defensive behaviour involving male–male rivalries.

Infidelity

Males are not sure of paternity and so fear signs of sexual **infidelity** in females, such as smiling at other men, which triggers sexual jealousy and initiates aggression to ensure sole access. Male sexual infidelity does not threaten females' certainty of maternity, but females are jealous of male emotional involvement with other women, where resources are spent on them, because the female prefers the resources to be spent on her and her children. Jealousy can also be initiated by the presence of younger, attractive women.

> **Typical mistakes**
>
> In questions that ask candidates about infidelity and/or jealousy, it is essential that answers are focused on how these factors relate to aggression. Many candidates offer well-written, knowledgeable answers about jealousy and infidelity without linking them to aggression. Such answers will not gain much credit.

> **infidelity** — the sexual and emotional unfaithfulness of romantic partners.

Buss et al. (1992) found that males had higher stress levels when viewing pictures of sexual infidelity, while females had higher stress levels when viewing pictures of emotional infidelity, suggesting that different environmental cues trigger aggression in males and females.

Goetz et al. (2008) found that men's violence against intimate partners punishes and deters sexual infidelity, its frequency being related to suspicions of infidelity.

- Harris (2003) found that Buss et al.'s findings are true of imagined scenarios, but in reality both genders feel threatened by emotional infidelity. The results from imagined scenarios might be explained as males being aroused by images of sexual infidelity, rather than feeling threatened.
- Critics feel that evolutionary explanations justify violence by men against women as natural and inevitable.

Explanations of group display in humans
Revised

Sport

Group displays help to determine dominance hierarchies over ownership of territory and aim to intimidate other groups.

- **War dances** — intimidate and motivate (e.g. the New Zealand *haka*) Supporter displays achieve the same ends, for example the wearing of club colours, face painting and the singing of club anthems. Such displays increase social identity, as do the use of dance troupes and mascots.
- **Territorial behaviour** — group displays mark out and defend territories, such as team supporters congregating in traditional areas.
- **Ritual behaviour** — much of the aggression shown between sports fans is ritualistic; posturing and verbal abuse occurs but little actual violence, suggesting a symbolic show of strength to limit injuries.

> **group displays** — ritualised displays (e.g. of aggression).

Schwarz and Barkey (1977) found that teams win more home games, due to social support of supporters, suggesting that group displays are a factor in success.

Morris (1981) studied Oxford United fans, home and away, finding their behaviour territorial and ritualised, which suggests that group displays serve a social purpose.

- Marsh (1982) believed that if ritual aggressive practices between fans were curtailed, violence rates would increase.

- The universal nature of war dances cross-culturally in sport suggests that the behaviour may have an evolutionary component related to ritualised aggression.

Lynch mobs

Lynch mobs involve unlawful group action resulting in death.

Evolutionary theory sees a dominant group's use of lynching against minorities as adaptive because it lessens the chances of minorities becoming stronger and reducing the status of the dominant group. Much lynching of blacks by white mobs in the USA was due to the perceived fear of black men impregnating white women, causing the reproduction of black genes at the expense of whites.

> **Blalock (1967)** found that as minority group size increases, majority groups work harder to retain dominance, supporting the evolutionary explanation of lynching.
>
> **Tolnay and Beck (1995)** reported that the fear of increased black power led white mobs to use lynchings as social control, which suggests that lynchings are an evolved adaptation to perceived threats.

- Evolutionary explanations are supported by perpetrators of lynchings having more reproductive success, leading to genes for such behaviour becoming more widespread.
- Dehumanisation is a powerful factor here, like debasing blacks as 'niggers', thus 'justifying' acts of aggression against them.

Typical mistakes

Candidates using material on lynch mobs to answer questions on evolutionary explanations of group displays in humans should be aware that many textbooks offer other non-evolutionary explanations of this phenomenon. The specification has changed and now focuses solely on evolutionary explanations. Therefore non-evolutionary explanations will gain credit only if used specifically as a comparison to evolutionary explanations.

Examiner's tip

A good way of incorporating IDA material into answers concerning group displays in sport — answers that are fully embedded into the topic and thus creditworthy — is to comment on possible alternative explanations. For instance, that although group displays may be a factor in aggression levels related to sports events, there are other explanatory factors too, including biological and cognitive ones. Giving brief, relevant examples would also be a good idea.

Now test yourself

Tested ☐

9 Outline the means by which evolutionary theory explains human aggression.

10 How can jealousy and infidelity be seen as explanations of aggression?

11 Assess the value of jealousy and infidelity as explanations of aggression through research support, IDA and other evaluative points.

12 In what ways are group displays evident in sport?

13 What evaluative points, including research support and IDA material, can be made concerning group displays in sport?

14 How does evolution explain lynch mobs?

15 To what extent does research and evaluation support the evolutionary view of lynchings?

Answers on p. 123

Exam practice

1 (a) Outline two social psychological theories of aggression.   [8]

   (b) Evaluate one of the theories outlined in 1(a).   [16]

2 Outline and evaluate explanations of institutional aggression.   [24]

3 (a) Outline the role of hormonal and/or neural mechanisms in aggressive behaviour.   [4]

   (b) Outline and evaluate the role of genetic factors in aggressive behaviour.   [20]

4 Discuss evolutionary explanations of human aggression.   [24]

5 (a) Outline two evolutionary explanations of group display in humans.   [8]

   (b) Evaluate one of the explanations outlined in 5 (a).   [16]

Answers and quick quiz 4 online

Online ☐

Examiner's summary

✔ Social learning theory sees aggression as learned through observation and imitation, while deindividuation sees aggression as occurring via loss of individual identity and the loosening of normal inhibitions.

✔ Institutional aggression perceives aggression as resulting from being in an institutionalised environment.

✔ Neural and hormonal mechanisms and genetic factors of aggression see aggression as arising through biological means.

✔ Evolutionary explanations see aggression as possessing an adaptive advantage, with gender differences in jealousy and infidelity related to mating behaviour.

✔ Group displays involve ritualised displays of aggression, which evolutionary explanations see as bestowing a survival value.

5 Eating

Eating behaviour

Attitudes to food and eating behaviour Revised

Eating is essential for survival. Many factors influence attitudes to food and eating, the three prime ones being **mood**, **cultural influences** and **health concerns**.

Mood

Emotional states affect eating practices, either in small ways or in ways that explain abnormal eating behaviour, such as binge eating.

> **Wansink et al. (2008)** offered popcorn and grapes to participants, finding that people watching a sad film ate more popcorn to cheer themselves up while those watching a comedy ate more grapes to prolong their mood.
>
> **Wolff et al. (2000)** found that female binge eaters had more negative moods on binge-eating days than female normal eaters, suggesting that negative moods are related to abnormal eating.

> **mood** — emotional states that affect practical behaviour (e.g. eating).
>
> **cultural influences** — practices that are transmitted by and to members of cultural groupings (e.g. eating practices).
>
> **health concerns** — attitudes generated by the desire to promote bodily health (e.g. eat in a nutritionally beneficial way).

Cultural influences

Different cultural and sub-cultural groups have different eating practices, transmitted to group members via reinforcement and social learning. Cultural attitudes to the health concerns surrounding food and eating also vary. Culture influences eating behaviour directly, but more usually it does so by moderating other variables to determine individual eating practices.

> **Stefansson (1960)** found that the Copper Eskimos, who lived on flesh and roots, were disgusted by sugar, suggesting that sweet tastes are not necessarily universal to all cultures.
>
> **McFarlane and Pliner (1987)** found that only sub-cultural groups who consider nutrition to be important prefer healthy food. But this is mediated by socioeconomic factors — if healthy food is expensive, low-income groups will not eat healthily.

Health concerns

The desire to eat nutritious food and avoid unhealthy diets affects attitudes and behaviour. There are differences between individuals and cultural groupings.

> **Monneuse et al. (1991)** found that people with preferences for high sugar content in dairy products chose items with lower sugar content, suggesting that health concerns do affect eating behaviour.
>
> **Tuorila and Pangborn (1988)** found that women had intentions to eat healthily, but that actual consumption of dairy products and high-fat foods was influenced more by the sensory qualities of food, showing that attitudes do not necessarily reflect behaviour.

- Research on mood states suggests that comfort foods should display nutritional information to stop depressed people eating badly; such habits can contribute to people becoming bulimic.

- Research findings could be used to create eating programmes that shape and maintain healthy dietary practices, such as the way information about healthy eating is presented and which groups are targeted.
- For a fuller understanding of eating behaviour, both nurture and nature need to be considered: that is, the effects of learning experiences and innate food preferences.

Success and failure of dieting — Revised

Dieting involves voluntary restriction of food intake. Wing and Hill (2001) defined success as 'successful long-term weight loss, involving the intentional loss of at least 10% of initial body weight and keeping it off for at least one year'.

Dieters differ in the extent to which eating is restrained and for how long, and these factors also affect success levels.

> **dieting** — restraint of eating that involves voluntary restriction of food intake.
>
> **calories** — the energy content of food.

Explanations for success

Success involves learning skills for weight maintenance. If weight loss is maintained for 2 years, the chances of long-term success increase dramatically.

- **Relapse prevention** — involves achieving a stable energy balance around a lower weight. It involves identifying situations in which 'lapses' occur and how to 'refocus' if they do.
- **Motivation** — financial incentives act as positive reinforcement, and social networks are beneficial in eliciting support from others. Role models create a positive social identity, crucial for success.
- **Goal-setting** — success requires achievable targets, with goal-setting consisting of short-term goals leading to the long-term goal. Initial targets are easy, increasing confidence and motivation. Dieters are involved in target setting, to create a sense of 'ownership'.

Miller-Kovach et al. (2001) reported that the social support methods offered by WeightWatchers® are superior to individual dieting regimes.

Bartlett (2003) found that dieting success occurs with a reduction of between 500 and 1000 **calories** per day, supporting the idea that achievable goal setting is a motivational force.

Explanations for failure

Unsustainable diets fail — initial weight loss slows and weight is regained. The more restrictive the diet, the more likely it is to fail. Unpleasant side effects, such as stress, create motivational loss and abandonment. Dieters perceive dieting as temporary, then return to old eating habits and regain weight.

The hormone ghrelin plays a biological role in failure, stimulating appetite and thus making hungry people even hungrier during dieting, increasing chances of abandonment. Cognitive factors also apply; a lessening of concentration is associated with failure.

Cummings et al. (2002) found that low-calorie diets stimulate appetite by increasing ghrelin production, reducing the chances of losing weight. The success of stomach-reduction surgery may be due to smaller stomachs producing less ghrelin.

Williams et al. (2002) found that people lacking concentration are unsuccessful, because they lose focus on targets and strategies, indicating cognitive factors to be important.

Examiner's tip

A useful IDA point concerning successful dieting could centre on how research findings may lead to strategies for dieting that successfully treat obesity. Such a point could also be used in questions about eating disorders if using material on obesity. In addition, Nolen-Hoeksema's findings about dieting and mental disorders could be used to make the point that low-fat dietary products should display warnings about such risks.

- Individual differences are also important. 'Low-restrainers' find dieting easy, while 'high-restrainers' find it difficult because they are hypersensitive to food cues and thus likely to abandon diets.
- Dieting can lead to mental disorders. Nolen-Hoeksema (2002) found that females on low-fat diets develop negative moods and so overeat, with 80% developing depression.

Now test yourself

Tested

1 Outline and evaluate how (i) mood (ii) cultural influences (iii) health concerns affect attitudes to eating. Include research evidence and IDA material in your evaluations.
2 Define (i) dieting (ii) successful dieting.
3 (a) Outline explanations for successful dieting.
   (b) What research support do these explanations have?
4 (a) Outline explanations for unsuccessful dieting.
   (b) What research support do these explanations have?
   (c) What other evaluative points can be made concerning dieting?

Answers on p. 123

Biological explanations of eating behaviour

The role of neural mechanisms

Revised

The hypothalamus is the hunger centre of the brain. The **ventromedial hypothalamus** (VMH) and the **lateral hypothalamus** (LH) feature in the **dual-control theory** and **set-point theory**.

The hypothalamus is part of the limbic system, linking the nervous system to the endocrine system. It acts like a 'thermostat' to initiate or stop eating behaviour.

Dual-control theory

This theory is a **homeostatic** view of hunger and satiety. When glucose levels fall, the LH is activated, causing hunger and motivating a person to eat, which releases glucose. This activates the VMH, leading to a feeling of satiety, and eating stops.

> **Hetherington and Ranson (1940)** found that **lesions** in the VMH lead to overeating and weight gain.
>
> **Anad and Brobeck (1951)** found that lesions in the LH lead to undereating and weight loss, supporting dual-control theory.
>
> **Stellar (1954)** found that stimulating the VMH decreases eating, but VMH lesions increase eating; while the LH, when stimulated and lesioned, produces the opposite effects, supporting dual-control theory.

- Lesioned VMH rats overeat and temporarily gain weight, after which body weight stabilises. Dual-control theory cannot explain this because lesioned VMH rats achieve satiety even though their satiety centre is supposedly absent.

neural mechanisms — the influence of brain components on behaviour (e.g. regulating eating behaviour).

ventromedial hypothalamus — brain region associated with the cessation of eating.

lateral hypothalamus — brain region associated with hunger and the onset of eating.

dual-control theory — a homeostatic view of eating, whereby hunger motivates eating, which in turn leads to satiety and cessation of eating.

lesions — damaged brain tissue.

set-point theory — each individual is orientated biologically to a specific body weight.

- Lesioned LH rats do not eat or drink and temporarily lose weight, after which eating ability is regained, even though they have supposedly lost their hunger centre. Dual-control theory cannot explain this.

Set-point theory

This theory explains the long-term effects of lesioning the VMH and LH, with the VMH and LH perceived as controlling body weight by a set-point mechanism. Lesioning the LH lowers the set-point for body weight, with body weight being maintained at a lower level than before. Lesioning the VMH heightens the set-point, body weight being maintained at a higher level than before.

> **Powley and Keesey (1970)** found that rats that had lost weight through starvation and then had lesions made to their LH did not lose further weight. This indicates that the rats had slimmed down to a new set-point before the lesions were made, supporting set-point theory.
>
> **Proc and Frohman (1970)** found that rats made obese through VMH lesioning and then force-fed to increase body weight lost weight when fed normally, supporting set-point theory, because the rats returned to their new increased set-point.

- Neural mechanisms are complex. Ungerstedt (1971) found that lesioning the nigrostriatal tract, an area outside the LH, also stops eating.
- Perceiving the VMH as a satiety centre and the LH as a hunger centre is simplistic. Lesions to the LH also produce disruptions to aggression levels and sexual behaviour.

Evolutionary explanations of food preference

Revised

Food preferences have evolved because they have an adaptive value. Most human evolution occurred during the **Pleistocene era** when food was only available periodically. Therefore humans evolved to favour energy-rich foods and store excess as fat for times of scarcity. We still exhibit these tendencies, even though food is available perpetually. Food preferences therefore reflect the need for energy, stored nutrition and the necessity to avoid toxins.

Sweet tastes indicate high-energy foods and non-toxicity and through natural selection became a universal food preference.

> **De Araujo et al. (2008)** found that mice that could not taste sweetness preferred sugar solution to non-calorific sweeteners, suggesting that the preference is based not on sweetness but on calorific content.

- A fondness for sweetness is common in the animal kingdom, lending support to it being an evolutionary preference.

Bitter tastes indicate toxicity. Plants produce toxins to discourage animals from eating them. It is therefore evolutionarily beneficial to develop an ability to detect and avoid bitter tastes.

> **Mennella (2008)** found children to be more sensitive to bitter tastes than adults, suggesting an innate preference, which explains why children do not like bitter-tasting vegetables and bitter medicines.

- 35% of children (but few adults) have a preference for sour tastes, suggesting that they are less food neophobic and will sample a greater variety of foods, incurring a selective advantage.

Salty tastes. Humans need sodium chloride — without it we would dehydrate and die. A high sodium concentration is required in the bloodstream to maintain nerve and muscle activity.

evolutionary explanation of food preferences — food preferences have a survival value and have occurred through natural selection.

Pleistocene era — the period of time over which most human evolution occurred (also known as the 'environment of evolutionary adaptiveness' — EEA).

Examiner's tip

A good IDA point to make concerning bitter taste preferences is that there is a practical application of the research in the production of children's medicines. These can have sweet tastes added to make them palatable, preventing children from vomiting due to the taste, suggesting toxicity, and thus not recovering from their illnesses.

Dudley et al. (2008) found that ants in inland, salt-poor environments prefer salty solutions to sugary ones, seemingly an adaptive response to maintain their evolutionary fitness.

- There are individual differences in salt preferences, which is puzzling because evolution would predict a standard universal preference.

Meat is high in protein and energy-rich fat. Group hunting skills made meat more available and cooking more palatable. Meat is associated with a growth in human intelligence. Hunting was dangerous and meat eating risky, because meat can be toxic and incur transmittable diseases.

Foley and Lee (1991) compared brain size with primate feeding strategies, concluding that meat eating led directly to the process of encephalisation (increased brain mass relative to body size). This suggests that evolution favoured meat eating in humans.

- Dunn (1990) reports that human dental structures and digestive systems are closer to those of herbivores than carnivores, and that true carnivores eat meat raw, guts and all, suggesting no evolutionary preference for meat eating.

Now test yourself

5 (a) Explain (i) dual-control theory (ii) set-point theory.
   (b) What research support do these theories have?
   (c) What other evaluative points can be made about these theories?
6 Explain why food preferences may have an adaptive value.
7 (a) Explain why (i) sweet tastes (ii) bitter tastes (iii) salty tastes (iv) meat eating may have evolved.
   (b) What evaluative points, including research evidence, can be made concerning the above food preferences?

Answers on pp. 123–124

Tested

Eating disorders

Psychological explanations

Revised

Psychodynamic explanation

Obesity is seen as due to unresolved conflicts, such as emotional deprivation during the oral stage of childhood, with the libido becoming locked on to oral gratification. Obesity is also linked to other factors explicable by psychodynamic means, such as depression.

Felliti (2001) reported on five cases of sleep-eating obesity (eating food while asleep). All had suffered abuse in childhood and their behaviour was interpreted as an unconscious anxiety reducer, backing up the theory.

- Most obese people have not suffered abuse and do not indulge in sleep eating, casting doubt on the explanation.
- Obesity is widespread, but there is no evidence of a parallel rise in unresolved childhood conflicts, casting doubt on the explanation.
- Cases of depression linked to obesity could be an effect of obesity rather than a cause.

Cognitive explanations

Cognitive theories see obesity as occurring through maladaptive thought processes, with information processing having an elevated focus for food-related stimuli.

Braet and Crombez (2001) found that obese children were hypersensitive to food-related words, suggesting an information-processing bias for food stimuli, leading to obesity.

Cserjesi et al. (2007) examined cognitive profiles of obese boys, finding them deficient in attention capabilities, suggesting that childhood obesity involves cognitive deficits.

psychodynamic explanation of obesity — that it results from unresolved childhood conflicts.

obesity — the condition of being chronically overweight.

cognitive explanation of obesity — that it results from maladaptive thought processes concerning food and eating.

- Attention deficits may be an effect of being obese. Elias (2003) found that early-onset, long-term obesity leads to a decline in cognitive functioning, weakening the cognitive explanation for obesity.
- The success of therapies based on the cognitive approach suggests that cognitive factors may be involved in developing obesity. O'Rourke et al. (2008) found that cognitive-behavioural therapy significantly improved weight loss.

Biological explanations
Revised

Neural explanations

The hypothalamus, identified with playing a role in the regulation of eating, is associated with the development of obesity. Specific neural circuits have been investigated, as well as associated hormones and neurotransmitters.

> **neural explanation of obesity** — that it results from brain mechanisms.

Stice et al. (2008) reported that obese people have fewer dopamine receptors in the brain. They overeat to compensate for having a poorly functioning dorsal striatum, leading to lessened dopamine signalling in the brain. This implies that the neurotransmitter dopamine is linked to obesity.

Reeves and Plum (1969) conducted a post-mortem on an obese female, finding that her VMH had been destroyed. This suggests that the hypothalamus is associated with the development of obesity.

- The evidence linking dopamine to obesity tends to be correlational, so it is not clear if dopamine is a cause or an effect of being obese.

Evolutionary explanations

Human eating habits are more suited to the Pleistocene era, during which food was not available universally. Humans evolved to find high-calorie foods desirable and to store excess energy as fat for times of scarcity. Humans also evolved to minimise physical activity to preserve fat stores. Therefore humans are not suited to a sedentary world of ever-available fatty foods and are vulnerable to overeating foods that were not present in their evolutionary past, because such foods do not trigger the neural mechanisms that control appetite.

> **evolutionary explanation of obesity** — that it results from a selective advantage in storing excess calories as fat.

The **thrifty gene model** believes that there was a selective advantage for people with insulin resistance because they could metabolise food more efficiently. This was advantageous in times of food scarcity, but now that food is always available it leads to obesity.

DiMeglio and Mates (2000) found that participants put on more weight when given liquid calories rather than an equal amount of solid calories, supporting the idea that liquid calories have caused the increase in obesity because we are not shaped by evolution to cope with them.

Rowe et al. (2007) studied Pima Indians who have high levels of obesity, concluding that they have a thrifty metabolism allowing them to metabolise food more efficiently. Once an advantage in times of food scarcity, it now leads to obesity, supporting the thrifty gene hypothesis.

- The thrifty gene hypothesis explains why people who do not have the gene are able to eat a lot and not put on weight.
- Evolutionary theory offers a plausible explanation for modern levels of obesity and why people find it difficult to lose weight. Humans are designed to consume as much as possible and lay down fat stores.

Examiner's tip

It is generally easier to create IDA material that is specifically embedded (relevant) in a topic if it concerns practical applications and ethical concerns. Therefore a good point to make concerning any explanation of obesity (or any eating disorder for that matter) is that increased knowledge about the condition may lead to effective treatments that properly address the serious effects of obesity.

8 Outline the following explanations of obesity: (i) psychodynamic (ii) cognitive (iii) neural (iv) evolutionary.

9 What evaluative points, including research evidence and IDA points, can be made about each of the above explanations?

Answers on p. 124

Exam practice

1	Outline and evaluate factors influencing attitudes to food and eating behaviour.	[24]
2	(a) Outline and evaluate explanations for the success of dieting.	[12]
	(b) Outline and evaluate explanations for the failure of dieting.	[12]
3	Outline and evaluate evolutionary explanations of food preference.	[24]
4	Discuss evolutionary explanations of food preference.	[24]
5	(a) Outline and evaluate one psychological explanation of one eating disorder.	[12]
	(b) Outline the neural explanation of one eating disorder.	[4]
	(c) Outline and evaluate the evolutionary explanation of one eating disorder.	[20]

Answers and quick quiz 5 online

Examiner's summary

✔ Several factors affect attitudes to food and eating behaviour, including mood, cultural influences and health concerns.

✔ Explanations for the failure of diets centre on restraint theory, as well as over-restrictive diets and cognitive and biological factors, while dieting success involves losing weight in a realistic and sustainable fashion.

✔ Neural mechanisms see eating as regulated by brain mechanisms, while evolutionary explanations see food preferences as possessing an adaptive advantage.

✔ Psychological explanations see obesity as arising from psychodynamic and cognitive means, while biological explanations see obesity as occurring through neural means and as having an evolved adaptive advantage.

6 Gender

Psychological explanations of gender development

Kohlberg's cognitive developmental theory
Revised

Kohlberg (1966) sees **gender** concepts as occurring through environmental interactions, restricted by cognitive capabilities at a given time. Kohlberg proposed three stages in which children attain increasingly sophisticated gender concepts, a new stage only appearing after thinking has matured to a certain point. Consequently, children understand gender differently at different ages, with gender concepts developing as children actively structure their social experiences (see Table 6.1). It is not, therefore, a passive social learning process occurring through observation and imitation.

gender — the social and psychological characteristics of males and females.

After **gender consistency** is reached, children start to develop gender concepts that suit their own gender.

Table 6.1 Kohlberg's stages of gender development

Approximate age	Stage	Description
2–3 years	Gender identity	Knowing who is a boy and a girl, including oneself
4–5 years	Gender stability	Knowing that gender is fixed and that boys become men and girls become women
5–7 years	Gender consistency	Knowing that gender is constant regardless of changes (e.g. haircuts, clothes etc.)

Frey and Ruble (1992) informed children that certain toys were either 'boy' or 'girl' toys. Boys who had achieved gender constancy chose 'boy' toys, even when uninteresting; girls of the same stage exhibited similar tendencies, but to a lesser degree.

Thompson (1975) found that by 2 years of age children could self-label and identify the gender of others. By 3 years, 90% showed gender identity, compared to 76% of 2 year-olds, showing the developmental nature of the concept.

- The theory concentrates on cognitive factors and therefore overlooks cultural and social influences, such as parents and friends.
- Children demonstrate and reward gender-appropriate behaviours in peers before they reach gender constancy, casting doubt on Kohlberg's idea of universal stages of development.

Gender schema theory
Revised

According to **gender schema theory** (Martin and Halverson, 1981; Bem, 1981) children develop gender concepts by cognitively processing information from social interactions, leading to the construction of gender schemas — organised groupings of related concepts.

Once a child has a basic gender identity, he/she accumulates knowledge about the **sexes** and organises this into a gender schema, which influences behaviour. In-group schemas form, concerning attitudes and expectations about the same gender, as well as out-group schemas about the other gender. This leads to favouring the same gender and actively ignoring the other gender. Toys, games and objects become categorised as boys' or girls' toys. Children now participate in same-sex activities and gender-consistent behaviour begins, with gender stereotypes reinforced due to only being exposed to same-sex concepts through social interactions. The theory predicts that, in addition to the development of gender understanding, there is an increase in sex-specific behaviour.

> **Masters et al. (1979)** found that children aged between 4 and 5 selected toys by their gender (boy/girl toy), rather than by which gender was seen playing with the toy, indicating the formation of gender schemas.
>
> **Aubry et al. (1999)** found that once a belief had taken hold that an item was for the opposite sex, a reduced preference for that item developed, implying that gender schemas do affect behaviour.

- Gender schema theory offers a plausible compromise between social learning and cognitive developmental theories.
- The theory explains why children's attitudes and behaviour concerning gender are rigid and lasting. Children focus on anything confirming and strengthening their schemas and ignore behavioural examples that contradict them.
- The theory neglects the influence of biological factors, assuming all gender-orientated behaviour is created through cognitive means.

gender schema — a means of understanding gender knowledge that changes with environmental experience.

sex — whether an individual is biologically male or female.

Now test yourself

1 Summarise the main points of (i) Kohlberg's theory, including his three stages (ii) gender schema theory, including developmental changes.

2 In what ways are the two theories similar and dissimilar?

3 Evaluate both theories in terms of their strengths and weaknesses. Include research evidence and IDA material in your evaluation.

Answers on p. 124

Tested ☐

Typical mistakes

Many candidates learn and revise topics such as psychological explanations of gender development as separate theories. However, an excellent means of creating evaluative material is to compare theories to draw out their similarities/differences and strengths/weaknesses. A question might even require direct comparison of theories. Have a go at Questions 2 and 3 in 'Now test yourself' above, and then attempt 'Exam practice' Question 2 at the end of this chapter.

Biological influences on gender

The role of hormones and genes

Revised ☐

Many gender differences are biological. Biological sex is determined by the sex chromosomes X and Y, with XX for females and XY for males. Sex chromosomes contain genetic material that controls development as a male or a female; during this process sex **hormones** are produced, which direct sexual development. The Sry gene on the Y chromosome controls whether gonads become ovaries or testes; only if the gene is present will testes appear. Testes produce hormones called androgens, preventing the development of female characterstics.

Testosterone is an androgen that causes the development of male sex organs and acts on the hypothalamus; without this the brain develops as

hormones — chemical messengers released into the blood stream from glands, associated with gender development.

female. Testosterone is associated with the masculinisation of the brain, (e.g. development of brain areas linked to spatial skills). Similarly, the female hormone oestrogen helps feminise the brain.

The hypothalamus of males and females differ, with the sexual diomorphic nucleus bigger in males, these differences possibly occurring through the action of sex hormones. During puberty, testes and ovaries help determine secondary sexual characteristics, distinguishing men from women.

Deady et al. (2006) found a relationship between high testosterone levels in female saliva and a low desire to have a family, suggesting that maternal urges are linked to hormone levels.

Koopman et al. (1991) found that genetically female mice lacking the Sry gene developed into males if the gene was implanted, demonstrating the important role of the Sry gene in determining gender.

If biological factors were responsible for sex differences, these would be apparent from an early age. However, there is little evidence of early behavioural differences between males and females. Therefore differences appearing later may be explicable by social factors.

There are ethical concerns in researching on people with abnormal conditions, such as congenital adrenal hyperplasia. Such participants are vulnerable to distress and psychological harm. Cost–benefit analyses may decide if such research is beneficial.

Evolutionary explanations of gender — Revised

Males and females have evolved different **gender role** behaviours due to different adaptive pressures.

- **Mating strategies** — males produce millions of sperm and can fertilise many females at little cost to themselves, but cannot be sure of paternity. Females have fewer reproduction opportunities and incur high costs but are certain of maternity. Therefore men seek to impregnate as many women as possible, while women seek genetically fit males willing to invest resources in them. Males compete aggressively and so have evolved to be bigger and stronger. Females compete to be seen as attractive.

- **Pair bonding** — monogamous pair bonding is advantageous. Females get protection and resources. Males ensure sexual fidelity and a level of paternal certainty.

- **Adaptive advantage of sex roles** — men hunted, while women undertook caring duties, farmed and prepared food, leading to bigger social groups and starvation avoidance.

- **Gender roles** — women evolved nurturing behaviours due to the constraints imposed by child-caring duties. Men possess greater strength so they show behaviours requiring power.

Holloway et al. (2002) found that human males are 1.1 times bigger than females, but in chimpanzees, where male competition is more intense, males are 1.3 times bigger, supporting the idea of gender size differences being due to evolutionary pressures.

Buss (1989) found that, cross-culturally, females seek males with resources and ambition, while males seek physical attractiveness and desire younger partners, supporting the idea that mating strategies evolved differently due to different environmental demands. (The idea that men place importance on chastity was only slightly supported, casting doubt on the explanation.)

> **evolutionary explanations of gender** — perceive it as serving an adaptive purpose with a survival value.
>
> **gender role** — culturally determined male and female behaviours.

Examiner's tip

A useful means of creating IDA material regarding the evolutionary explanation of gender is to comment on how some criticise the approach as being deterministic in perceiving gender differences as biologically inevitable. Similarly a relevant IDA point concerning the biosocial approach would be to comment on how the model is an example of the way in which psychological approaches can work in unison and should not, therefore, be seen as a single, exclusive explanation of human behaviour.

- Even if gender roles have evolved, it does not mean they are desirable; men are negatively affected by jealousy and rejection.
- Evolutionary theory provides plausible explanations for physical differences between males and females, and why men are promiscuous and women choosy in sexual behaviour.

The biosocial approach

Biosocial theory sees gender as determined by biological and social factors working together to produce masculine and feminine behaviours and identities. Gender is not therefore explicable by biology alone; gender dysphoria indicates that biological sex does not necessarily reflect gender.

The theory sees the perceptions of biological sex as leading to gender identity and gender role behaviour. Babies are labelled as males or females and this labelling has consequences for how children are perceived, with boys and girls treated differently (e.g. in how they are handled). So gender is socially constructed and differs across cultures and over time.

While biological explanations see gender behaviours as biological and therefore fixed and constant, the biosocial model views them less rigidly. This means it is possible for individuals to change and develop in ways not confined by traditional views of gender behaviour and identity.

> **biosocial approach** — the perception of gender identity as arising from the interaction of environmental and biological influences.

> **Wetherell and Edley (1999)** found several styles of adult masculinity, for example 'unconventional' and 'sporty', indicating that gender role is not fixed exclusively by biology, supporting the biosocial view of gender behaviour flexibility.
>
> **Smith and Lloyd (1978)** dressed babies in non-specific gender clothes and labelled them with either boys' or girls' names. Participants played with them in ways consistent with gender labelling, supporting biosocial theory, which sees gender labels directing how children are perceived and treated.

- Individuals given reassignment surgery and raised as opposite genders to biological sex often produce contradictory results, possibly due to researcher bias. Reiner and Gearhart (2003) found that 16 males born without penises, given reassignment surgery and raised as females exhibited male tendencies, ten deciding to become male again. Money (1991), however, found 250 cases of people happy with gender reassignment.
- The model does not see gender behaviour as innate and fixed, meaning that gender identity could be developed in new and positive ways.

Gender dysphoria

Gender dysphoria is a mainly male psychiatric disorder, occurring when individuals want to change biological gender. Indications of the condition occur fairly early, with children unhappy wearing clothes of their biological gender, or playing gender stereotypical games. Later behaviour may involve assuming the gender role of the desired sex. Masculinising or feminising hormones can be taken to alter physical features, the ultimate remedy being gender-reassignment surgery.

> **gender dysphoria** — unhappiness with one's biological sex.

Psychological explanations centre on maladaptive learning experiences, maladaptive cognitive processes and psychodynamic fixations in childhood. Biological explanations are increasingly favoured, centring on the idea of genetic sex not matching gender during pregnancy, through additional hormones present in the mother, or by insensitivity to the mother's hormones (androgen insensitivity syndrome), leading to the development of female genitals but with male genes.

> **Rekers (1995)** reported no evidence of dysphoric boys showing evidence of biological causes, but found a common factor of a lack of stereotypical male role models, suggesting a psychological cause.
>
> **Hare et al. (2009)** found a relationship between gender dysphoria and variants of the androgen receptor gene, implying that the gene is involved in a failure to masculinise the brain during development in the womb, supporting a biological explanation.

- Research in this area is dependent on case studies, which are often affected by memory bias and selective recall.
- Individuals with the condition often do not perceive it as a disorder, but believe that gender characteristics are a social construction with no relation to biological sex.
- Although gender confusion in childhood can indicate gender dysphoria, only a minority exhibit the condition into adulthood.

Typical mistakes

Candidates might perceive gender dysphoria as a separate topic and use material about the condition to answer specific questions. However, material on gender dysphoria can also be used to answer general questions on the biosocial approach, because the specification regards the condition as a part of the biosocial approach.

Examiner's tip

A relevant IDA point to make regarding gender dysphoria is the social sensitivity of researching the condition. Identification of genes possibly associated with gender dysphoria has caused concerns about foetal gene screening with a view to aborting 'at-risk' pregnancies.

Now test yourself

Tested ☐

4 Outline how hormones and genes can influence gender development.
5 Does research on hormones and gender favour a biological or environmental view of gender development?
6 In what ways have males and females evolved different gender role behaviours?
7 What degree of support is there for evolutionary explanations?
8 Explain how the biosocial approach perceives the development of gender.
9 What research support is there for the biosocial approach?
10 What other evaluative points can be made concerning the biosocial approach?
11 What is meant by gender dysphoria?
12 (a) How can gender dysphoria be explained?
   (b) Does research suggest a psychological or biological explanation?
13 What other evaluative points can be made concerning gender dysphoria?

Answers on p. 124

Social influences on gender

Social influences

Revised ☐

Parents

Parents reinforce children's gender behaviour through expectations of what is and is not appropriate. When children demonstrate gender-appropriate behaviour, it is reinforced by rewards of praise and attention. Parents act as gender role models too, demonstrating gender-appropriate behaviours to be observed and imitated. Children, by a gradual immersion, adopt their parents' gender schemas.

> **social influences on gender** — the action of socialising agents, such as parents, schools and the media, on gender.

Eccles et al. (1990) reported that parents encouraged children to play with gender-stereotypical toys, supporting the idea that parents reinforce gender roles.

Fagot and Leinbach (1995) compared children of 'traditional' families, where fathers worked and mothers nurtured children, with 'alternative' families, where parents shared childcare. 'Traditional' family children displayed more gender role stereotyping and used gender labels earlier, suggesting that parents act as gender role models.

- Parents exert influence over children's gender concepts and behaviour when they are young, but peers become more important as gender role models in later childhood.

Schools

Teachers moderate parent and peer influences by reinforcing less gender-stereotypical attitudes and behaviour, but also enforce gender stereotypes, (e.g. through separate dress codes for genders). Teaching materials also exert an influence. Primary school teachers are generally female, which may explain why boys do worse, perceiving learning to be for girls.

In secondary education men and women teachers teach gender-stereotypical subjects (e.g. men teaching maths) and pupils regard subjects as 'girl' or 'boy' subjects. These influences are reinforced and policed by parents, peers and teachers.

Renzetti and Curran (1992) report that teachers reinforce boys through praise for instances of 'cleverness'. Girls receive praise for 'neatness', supporting the view that teachers enforce gender stereotypes.

Colley (1994) found that secondary school pupils view subjects as either masculine or feminine, demonstrating that social influences are apparent in schools.

- Fagot (1995) found that teachers reinforce female behaviours in boys and girls, but that only girls learn them, suggesting that cognitive rather than behavioural factors are stronger.

Cultural influences   Revised ☐

If similarities are found in gender roles across cultures, it suggests that they are biological in nature, while if differences are found, it suggests they are socially constructed.

Barry et al. (1957) found that nurturing was a dominantly feminine characteristic, while self-reliance was the same for males in non-Westernised cultures. These findings reflect those from Western cultures, suggesting a biological basis to gender roles.

Mead (1935) conducted research into gender differences between tribes in Papua New Guinea. With the Arapesh, both genders exhibited caring personas; with the Tchambuli, men demonstrated female behaviours, while women exhibited male behaviours; in the Mundugumor, both sexes showed aggressive personalities. This implies that gender roles are socially constructed rather than being biological in nature.

Williams and Best (1990) found universal agreement across cultures about which characteristics were masculine and which feminine, men being perceived as dominant and independent, and women as caring and sociable. Children exhibited the same attitudes, implying that attitudes to gender roles are universal and biological in nature.

- Collectivist cultures hold clearer views than individualistic cultures about which gender roles are male and female.

- A methodological problem with **cross-cultural gender studies** is that it is difficult to obtain identical samples and researchers can be biased to their own cultural viewpoints.

- Globalisation may be contributing to the lessening of cultural differences and there has been a reduction in the differences between masculine and feminine gender roles, implying that social influences are stronger than biological ones.

> **cross-cultural gender studies** — research studies comparing the gender roles of people from different cultural groupings.

- There is a possibility that Mead exhibited researcher bias and she did subsequently change her views, stating that gender behaviours can be biological in nature.

Examiner's tip

A relevant IDA point to make concerning cross-cultural research into gender roles is to comment on how findings from cross-cultural studies can be related to the nature/nurture debate. If gender roles, behaviours and attitudes are universal, this suggests that they are innate and due to nature, while if cultural differences are found, it is indicative of nurture influences.

Now test yourself

Tested ☐

14 Explain how (i) parents (ii) schools can exert social influences on gender.
15 (a) What degree of research evidence is there for parents and schools exerting social influence on gender?
   (b) What other evaluative points can be made concerning these factors?
16 Why are cross-cultural studies of gender role conducted?
17 What do cross-cultural studies suggest about how gender roles are constructed?
18 What other evaluative points can be made concerning cross-cultural studies of gender role?

Answers on p. 124

Typical mistakes

A common mistake is to create identical descriptions regardless of marks available, but the descriptive parts of questions can be worth variable amounts and candidates should produce answers that reflect this. Question 3(a) below has 4 marks available for outlining evolutionary explanations of gender, but it is quite possible that this question could have 8 marks for the same requirement, and candidates should therefore produce appropriate amounts of material to gain the marks on offer.

Exam practice

1 (a) Outline gender schema theory and Kohlberg's cognitive theory of gender development. [8]
  (b) Evaluate one of the theories outlined in (a). [16]
2 Critically compare gender schema theory and Kohlberg's cognitive theory of gender development. [24]
3 (a) Outline evolutionary explanations of gender. [4]
  (b) Consider the role of hormones and genes in gender development. [16]
4 Discuss the biosocial approach to gender development. [24]
5 (a) Outline and evaluate explanations of gender dysphoria. [12]
  (b) Outline and evaluate social influences on gender. [12]
6 (a) Outline social and cultural influences on gender. [4 + 4]
  (b) Evaluate cultural influences on gender. [16]

Answers and quick quiz 6 online

Online ☐

Examiner's summary

✔ Kohlberg's theory sees gender identity as occurring in set stages, while gender schema theory sees gender knowledge changing with environmental experience.

✔ Biological influences perceive hormones and genes as affecting gender development, with evolutionary explanations seeing gender roles as possessing an adaptive advantage, while the biosocial approach sees gender as being determined by both biological and social factors.

✔ Social influences on gender include those of parents and schools, while cultural influences suggest a role for both biological and environmental factors in determining gender roles.

7 Intelligence and learning

Theories of intelligence

Psychometric theories Revised

Psychometric theories perceive **intelligence** as a set of abilities measurable by mental tests, and believe that intellectual differences between individuals are determinable. Psychometric theories differ in the number of basic factors that intelligence consists of.

Spearman's two-factor model

Spearman believed that there is a common factor explaining why individuals score similarly on tests of different abilities. Using **factor analysis**, he identified two basic factors that intelligence tests measure: general intelligence (g) — an innate factor underpinning all mental abilities, shared by individuals in differing amounts, and specific abilities (s) — a factor concerning specific skills that individuals possess.

> **Johnson and Bouchard (2005)** using factor analysis, found a single, higher-order factor of intelligence, which implies that general intelligence exists and contributes to all forms of intelligence.
>
> **Kitcher (1985)** found no single measure of intellectual ability, suggesting that general intelligence is a myth.

- Spearman's work inspired focus on and interest in the study of intelligence and led to the introduction of factor analysis into psychology. Spearman's theory was not widely accepted, multi-factor theories becoming more popular.

Guildford's structure of intellect model

Guildford (1967) believed that there were 120 separate mental abilities. Using factor analysis, Guildford proposed that intellectual abilities were divisible into five types of operation (types of thinking being used), four types of content (what is being thought about) and six kinds of product (types of answer required). He devised tests measuring each ability.

> **Guildford (1985)** created tests to measure 70 separate mental abilities. However, scores achieved on these tests were often similar; suggesting that they're measuring the same ability and so there could be fewer than 120 different mental abilities.

- Spearman used schoolchildren, with widely ranging intellects, while Guildford used college students who have a narrower range of intelligence. This contributed to finding different numbers of basic factors.

> **psychometric theories** — approaches that seek to reduce intelligence to its basic parts and measure them.
>
> **intelligence** — understanding the essentials of a situation and responding appropriately to them.
>
> **factor analysis** — a statistical technique used by psychometricists, which attempts to reduce large amounts of data to a basic number of factors.

Typical mistakes

Candidates often view psychometric and information-processing theories as separate from one another, restricting the marks they gain for evaluation on questions in this area. Comparing both types of theory is a good way of drawing out their differences/similarities, as well as strengths/weaknesses. Making such a comparison successfully will score high-level evaluative marks.

Information processing theories

Revised

These theories take a cognitive approach, perceiving intelligence as dependent on the stages gone through to create solutions to problems. Intelligence is seen as a set of mental representations of information and the set of processes acting on them (e.g. speed of processing).

> **information processing theories** — an approach that perceives the mind as using logical rules and strategies to process and make sense of incoming sensory data.

Sternberg's triarchic theory of intelligence

Sternberg (1977) saw 'street smart' intelligence as how well someone copes with their environment. Intelligence has three facets (sub-theories):

- **Analytical intelligence** — intelligence measurable through academic problems, involving three components: metacomponents, performance components and knowledge acquisition components.

- **Creative intelligence** — deals with the relationship between intelligence and experience. Involves how well tasks are performed in regard to level of experience, with two parts: novelty and automation. Creative intelligence is associated with *synthetic giftedness*, an ability to create new ideas and solve novel problems.

- **Practical intelligence** — deals with the relationship between intelligence and the external world, involving three processes — adaptation, shaping and selection — to create a 'fit' between individuals and their environment. Practical intelligence is associated with *practical giftedness*, an ability to apply new ideas and analytical skills to practical situations.

Merrick (1992) used the Cognitive Abilities Self-Evaluative Questionnaire to find individuals with all three types of intelligence detailed by Sternberg, supporting the components of his theory.

- Gottfredson (2003) criticised the theory as non-scientific, believing practical intelligence to be merely task-specific knowledge — skills learned to cope with particular environments.

Case's information processing theory

Case (1985) described how information-processing ability is related to the degree of M-space (mental capacity), information-processing ability developing over time due to three factors: brain maturity, cognitive strategies and metacognitive skills.

Chi (1978) found that child chess players using metacognitive skills recalled more positions than adults who did not have the same skills, supporting Case's theory.

- The theory is objective, seeing intelligence as measurable due to the capacity of M-space being determinable.

Examiner's tip

A relevant IDA point to make concerning Sternberg's theory is that teaching methods based on Sternberg's theory are superior to more conventional methods in improving reading ability, which not only lends support to the theory but demonstrates its practical application. Similarly Guildford's structure of intellect model has practical applications in personnel selection and placement.

Now test yourself

Tested

1 Outline (i) Spearman's two-factor model (ii) Guildford's structure of intellect model.
2 What evaluative points, including IDA material, can be made about psychometric theories?
3 Outline (i) Sternberg's triarchic theory (ii) Case's theory.
4 What evaluative points can be made concerning information processing theories?

Answers on p. 124

Animal learning and intelligence

Classical conditioning

Pavlov (1927) noticed that dogs salivated before food was presented, as other environmental features became associated with feeding, such as sighting food bowls. The dogs learned to produce a natural reflex (salivation) to stimuli not associated with that response. Pavlov then paired food presentation with the sound of a bell, getting the dogs to salivate to the sound of the bell alone (see Table 7.1).

classical conditioning — learning occurs through association of a neutral stimulus with an involuntary unconditioned stimulus.

operant conditioning — learning occurs through reinforcement of behaviour, increasing the chances of the behaviour recurring.

Table 7.1 Pavlov's classical conditioning

Before learning	food (unconditioned stimulus, UCS) → salivation (unconditioned response, UCR)
During learning	food (UCS) + bell (neutral stimulus) → salivation (UCR)
After learning	bell (conditioned stimulus, CS) → salivation (conditioned response, CR)

The conditioning process is generalisable, by slightly varying a conditioned stimulus (CS) to produce weaker forms of the conditioned response (CR), while discrimination occurs when an unconditioned stimulus (UCS) is paired with a specific CS and the CR only occurs with this pairing. If a CS is continually given without the UCS, the CR weakens and becomes extinct, though if a rest period is given, re-presentation of the CS revives the CR.

Operant conditioning

Operant conditioning is based on Thorndike's (1911) law of effect, which sees behaviours resulting in pleasant outcomes as being repeated in similar circumstances. Reinforcements increase the chances of behaviours recurring, while punishments decrease the chances.

Skinner (1938) used a Skinner box where animals were reinforced with food pellets for producing desired behaviours. Accidentally producing certain actions, such as pressing a lever, caused food pellets to be released. Gradually animals learned to associate behaviours with reinforcements, producing the behaviour every time.

There are four possible outcomes of behaviour:

1 positive reinforcement, receiving something pleasant (e.g. food)
2 negative reinforcement, not receiving something unpleasant (e.g. not doing chores)
3 positive punishment, receiving something unpleasant (e.g. being grounded)
4 negative punishment, not receiving something pleasant (e.g. not getting a promised treat)

The role of simple learning in behaviour

Animals use conditioning to learn about their environment and adapt to changing environments. Animals use classical conditioning to learn whether food sources are safe, although *biological preparedness*, where the tendency to learn associations depends on biological predispositions, also plays a role.

Operant conditioning allows animals to interact with their environment and, by trial and error learning, to shape behaviour via reinforcement and punishment processes (e.g. finding food and avoiding danger).

Baker (1984) showed how pigeons use trial and error learning to use landmarks to navigate.

Fisher and Hinde (1949) found that animals learn behaviours resembling innate ones. Blue tits seemingly used imitation to drink cream from milk bottles, but this artificial behaviour was easily learned because it resembled their natural behaviour of stripping tree bark.

Garcia and Koelling (1966) showed how rats learn taste aversions by classical conditioning. Exposed to radiation, they associated the sickness they felt with the taste of their feeding bottle, refusing to drink from it.

Breland and Breland (1961) demonstrated instinctive drift, where animals revert to natural behaviours. Pigs trained to put tokens in a piggy bank to get rewards preferred to root in the ground with them.

- Classical conditioning cannot explain how new behaviours arise, but operant conditioning, via reinforcements, can, as well as explaining complex behaviours.
- Animals also use social learning via observation and imitation.
- Operant conditioning cannot explain latent learning, where learning occurs without reinforcement. Tolman (1930) showed that rats learned to navigate a maze without being reinforced, but only demonstrated this when given the incentive of a reward.

Examiner's tip

It is generally easier to create embedded (relevant) IDA material that concerns practical applications and ethical concerns. For instance, that findings from research into simple learning suggest practical applications in the training of wild and domestic animals, but that some uses of conditioning may be unethical, such as training animals for warfare.

Intelligence in non-human animals
Revised

Animal intelligence is associated with the capacity to survive and reproduce and is a hierarchy of learning processes, species differing in the degree of behaviour learned.

Social learning

Social learning refers to behavioural processes affecting what animals learn via social interactions. Several forms exist: imitation, where behaviour is observed and directly copied; enhancement, where attention is directed to particular environmental features to solve problems; emulation, where the consequences of behaviour are reproduced and tutoring, where models encourage, punish or provide behavioural examples, at a cost to the models.

social learning — learning occurs through the observation and imitation of others.

Whiten (1999) found that in chimpanzee colonies, different population-specific behaviours arose in using twigs to eat ants, suggesting that such behaviours are learned by direct imitation.

Nagell (1993) suggested that snow monkeys' apparent imitation of washing potatoes was actually due to attention being focused onto the potatoes and the water, enhancing the chances of the skill being learned by trial and error.

Tomasello et al. (1987) found that chimpanzees emulated a model using a rake to get food. The chimpanzees did not imitate particular actions but developed their own technique, suggesting that they try to attain the consequences of the behaviour.

Rendell and Whitehead (2001) found that adult orcas act as tutors by delaying the killing and eating of prey, so youngsters may practise their hunting skills.

- Examples of tutoring are disputed. Adult orcas may not be delaying killing in order for youngsters to learn, but simply be 'playing with their food'.
- Due to subjective interpretation, it is not clear if behaviour arises via imitation or enhancement.

Machiavellian intelligence

Intelligent individuals look after their own interests, by using deception or forming coalitions, but without disturbing social cohesion.

> **Nishida et al. (1992)** reported that alpha males do not share food with rivals, but do with non-rivals so they will assist in power struggles.
>
> **Whiten and Byrne (1988)** showed how young baboons use deceit to get their mothers to chase adults away from foodstuffs so they may eat them.

- Evidence suggests that Machiavellian intelligence exists in primates, especially those living in large social groups with high social complexity and an ability to memorise socially relevant information.
- The evolution of advanced cognitive abilities necessary for Machiavellian intelligence has not as yet been adequately explained.

machiavellian intelligence — the ability to serve one's own interests by manipulation of, or cooperation with, others, in a way that does not upset the social cohesion of a group.

Examiner's tip

A relevant IDA point to make concerning animal intelligence is that research in this area focuses on behaviour that enhances survival and reproduction and therefore can be placed in the evolutionary approach, which sees intelligence as an adaptive feature shaped by natural selection. A relevant ethical point is that research on wild animals is ethical as long as it does not lower their fitness (e.g. affecting their ability to forage or reproduce).

Now test yourself

Tested ☐

5 Outline the main characteristics of (i) classical conditioning (ii) operant conditioning.
6 What have psychologists discovered about the role of simple learning in the behaviour of non-human animals?
7 What evaluative points can be made about the role of simple learning in the behaviour of non-human animals?
8 (a) What is meant by (i) imitation (ii) enhancement (iii) emulation (iv) tutoring?
   (b) Give details of a relevant research study for each of these.
9 (a) What is meant by Machiavellian intelligence?
   (b) What evidence is there that animals use Machiavellian intelligence?

Answers on pp. 124–125

Human intelligence

Evolutionary factors

Revised ☐

Human intelligence evolved due to the demands of ever-changing environments creating selective pressure for increased intellect.

Ecological demands

Milton (1988) believes that developing mental maps helped fruit-eaters to know when and where to find food by monitoring the availability of fruits. Gibson (1987) proposed the food extraction hypothesis, seeing the need to find hidden foods as driving the evolution of intelligence. Cognitive processing, manual dexterity and tool use were necessary, creating selective pressure for a larger cortex.

evolutionary factors in intelligence — influences affecting the development of intelligence that convey an adaptive advantage and occur through natural selection.

ecological demands — features of the environment that provide a survival value.

Dunbar (1992) found no relationship between the amount of fruit in an animal's diet and the size of its neocortex. However, only small amounts of fruit are needed for necessary nutrition.

Boesche et al. (1992) found that chimpanzees' use of tools to open nuts closely matched archaeological evidence of early humans, supporting Gibson's hypothesis.

- Milton does not explain why fruit-eaters need a high-quality diet. Did energy fuel a larger brain, or did brains grow to develop skills to find fruit?
- Many species have maps for stored food items, so it seems unlikely that developing mental maps produces cognitive evolution.

Social complexity hypothesis

Social living has advantages, but conflicts arise. Intelligent individuals can solve such problems. Advanced abilities in social cognition are evident in those living in large, complex groups, such animals possessing large frontal cortexes.

Holekamp and Engh (2003) found a relationship between brain size and complexity of social living in carnivores, supporting the hypothesis.

Ehmer et al. (2001) found larger brain structures in female paper wasps living in social colonies than in solitary females, supporting the hypothesis.

- Observations of animals involve subjective interpretation that may be subject to researcher bias.
- An important ethical issue when performing studies on wild animals is the need to avoid lowering their fitness.

Typical mistakes

The specification for intelligence is clear in its requirements for candidates to concentrate sometimes on humans and at other times on non-human animals (for instance, simple learning and its role in the behaviour of non-human animals and evolutionary factors in the development of human intelligence). Candidates should therefore take care to shape material specifically to these requirements when answering exam questions.

social complexity — the degree of organisation and order among animal social groupings.

Genetic and environmental factors

Revised

IQ tests claim to measure intelligence. Using twin and adoption studies, if differences in IQ are genetic, people with close genetic relationships should have similar IQs. Also IQ levels should not be affected by experience, and attempts to increase IQ by enrichment should not work. Attempts have also been made to identify specific genes. Research findings have not drawn clear conclusions and attract controversy.

environmental factors — developmental influences acquired via experience.

genetic factors — developmental influences of intelligence transmitted through heredity.

Genetic factors

Twin studies examine the relationship between people's genetic similarity and IQ scores. High correlations support the genetic argument.

Bouchard and McGue (1981) found that identical twins had a much higher concordance rate than less related individuals. However, identical twins often have identical environments.

- If intelligence were entirely genetic then concordance rates for identical twins would be 100%. As they aren't, environment must play a role.

Adoption studies are concerned with the idea that if intelligence is genetic, adopted children should have IQ scores closer to their biological parents than their adopted ones.

Petrill and Deater-Deckard (2004) found that mothers were closer in IQ terms to biological than adopted children. However, IQ performance was related to age when adopted and time spent in the adoptive home, suggesting that environment also plays a role.

- Important factors are often not controlled and IQ scores of biological parents are difficult to confirm.
- Just like twin studies, adoption studies do not allow clear conclusions to be drawn.

In **gene identification** attempts are made to identify specific genes involved in the inheritance of intelligence. Individual genes may only have slight influences, but collectively exert great influence.

> **Lahn et al. (2004)** identified a gene, ASPM, linked to higher intelligence. ASPM affects the expansion of the cerebral cortex, explaining how genes influence intelligence.

- Gene identification could help to understand not only intelligence but also learning disabilities and intellectual decay, leading to effective therapies.

Environmental factors

Family influences. IQ is affected by how much social stimulation occurs.

> **Zajonc and Markus (1975)** found that as families grow in size, less stimulation is given to later children and their IQ is lower. However, the effect was small.

- Research implies that the fall in American IQ levels is due to having larger families and the reduced social stimulation that then occurs.

Enrichment. If intelligence is genetic, enrichment should not increase IQ.

> **Atkinson (1990)** reviewed several enrichment programmes, finding that parental involvement, leading to stimulation at home, raised IQ levels and social skills.

- Parental involvement is a key factor in boosting children's confidence and motivation to do well.
- In general, enrichment programmes boost intellectual performance, especially in the short term.

Cultural influences

IQ tests are biased in favour of the culture they represent, testing the skills and knowledge of that culture. Attempts were made to create culture-free tests where questions were not culturally based, thus allowing fair comparison of people. Poverty is a cultural factor with minority cultural groups often living in impoverished conditions, which can affect IQ levels.

> **Williams (1972)** devised the Black Intelligence Test for Cultural Homogeneity (BITCH) based on black culture. Black people, who score poorly on traditional white-cultural tests, did well, while white people scored poorly, suggesting that IQ tests are culturally biased.

- Culture-free tests are culturally biased because testing is itself a cultural concept.
- Vernon (1969) believes that intelligence refers to different things in different cultures and is not something we all share in differing amounts measurable by IQ tests.

> **Typical mistakes**
>
> Candidates often perceive genetic and environmental factors as separate from each other. However, a good way of accessing high-level evaluation marks when answering questions in this area is to use both types of factor, as long as they are shaped to the requirements of the question to illustrate to what extent intelligence is genetic or environmental.

> **cultural influences —** development factors of intelligence originating from cultural groupings.

Now test yourself

Tested

10 Outline evolutionary factors in the development of human intelligence.

11 (a) What research evidence is there to support these factors?

   (b) What other evaluative points can be made?

12 Outline genetic and environmental factors associated with IQ test performance.

13 (a) What research evidence is there to support these factors?

   (b) What other evaluative points can be made?

14 (a) Outline the influence of culture on IQ test performance.

   (b) What evaluative points can be made concerning the cultural nature of IQ?

Answers on p. 125

Exam practice

1 Outline and evaluate psychometric theories of intelligence. [24]

2 (a) Outline two information processing theories of intelligence. [8]

   (b) Evaluate one theory outlined in (a). [16]

3 Discuss simple learning and its role in the behaviour of non-human animals. [24]

4 Discuss intelligence in non-human animals. [24]

5 Outline and evaluate evolutionary factors in the development of human intelligence. [24]

6 (a) Outline genetic or environmental factors associated with intelligence test performance. [4]

   (b) Outline and evaluate the influence of culture on intelligence test performance. [20]

Answers and quick quiz 7 online

Online

Examiner's summary

✔ Psychometric theories attempt to measure intelligence, while information processing theories focus on the cognitive processes involved in intelligence.

✔ Simple learning sees animal intelligence as determined through classical and operant conditioning, while higher forms of animal intelligence are seen as involving social learning and Machiavellian intelligence.

✔ Evolutionary factors of human intelligence, such as ecological demands and the social complexity

hypothesis, see an adaptive advantage to developing intelligence.

✔ Genetic and environmental factors concern the degree to which intelligence test performance is determined by innate and learned influences, while cultural influences examine the degree to which intelligence is culturally produced.

8 Cognition and development

Development of thinking

Theories of cognitive development Revised

Cognitive development theories attempt to explain the growth of mental abilities. Some theories see thought processes as undergoing qualitative changes as children age, with biological processes directing these changes. Other theorists believe that learning experiences are a major influence, with the relative influence of innate and environmental factors being a key issue.

Piaget

Piaget's theory of biological maturation sees *qualitative* differences between adult and child thinking, with a set sequence of developmental stages (see Table 8.1), children only progressing to the next stage when they are biologically ready.

Infants have basic reflexes and innate **schemas**. If new experiences fit existing schemas, they're **assimilated**. If they do not, they create disequilibrium (see below) and **accommodation** occurs where existing schemas change to fit new experiences. Assimilation and accommodation are **invariant processes** (remain the same). Schemas and **operations** are **variant structures** (change as individuals develop).

A desire for **equilibrium** drives development, new experiences pushing children into **disequilibrium**.

> **schemas** — ways of understanding the world.
>
> **assimilation** — fitting new environmental experiences into existing schema.
>
> **accommodation** — altering existing schema to fit in new experiences.
>
> **operations** — strings of schemas assembled in a logical order.
>
> **equilibrium** — a pleasant state of balance.
>
> **disequilibrium** — unpleasant state of imbalance that motivates to return to equilibrium.

Table 8.1 Piaget's developmental stages of thinking

Stage of development	Description
Sensorimotor stage (0–2 years)	New schemas arise from matching sensory to motor experiences Object permanence develops
Pre-operational stage (2–7 years)	Internal images, symbols and language develop Children influenced by how things seem, not logic
Concrete operational stage (7–11 years)	Development of conservation (use of logical rules), but only if situations are concrete, not abstract Decline of egocentrism
Formal operational stage (11+ years)	Abstract manipulation of ideas (concepts without physical presence) Not achieved by all

Piaget (1954) found that 3–4-month-old babies do not look for items out of view, suggesting that they have no object permanence.

Bower and Wishart (1972) disagree, stating that 1-month-old babies show surprise when items disappear.

Piaget and Inhelder (1956) suggested that children under 7 were egocentric, choosing the view they see of a model of mountains, rather than the doll's view.

Exam practice answers and quick quizzes at **www.therevisionbutton.co.uk/myrevisionnotes**

- Cross-cultural evidence suggests that the sequence of development is invariant and universal (except formal operations), and that it is a biological process of maturation.
- Due to poor methodology, Piaget underestimated what children could do.
- Piaget's theory was a starting point for subsequent theories and research.

Vygotsky

Vygotsky saw cultural knowledge as central to development. Knowledge and thinking are socially constructed through the interaction of children with people from their culture. Culture changes elementary mental functions (innate capacities, e.g. attention) into higher mental functions, such as comprehension of language. Culture teaches children what and how to think; there are several ways in which culture influences cognitive development.

Cultural influences and experts push children through the **zone of proximal development** (ZPD) onto tasks beyond their current ability.

Scaffolding involves being given clues rather than answers. Learning involves shared social activities, but eventually individuals self-scaffold and learning becomes an individual, self-regulated activity.

Semiotics help cognitive development through language and other cultural symbols. These act as a medium for knowledge to be transmitted, turning elementary mental functions into higher ones.

First, children use pre-intellectual language for social and emotional purposes and pre-linguistic thinking occurs without language.
From 2 years of age, language and thought combine.

- Social speech (0–3 years) — pre-intellectual language.
- Egocentric speech (3–7 years) — self-talk/thinking aloud.
- Inner speech (7+ years) — self-talk becomes silent and internal, and language is used for social communications.

From research Vygotsky proposed four stages of concept formation (see Table 8.2).

Table 8.2 Vygotsky's four stages of concept formation

Stages of concept formation	Description
Vague syncretic	Trial and error formation without comprehension (similar to Piaget's pre-operational stage)
Complex	Use of some strategies, but not systematic
Potential concept	More systematic with one attribute being focused on at a time (e.g. weight)
Mature concept	Several attributes are dealt with systematically (e.g. weight and colour) Similar to Piaget's formal operations

Berk (1994) found that children talked to themselves more when doing difficult tasks, supporting the idea of egocentric speech.

Wertsch et al. (1980) found that the amount of time under-5s spent looking at their mothers when assembling jigsaws decreased with age, supporting the idea of increased self-regulation.

- There is a lack of research support, but as the theory focuses on processes rather than outcomes, it is harder to test.
- The theory is more suited to collectivist cultures, which lay more stress on social learning.

Typical mistakes

Many candidates study and revise theories of cognitive development as separate concepts. However, a good way of accessing higher-level marks for evaluation is to compare Piaget's and Vygotsky's theories to draw out their similarities/differences, as well as their strengths and weaknesses.

zone of proximal development — the distance between current and potential intellectual ability.

scaffolding — tuition given by more knowledgeable others.

Piaget

Concept of readiness. Children are not capable of learning until they are ready, limiting what can be learned at certain times. Teachers should teach age-related material in the order of development.

Discovery learning. Learning is child-centred; children interact with their environment and construct knowledge through **discovery learning**. Teachers create disequilibrium, making children accommodate new experiences and develop schemas.

Role of the teacher. Children's stages of development are assessed and suitable tasks are given to challenge them, creating disequilibrium. Relevant materials are provided at different ages. Opportunities for group learning are given as learning occurs from conflicting views, and peer interactions have social as well as cognitive value.

> **Modgil et al. (1983)** found that discovery learning leads to poor reading and writing skills in children who need assistance, which suggests that it is not for all children.
>
> **Danner and Day (1977)** found that coaching 10 and 13 year olds had no effect, supporting Piaget's concept of readiness. However, it did assist 17 year olds, suggesting that tuition helps at a later stage of development.

- Piaget never intended his theory as an educational tool; it was others who put it to this use.
- Walkerdine (1984) believes that educationalists used Piaget's theory as a convenient vehicle to justify changes they wanted to make.

Discovery learning — learning that occurs through active exploration.

Vygotsky

Cooperative and collaborative thinking. Knowledge is socially constructed by learners working collectively on a common task. Individuals depend on and are accountable to each other, helping individuals to work better on their own.

Peer tutoring. Allowing peers to be tutors creates a beneficial learning experience for the tutor as well as the learner.

Expert tutoring. This is an effective teaching tool if the boundaries of a child's zone of proximal development are taken into account.

Scaffolding. Experienced people assist development, providing general and specific tutoring, and enabling individuals to achieve. Eventually, scaffolding becomes self-instruction.

> **Cloward (1967)** found peer tutoring to be of greater benefit to tutors than designated learners, demonstrating the benefit of the method.
>
> **Gokhale (1995)** tested students on critical thinking, finding that those undertaking collaborative learning outscored those studying alone, supporting the idea of cooperative learning.

- Learning via cooperative groups needs monitoring or some individuals dominate and others coast.
- Vygotsky's approach works less well in individualistic settings, with their emphasis on competitiveness and autonomy.

Typical mistakes

Candidates tend to evaluate research studies in terms of methodology. However, this is often done in an ineffectively general way (e.g. 'shows causality'; 'can be replicated' etc.). If the requirement is to evaluate an explanation, you are much better off using research evidence to show the degree of support given to the explanation.

Tested

Now test yourself

1 Outline the key points of (i) Piaget's theory (ii) Vygotsky's theory, highlighting their similarities and differences.
2 For both theories compile a list of evaluative points assessing their degree of support.
3 Describe the ways in which both theories have educational applications.
4 What evaluative points can be made concerning the application of both theories to education?

Answers on p. 125

Development of moral understanding

Kohlberg's theory of moral understanding

Revised

Kohlberg (1966) sees **morality** developing in innate stages in a set order when biological maturation is ready, with disequilibrium playing a part, as experiences which fail to fit existing schemas challenge current moral thinking. Women are less morally developed, being restricted to domesticity.

Each moral stage involves different kinds of thinking to reach moral decisions, the focus on how moral thinking occurs. Moral behaviour results from moral thinking.

Kohlberg used **moral dilemmas** with no 'right' or 'wrong' answers. One involved a chemist who will not give Heinz a drug to save his dying wife, because he cannot afford it. Is Heinz right to steal the drug? Kohlberg was interested not in whether participants think it is right to steal but in the reasoning behind their answers. From this he created three levels of morality, each one containing two stages (see Table 8.3).

Table 8.3 Kohlberg's three levels of morality

Level of morality	Description
Pre-conventional (age 6–13)	Stage 1: morality based on outcomes (e.g. punishments), rather than intentions
	Stage 2: moral rules followed when it benefits us
Conventional (age 13–16)	Stage 3: morality based on 'being good' and maintaining trust and loyalty of others
	Stage 4: morality based on what's best for society, fulfilling our duty
Post-conventional (age 16–20)	Stage 5: social order seen as paramount, with realisation that bad rules can be changed
	Stage 6: adherence to a personal set of moral rules

Kohlberg (1969) tested moral reasoning in several cultures and found the same sequence of moral development, suggesting that transition through the stages occurs as an innate biological process.

Kohlberg (1975) gave students a chance to cheat on a test, finding that 15% with post-conventional morality cheated, while 70% with pre-conventional morality did, supporting the prediction.

Fodor (1972) compared delinquents' and non-delinquents' levels of morality, finding non-delinquents at a higher level, supporting the notion that moral thinking reflects actual moral behaviour.

Typical mistakes

With questions that require candidates to outline and evaluate theories, such as Kohlberg's theory of moral understanding, many candidates spend a lot of time on the outline. Remember that two-thirds of the marks are for evaluation and so the majority of time should be spent on evaluative material.

morality — the rules by which a society adjudges what kinds of behaviour, beliefs and attitudes are acceptable.

moral dilemmas — hypothetical stories used to assess levels of moral reasoning.

Examiner's tip

Kohlberg's theory presents a good opportunity to make a relevant IDA point concerning the accusation of gender bias. He saw morality based on principles of justice, while Gilligan argues that women operate on principles of care. Kohlberg's negative rating of female morality may be a result of being assessed by male-created standards and methodological faults, such as using only male participants.

- As only 12% of adults reach post-conventional morality, Atkinson et al. (1990) argued that it is more of a philosophical ideal than a normal developmental sequence.
- Moral dilemmas are not real-life scenarios; people behave differently from their moral reasoning if actually placed in such situations. Gilligan (1982) questioned women deciding whether to have abortions and found different patterns of moral thought from Kohlberg, although this may be due to using females rather than males.

Now test yourself

Tested

5 Describe how Kohlberg explains the development of morality.

6 What are moral dilemmas and how were they used to formulate Kohlberg's theory?

7 Outline Kohlberg's three stages of morality.

8 Compile a list of the strengths and weaknesses of Kohlberg's theory.

Answers on p. 125

Development of social cognition

Development of the child's sense of self

Revised

Self-recognition is important for social interaction and is assessed by the mirror test, which assesses whether participants put in front of a mirror can detect a mark placed on their face while asleep. Some can do this at 15 months and the majority by 2 years of age. For individuals to comprehend whom the image is of there must be a mental representation of self.

Mans et al. (1978) showed that self-recognition in Down's syndrome children was delayed, but by 4 years of age 89% could do it, suggesting that self-awareness is related to cognitive development.

Certain emotions, such as embarrassment, are **self-referential**, that is they convey a sense of self-awareness, involving thinking about oneself in relation to others.

Lewis et al. (1989) found that when children are asked to dance in front of adults they display embarrassment at around the same age that they demonstrate self-recognition.

The sense of **self-esteem** — the ability to self-evaluate — is dependent on assessing the difference between the actual and ideal self. It differs between individuals and across situations.

Vershueren et al. (2001) found that children between 4 and 5 years of age have a sense of self-esteem related to attachment, with securely attached individuals having higher levels of self-esteem.

Theory of Mind

The comprehension of another's thoughts and emotions — the **Theory of Mind** (ToM) — is perceived as indicating intelligence. It is assessed with the Sally-Anne test, which looks for realisation of false beliefs. ToM develops around 4 years of age and its processing is associated with the functions of

theory of Mind — the ability to attribute mental states to oneself and others.

the amygdala and basal ganglia. With ToM development comes the ability to manipulate and deceive by hiding emotions and intentions.

> **Avis and Harris (1991)** found that children in developed and non-developed countries realise at 4 years of age that people have false beliefs, supporting the idea of biological maturation.

- A lack of ToM is similar to Piaget's idea of egocentrism, coinciding at similar ages, suggesting the two concepts to be linked.
- A sizeable number of autistic children pass the Sally-Anne test, suggesting that lack of ToM is not the key factor in autism.

Perspective taking

Revised

The idea of **perspective taking** concerns the ability to assume another's perspective and understand their thoughts and feelings. Selman (1980) proposed **role-taking theory**, where adopting the perspective of another allows comprehension of feelings, thoughts and intentions. The theory has five levels (see Table 8.4) and was developed through **interpersonal dilemmas**, such as whether expert tree-climber Holly, who has promised she will not climb trees, should do so to save a kitten.

With maturity children take more information into account, realising that people react differently to identical situations. They analyse people's perspectives from the viewpoint of objective, neutral bystanders, realising that different cultural and societal values affect the perception of bystanders.

> **perspective taking** — the ability to understand from another's point of view.

Examiner's tip

A strong IDA point can be made concerning perspective taking by discussing its practical applications as a means of conflict resolution. Walker & Selman (1998) used perspective taking to reduce aggression levels by getting individuals to empathise with others' feelings and opinions. It is also worth pointing out that research in this area is culturally biased. Quintana et al. (1999) criticised Selman's work as disregarding the development of perspective taking in ethnic sub-cultural groupings.

Table 8.4 Selman's five levels of perspective taking

Level of perspective taking	Description
Undifferentiated (age 3–6)	Recognises that self and others have different thoughts and feelings, but often confuse the two
Social informational (age 5–9 years)	Recognises that different perspectives arise because people have access to different information
Self-reflective (age 7–12 years)	Perceives others' feelings, thoughts and behaviour from their perspective
Third party (age 10–15)	Steps outside two-person situations, viewing them from third-party, neutral viewpoints
Societal (14–adult)	Understands that third-party perspectives are influenced by societal value systems

> **Schultz and Selman (1990)** found that the transition from self-centred perspectives to perceiving from others' perspectives is related to the development of enhanced interpersonal negotiation skills and concern for others, suggesting that perspective is important in social maturation.

> **Underwood and Moore (1982)** found that the ability to perspective take positively correlated with pro-social behaviour, suggesting that perspective taking enhances social relationships.

- The theory is used to resolve conflicts. Walker and Selman (1998) used perspective taking to reduce violence levels by getting individuals to empathise with others' feelings and viewpoints.
- Selman's role-taking theory and use of dilemmas provides researchers with an objective means of assessing social competence.

Biological explanations of social cognition
Revised

Biological factors interact with environmental variables, producing individual differences in social competence. Although learning experiences are necessary for normal development, without innate neural systems processing social stimuli, it is difficult to explain the universality and speed of social learning. Brain imaging studies indicate that a network of brain areas linking the medial prefrontal and temporal cortex form the neural substrate of mentalising, allowing representation of one's own and others' mental states.

Mirror neurons are brain nerves active when specific actions are performed or observed in others, allowing observers to experience actions as if they were theirs, and permitting the perception of feelings and thoughts of others by empathising with and imitating them and having a ToM.

social cognition — the understanding of information relating to members of the same sex.

mirror neuron system — a network of nerves in the brain that allows individuals to experience the actions of others as if their own.

Rizzolato and Craighero (2004) used brain scanning to find a network of neurons in the frontal and parietal brain areas working as mirror neurons.

Gallese (2001) using fMRI scanning found that the anterior cingulate cortex and inferior frontal cortex are active when individuals experience emotions or observe others experiencing identical emotions, suggesting a type of mirror neuron activity.

Stuss et al. (2001) reported that individuals with damaged frontal lobes were unable to empathise with and read others' intentions and were easily deceived, suggesting a biological link to social cognition.

- A methodological problem is that it is not possible to study the actions of single mirror neurons in humans.
- Social cognition only exists in higher animals, suggesting that it has a biological basis which evolved due to its adaptive advantage.
- Jacob and Jeannerod (2004) argue that a mirror neuron system is too simplistic. It cannot explain how the same actions performed in others can be interpreted differently by an observer in different contexts.

Examiner's tip

Biological explanations of social cognition present an opportunity to make the IDA point that such explanations are reductionist because they perceive only biological processes, such as mirror neurons, are at work, thus neglecting important non-biological factors, such as cognitive processes.

Research into mirror neurons indicates a possible biological explanation for autism and therefore the possibility of developing methods to counteract the condition.

Now test yourself
Tested

9 Describe factors that contribute to the development of the child's sense of self.
10 What degree of research support do these factors have?
11 What is meant by perspective taking?
12 Outline Selman's levels of perspective taking.
13 What evaluative points can be made concerning perspective taking?
14 How is social cognition explained biologically?
15 How might mirror neurons contribute to social cognition?
16 What evaluative points can be made concerning social cognition?

Answers on p. 125

Exam practice

1 Critically compare Piaget's and Vygotsky's theories of cognitive development. [24]
2 (a) Outline the development of perspective taking. [8]
   (b) Consider the applications of cognitive development theories to education. [16]
3 Discuss Kohlberg's theory of moral understanding. [24]
4 (a) Outline the development of the child's sense of self. [4]
   (b) Outline and evaluate biological explanations of social cognition. [20]

Answers and quick quiz 8 online

Online

Examiner's summary

✔ Piaget saw cognitive development as a series of innate, set stages, while Vygotsky saw cognitive development as a cultural construct occurring through social experience.

✔ Both Piaget and Vygotsky's theories have practical applications in education.

✔ Kohlberg saw moral development occurring gradually in innate, set stages.

✔ The child's sense of self is seen as developing through self-recognition, self-referential emotions and a sense of self-esteem, with the development of a Theory of Mind essential in the ability to attribute mental states to oneself and others.

✔ The development of children's understanding of others involves developing the ability to see other peoples' perspective.

✔ The mirror neuron system perceives a biological foundation to empathising with and imitating others.

9 Psychopathology

Students are required to study one mental disorder — schizophrenia, depression, phobias or obsessive-compulsive disorder (OCD). For the chosen disorder there is a requirement to know its clinical characteristics and relevant issues of classification and **diagnosis**, including reliability and validity. Students also need knowledge of both the biological and psychological explanations of their chosen disorder, as well as biological and psychological therapies. All relevant ones are valid as none is explicitly specified.

Classification and diagnosis

To diagnose mental disorders clinicians use classification systems based on the idea that groups of symptoms can be classed together as separate **syndromes**, allowing diagnosis, treatment and cure. **DSM-IV** and **ICD-10** are the main systems in worldwide use.

Reliability of diagnosis concerns the *consistency* of symptom assessment, affecting classification and diagnosis in two ways:

- **test–retest reliability** — occurring when a clinician makes the same consistent diagnosis on separate occasions from the same information
- **inter-rater reliability** — occurring when several clinicians make identical, independent diagnoses of the same patient

Validity of diagnosis concerns the *accuracy* of diagnosis and is assessed in several ways:

- **reliability** — a valid diagnosis has first to be reliable
- **predictive validity** — if diagnosis leads to successful treatment, validity is assumed
- **descriptive validity** and **aetiological validity** — to be a valid diagnosis all patients with a disorder should have the same cause

> **diagnosis** — identification of the nature and cause of illness.
>
> **DSM-IV** — diagnostic classification system produced in the USA.
>
> **ICD-10** — diagnostic classification system produced by the World Health Organization.
>
> **reliability** — consistency of diagnosis.
>
> **validity** — accuracy of diagnosis.

Schizophrenia

Clinical characteristics — Revised

Schizophrenia affects thought processes and the ability to determine reality. 1% of people worldwide are schizophrenic.

Some patients have only one episode, others have persistent episodes but live normal lives through the use of medication, while some remain disturbed.

Type I is an acute type characterised by positive symptoms, such as thought disorders. **Type II** is a chronic type characterised by negative symptoms, (e.g. apathy) with poorer prospects for recovery.

> **schizophrenia** — mental disorder characterised by withdrawal from reality.
>
> **type I schizophrenia** — acute form, characterised by positive symptoms and responsive to medication.
>
> **type II schizophrenia** — chronic type, characterised by negative symptoms and unresponsive to medication.

Diagnosis requires two or more symptoms for more than 1 month and reduced social functioning.

Symptoms are positive, where distortion of normal functioning occurs, or negative, with a lessening of normal functioning. With **chronic onset** schizophrenia, individuals gradually withdraw, losing motivation over time. **Acute onset** schizophrenia occurs suddenly after stressful incidents.

Schizophrenia occurs between 15 and 45 years of age, with equal proportions of males and females, though males show earlier onset.

Symptoms of schizophrenia

Passivity experiences and thought disorders — thoughts and actions are perceived as under external control. Sufferers may believe that thoughts are inserted, withdrawn or broadcast to others.

Auditory hallucinations — sufferers experience internal voices, forming running commentaries, or discussing sufferers' behaviour.

Primary delusions — sufferers may experience delusions of grandeur, thinking they are someone important. Delusions may become delusions of persecution, sufferers believing that someone is 'after them'.

Thought-process disorders — sufferers wander off the point, muddle their words, or invent new ones.

Disturbances of effect — sufferers appear indifferent, exhibit inappropriate emotional responses, or display mood changes.

Psychomotor disturbances — sufferers exhibit statue-like poses, tics and twitches, or repetitive behaviours.

Lack of volition — sufferers are unable to make decisions, have no enthusiasm and do not display affection.

Sub-types of schizophrenia

Paranoid — characterised by delusions of grandeur and/or persecution. Less noticeable disturbance than other types.

Catatonic — sufferers are excitable, or mute with frozen poses, or alternate between these two states. Negativism occurs, sufferers doing the opposite of what they are told. Hallucinations and delusions are less obvious.

Disorganised — onset occurs in the early to mid-twenties, sufferers experience auditory hallucinations, delusions, thought-process disorders, bizarre behaviour and disturbances of mood.

Residual — sufferers exhibited symptoms previously, but not presently. Negative symptoms are experienced during the past year. Sufferers display mild positive symptoms.

Undifferentiated — a category for schizophrenics not fitting other types, or with symptoms of several sub-types.

Simple — appears in late adolescence with gradual onset. There is an increase in apathy and social deterioration, with a decline in academic/occupational performance.

Examiner's tip

When revising for the Unit 4 examination, ensure that you have prepared material for both a short and a longer version of answers requiring an outline. Sometimes an outline may be worth just 4 marks, but at other times 8 marks. A different amount of material would therefore be required for these questions. For instance, look at Questions 1(a) and 6(a) in the 'Exam practice' section.

Post-schizophrenic depression — a sub-type for schizophrenics meeting criteria in the last year, though not at present, exhibiting severe and prolonged depressive symptoms.

Issues surrounding classification and diagnosis — Revised

Reliability

Beck et al. (1962) reported a 54% concordance rate between experienced practitioners' diagnoses.

Söderberg et al. (2005) reported a concordance rate of 81% using DSM-IV-TR, the most up-to-date form of the DSM classification system, suggesting that classification systems became more reliable over time.

Read et al. (2004) reported test–retest reliability of schizophrenia diagnosis to have only a 37% concordance rate, suggesting that reliability is low.

- The DSM classification system (used in the UK) is more reliable than the ICD (used in the USA), because of the amount of specificity in the symptoms outlined for each category.

- Even if reliability of diagnosis based on classification systems is poor, it allows practitioners to have a common language, permitting communication of research ideas and findings, and leading to better understanding of schizophrenia and effective treatments.

- Evidence suggests that reliability of diagnoses improves as classification systems are updated.

Validity

> **Typical mistakes**
>
> Many candidates answering questions on reliability and validity in diagnosis of schizophrenia describe what is meant by reliability and validity (even outlining different types of reliability and validity), believing this to be a good, detailed answer. However, unless the descriptions are made fully relevant to schizophrenia, such answers will gain little credit.

Hollis (2000) applied DSM classification diagnoses to case notes, finding that the diagnosis of schizophrenia had a high level of stability. This suggests that diagnoses are valid.

Heather (1976) reported that few causes of mental disorders are known and that there is only a 50% chance of predicting what treatment patients will receive based on diagnosis, suggesting that diagnosis is not valid.

Jansson and Parnas (2007) reviewed studies that applied different definitions of schizophrenia to the same patient samples. Both ICD-10 and DSM-IV showed reliability, but both were weak on measures of validity, casting doubt on the idea that schizophrenia is a separate condition.

- Bentall (2003) claimed that diagnosis of schizophrenia reveals nothing about the causes, implying that diagnosis is invalid. Diagnosis also reveals nothing about prevalence rates, which differ widely from rural to urban environments, again suggesting diagnosis to be invalid.

- Cochrane (1977) reported that the incidence of schizophrenia in the West Indies and the UK is 1%, but that people of Afro-Caribbean origin are seven times more likely to be diagnosed as schizophrenic when living in the UK, suggesting that Afro-Caribbean people living in the UK either have more stressors leading to schizophrenia, or receive invalid diagnoses due to cultural bias.

Biological explanations of schizophrenia — Revised

Evidence suggests that biological factors play a major contributory role. Findings from twin, family, adoption and gene mapping studies suggest a genetic component, making some individuals more vulnerable.

Torrey et al. (1994) found that if one identical twin develops schizophrenia, there is a 28% chance that the other twin will too, suggesting a genetic influence.

Kety and Ingraham (1992) found schizophrenia to be ten times higher among genetic than adoptive relatives, also suggesting a genetic role.

- Hedgecoe (2001) believes scientists construct schizophrenia as a genetic disease by using evidence in a biased way to produce a narrative about schizophrenia that prioritises **genetic explanations**.
- Varma and Sharma (1993) believe that family studies can identify samples for further research that have an increased probability of carrying the schizophrenic genotype.

Evolutionary explanations suggest an adaptive value to schizophrenia. Stevens and Price (1997) proposed the **group-splitting hypothesis**, where those possessing schizophrenic qualities make ideal leaders when groups split due to environmental pressures.

> **genetic explanations** — see schizophrenia as transmitted by hereditary means.
>
> **evolutionary explanations** — perceive schizophrenia as having an adaptive purpose.
>
> **biochemical explanations** — see schizophrenia as determined by neurotransmitters and hormones.

> **Peters et al. (1999)** studied religious cults, finding leaders were charismatic and possessed delusional beliefs, supporting the group-splitting hypothesis.
>
> **Storr (1997)** cites examples of group leaders possessing schizotypal, paranoid, psychopathic qualities, for example Adolf Hitler.

- Although some leaders possess schizophrenic qualities, the majority do not, even in new, breakaway social groupings, weakening support for the theory.

Biochemical explanations of schizophrenia centre on the idea that excess dopamine leads to its onset and that many anti-schizophrenic drugs inhibit dopamine activity. Davis et al. (1991) suggest that high levels of dopamine in the mesolimbic dopamine system are associated with positive symptoms, while high levels in the mesocortical dopamine system are associated with negative symptoms. The neurotransmitter glutamate also attracts attention, due to reduced function of NMDA glutamate receptors in schizophrenics.

Typical mistakes

In questions worth 24 marks requiring an outline and an evaluation (e.g. 'outline and evaluate psychological explanations of schizophrenia'), the outline is worth 8 marks while the evaluation is worth 16 marks. Many candidates spend too much time on the outline. Only one-third of your time should be spent on the outline and two-thirds on the evaluation.

> **Iversen (1979)** reported that dead schizophrenics have an excess of dopamine in their limbic systems, supporting the explanation.
>
> **Javitt et al. (2000)** found that glycine (a glutamate receptor agonist) reduced schizophrenic symptoms, supporting the glutamate theory.

- Healy (2000) believes that pharmaceutical companies were keen to see the dopamine theory promoted because they make profits from manufacturing anti-schizophrenic drugs that inhibit dopamine production.
- Excess dopamine could be an effect rather than a cause of schizophrenia.

Psychological explanations of schizophrenia

Revised ☐

Although evidence indicates that biological factors are important in the development of schizophrenia, it is generally accepted that psychological factors are involved too.

Psychodynamic

Psychodynamic explanations propose that schizophrenics have experienced either interpersonal regression or interpersonal withdrawal, with stress seen as a contributory factor and emphasis on the personality characteristics of parents, the interactions between parents and children, and family structures.

> **psychodynamic explanations** — see the origins of schizophrenia in repressed childhood conflicts.

Read et al. (2005) reviewed studies of schizophrenia, finding links between sexual abuse in childhood and the later development of schizophrenia. Schizophrenia was the most common mental disorder for victims of sexual abuse, supporting the psychodynamic explanation.

● There is little empirical data to back up the psychodynamic theory, most of the evidence coming from subjective analyses of case studies, which rely on honesty and accuracy of recall during psychoanalysis.

Cognitive

Cognitive explanations see schizophrenia as linked to maladaptive thinking, and symptoms such as disorganised thinking suggest a cognitive input. Frith (1992) suggests that the positive symptoms of schizophrenia, such as delusions, are meta-representation problems where there is an inability to distinguish external speech from internal thoughts. Conversely, negative symptoms, such as disorganised thinking, are problems of central control, where there is a failure to distinguish between behaviour of conscious intent and automatic response.

> **cognitive explanations** — see schizophrenia as determined through irrational thought processes.
>
> **sociocultural explanations** — see schizophrenia as determined through family and social environments.

Bentall et al. (1991) found that schizophrenics struggled to identify words belonging to certain categories (e.g. birds), which they had read earlier, had created themselves or had not seen before, supporting Frith's theory of schizophrenics having meta-representation problems.

● Kane and Lencz (2008) proposed that the inclusion of cognitive impairment in the diagnostic criteria for schizophrenia would improve the validity of diagnosis and treatments by targeting cognitive enhancement as a primary goal.

Sociocultural

Sociocultural explanations see the maintenance of schizophrenia linking to the degree of expressed emotion within families (e.g. hostility), which predicts relapse in schizophrenics.

The **double-bind theory** sees schizophrenia as a learned response to conflicting messages and mutually exclusive demands during childhood, leading to disorganised thinking and communication. **Social causation** perceives lower social classes as subject to more stressors, causing heightened levels of schizophrenia.

Leff (1976) reported a relapse rate of 51% for schizophrenics returning to homes with high expressed emotion compared with 13% for schizophrenics returning to homes with low rates of expressed emotion.

● Social-cultural factors may be effects rather than causes (e.g. expressed emotions may occur within families due to the stresses and conflicts associated with living with schizophrenics, rather than contributing to the condition's onset).

> **Examiner's tip**
>
> When evaluating biological and psychological explanations of schizophrenia, a good way of accessing higher-level marks for evaluation is to refer to associated therapies. If therapies have research support in terms of their effectiveness, then this can be argued to support the theoretical foundations of the explanations they are based on.

Biological therapies for schizophrenia ⎯ Revised ☐

Electro-convulsive therapy

Cerletti (1935) believed that inducing epileptic fits through **electro-convulsive therapy** (ECT) could have a positive outcome for schizophrenics. This proved not to be the case, but ECT was reintroduced and has emerged as more effective than placebos, although not as

> **electro-convulsive therapy** — the application of electrical voltages across the brain, to treat schizophrenia.

effective as drugs. ECT works best applied bilaterally (to both sides of the head). Treatments are given in conjunction with anaesthetics and muscle relaxants.

Tharyan and Adams (2005) reviewed studies of ECT, concluding that it was effective in the short term, and better than no treatment, but not as effective as antipsychotic drugs.

Tang et al. (2002) found ECT effective in treating schizophrenics non-responsive to antipsychotic drugs, suggesting that the treatment provides relief to such patients.

- 50% of schizophrenics who respond positively to ECT relapse within 6 months, suggesting that it is not a long-term solution.
- Unilateral ECT treatment produces fewer side effects, such as short-term memory loss, but is not as effective. Memory generally returns to normal, but 1% of people treated suffer severe memory loss.

> **drug therapy for schizophrenia** — chemical treatment through tablets and intravenous means.

Drug therapy

The prime treatment for schizophrenia is antipsychotic drugs, which reduce symptoms so that some degree of functioning becomes possible. Drugs do not offer a cure. There are first- (typical) and second-generation (atypical) antipsychotic drugs. Typical varieties, such as chlopromazine, arrest dopamine production by blocking receptors in synapses that absorb dopamine, thus reducing positive symptoms, such as auditory hallucinations. Atypical antipsychotics, such as clozapine, act on serotonin and dopamine production systems, affecting negative symptoms, such as reduced emotional expression.

Some sufferers take antipsychotic drugs as a one-off treatment, while others take regular doses to prevent schizophrenia reappearing. A sizeable minority of schizophrenics do not respond to drugs.

> **Typical mistakes**
>
> Many students study and revise biological and psychological therapies of schizophrenia as separate from each other. However, a good way of accessing higher levels of marks for evaluation is to compare the therapies, drawing out their appropriateness and effectiveness by contrasting their strengths and weaknesses. Questions might ask for such a comparison. For instance, look at Question 5 in the 'Exam practice' section.

Kahn et al. (2008) found that antipsychotic drugs are generally effective for over a year, but that second-generation drugs were more effective than first-generation ones.

Davis et al. (1989) performed a meta-analysis of studies comparing antipsychotics with placebos, finding drugs to be more effective. 70% of sufferers treated with antipsychotics improved after 6 weeks, while 25% improved with placebos, suggesting that antipsychotics are beneficial.

- Antipsychotics are relatively cheap, easy to administer and help many sufferers, allowing them to live relatively normal lives outside institutions.
- Although antipsychotics can produce relatively minor side effects, such as constipation, some sufferers incur serious neurological symptoms leading to coma and death.

Psychological therapies for schizophrenia
Revised

Behavioural therapy

There is little evidence that schizophrenia is learned, but successful treatment is attained through **token economies** — behavioural change being achieved by awarding tokens for desired actions. These reinforcers are exchanged for goods or privileges. Negative symptoms, such as poor motivation, are reduced and nurses view patients more positively, which benefits the patients.

> **behavioural therapies** — treatments that modify maladaptive behaviours, including those shown in schizophrenia.

McMonagle and Sultana (2000) found that participating in token economies reduced sufferers' negative symptoms, though it is unclear whether behavioural changes are maintained after treatment.

Upper and Newton (1971) found that weight gain associated with antipsychotics was addressed by taking part in token economies. Chronic schizophrenics achieved a target of 1.5 kg of body weight loss a week.

- The behavioural changes achieved through taking part in token economies disappear when the tokens are withdrawn, suggesting that such treatments address the effects of schizophrenia rather than its causes.
- Token economies focus on shaping and positively reinforcing desired behaviours, not on punishing undesirable behaviours.

Cognitive-behavioural therapy

Cognitive-behavioural therapy (CBT) is the main psychological treatment for schizophrenia, although antipsychotics are also used to reduce psychotic thought processes. The idea is that beliefs, expectations and cognitive assessments of self, the environment and the nature of personal problems affect how individuals perceive themselves and others, how problems are approached and how successful individuals are in coping and attaining goals. CBT aims to identify and alter irrational thinking. Drawings are employed to display links between sufferers' thoughts, actions and emotions; comprehension of the origins of their symptoms is useful in reducing sufferers' anxiety levels.

cognitive-behavioural therapy — treatment of schizophrenia that modifies thought patterns to alter behavioural and emotional states.

Examiner's tip

When studying and revising biological and psychological explanations of schizophrenia, as well as biological and psychological therapies for schizophrenia, ensure that you have covered two of each. Sometimes questions will ask specifically for one explanation/ therapy, but if the question asks for explanations/therapies, then two will be required.

Turkington et al. (2006) found CBT to be highly effective in treating schizophrenia, and suggested that it should be used as a mainstream treatment wherever possible.

Tarrier (2005) found evidence of reduced symptoms, especially positive ones, and lower relapse rates, suggesting CBT to be an effective treatment.

- For CBT to be effective, training is essential, successful treatment being dependent on developing empathy, respect, unconditional positive regard and honesty between patient and practitioner.
- CBT is not suitable for everyone, especially those thought to be too disorientated or agitated, who refuse medication, or are too paranoid to form trusting alliances with practitioners.

Depression

Clinical characteristics — Revised

Symptoms of depression

Constant depressed mood — feelings of sadness, reported by sufferers or observed by others.

Lessened interest — diminished concern with and/or lack of pleasure in daily activities, reported by sufferers or observed by others.

Weight loss — significant decrease (or increase) in weight and/or appetite.

Sleep pattern disturbance — constant insomnia or oversleeping.

Fatigue — loss of energy and displacement of energy levels, for example becoming lethargic or agitated.

Reduced concentration — difficulty in paying attention, slowed thinking and/or indecisiveness, reported by sufferers or observed by others.

Worthlessness — constant feelings of reduced worth and/or inappropriate guilt.

Focus on death — constant thoughts of death and/or suicide.

At least five symptoms must be apparent every day for at least 2 weeks for **depression** to be diagnosed, with impairment in general functioning unaccountable by other medical conditions. One of the five symptoms should either be a constant depressed mood or lessened interest in daily activities.

Sub-types of depression

Unipolar depression (major depression) is differentiated from **bipolar depression** by its manifestation of pure depression without manic episodes.

Bipolar depression (manic depression) involves different types of episode, including depressive ones, plus manic episodes where sufferers are aroused and have trouble concentrating, while simultaneously displaying elevated self-esteem and excessive involvement in pleasurable but harmful activities, such as taking drugs.

> **depression** — a mood disorder characterised by feelings of despondency and hopelessness.
>
> **unipolar depression** — a form of depression occurring without alternating periods of mania.
>
> **bipolar depression** — a mood disorder characterised by alternating periods of depression and mania.

Issues surrounding classification and diagnosis
Revised

Reliability

Most people's moods vary over time, so reliable diagnosis is difficult. Another problem is assessing the degree of depression.

Diagnosis was originally performed by clinical interviews, but use is increasingly made of depression inventories.

Einfeld et al. (2002) found high levels of agreement between skilled clinicians in diagnosing depression, implying a high degree of inter-rater reliability.

Sato et al. (1996) assessed the test–retest reliability of the Inventory to Diagnose Depression, Lifetime Version, finding a concordance rate of 77%, suggesting that using inventories to diagnose depression is highly reliable.

● A problem in assessing the reliability of diagnosing depression over time is that patients may improve in condition between diagnoses.

● Chao-Cheng et al. (2002) raises the possibility of self-diagnosing depression through internet self-assessments. Jürges (2008) reports that the problem with self-assessments is that patients underestimate changes in self-ratings of health, reducing the reliability of this diagnostic method.

Validity

Zigler and Phillips (1961) reported that symptoms of depression are found equally in patients assessed as neurotic and as having bipolar disorder, as well as in 25% of diagnosed schizophrenics, implying low diagnostic validity of depression.

Sanchez-Villegas et al. (2008) assessed the validity of the Structured Clinical Interview, finding that 74.2% of depressives were accurately diagnosed, suggesting the diagnostic method to be valid.

Typical mistakes

When answering questions on reliability and validity in depression, many candidates describe what is meant by reliability and validity (or even outline different types of reliability and validity) believing this to be a good, detailed answer. However, unless the descriptions are made fully relevant to the reliability and validity of *depression*, such answers will gain little credit.

- Validation of diagnostic scales is important in proving such criteria valid in themselves, but also because such diagnostic scales are then used to assess further the validity of other diagnostic measures.
- A significant obstacle to treating depression is the failure to diagnose symptoms. Burrows et al. (1995) found that healthcare providers under-diagnosed depression in 56% of nursing home residents.

Biological explanations of depression
Revised

Biological explanations of depression are supported by hereditary factors, the uniformity of symptoms across genders, ages and cultural groups, and the effectiveness of biological therapies, although environmental factors are important too.

Genetic explanation

Findings from twin, family, adoption and gene mapping studies suggest a genetic component in depression, making some individuals more vulnerable than others.

> **genetic explanation** — sees depression as transmitted by hereditary means.

Sevey et al. (2000) found a concordance rate for bipolar disorder of 69% in identical twins, but only 20% in non-identical twins. As MZ twins share 100% genetic similarity compared to 50% in DZ twins, this suggests a genetic influence.

Wender et al. (1986) found that adopted children who develop depression were more likely to have a biological parent with the disorder, even though adopted children are raised in different environments, implying that biological factors are more important than environmental ones.

Caspi et al. (2005) used gene mapping to find a relationship between depression and abnormalities in the 5-HTT gene, suggesting a genetic link. As 5-HTT is associated with the manufacture of serotonin, this implies a link between genetics and biochemical factors.

- Findings from studies involving genetics suggest evidence for the diathesis-stress model, where individuals inherit different levels of genetic predisposition to developing depression, but ultimately it is environmental triggers that determine whether individuals develop the disorder.
- Twin and family studies suggest a genetic factor in the onset of depression, but often do not consider the influence that social class and sociopsychological factors between family members have.

Biochemical explanation

Biochemical explanations centre on the idea that abnormal levels of neurotransmitters and hormones cause depression. Attention focuses on monoamine neurotransmitters such as serotonin, noradrenaline and dopamine, low levels being found in depressives' brains. Antidepressant drugs work by increasing the production of monoamines. Certain depressions, such as post-natal depression, are also associated with hormonal changes.

> **biochemical explanations** — see depression as determined by neurotransmitters and hormones.

Mann et al. (1996) found that major depression results from serotonin deficiency or insufficient serotonin receptors, suggesting a biochemical cause to depression.

Zhou et al. (2005) found that selective serotonin reuptake inhibitors work by increasing dopamine levels in depressives, implying that the neurotransmitter is involved in the causation of depression.

Chen et al. (2006) reported that declines in the level of the hormone insulin following childbirth are responsible for post-natal depression.

- A problem with biochemical explanations is whether fluctuations in neurotransmitter and hormonal levels are a cause or an effect of depression.

Typical mistakes

Candidates answering 24-mark questions requiring an outline and an evaluation (e.g. 'outline and evaluate psychological explanations of depression') often spend too much time on the outline, leaving little time for the evaluation. The outline is worth only 8 marks while the evaluation is worth 16 marks, so only one-third of the time should be spent on the outline and two-thirds on the evaluation.

Exam practice answers and quick quizzes at **www.therevisionbutton.co.uk/myrevisionnotes**

- It may be possible to prevent post-natal depression by increasing the amount of carbohydrates eaten, because carbohydrates stimulate the production of insulin.

Psychological explanations of depression   *Revised*

Although evidence indicates that biological factors play a role in the onset of depression, it is generally accepted that psychological factors are involved too.

Psychodynamic

Freud (1917) believed that depression was related to childhood experiences of loss and that depression in adulthood was delayed regret for this loss. Children experience anger over loss and, being unable to express this, regress it. Similar loss in adult life causes people to re-experience childhood loss.

Bowlby (1973) also offered a **psychodynamic explanation** for depression, that experiencing separation from a mother figure in early childhood led to an enhanced vulnerability to depression in later life.

> **psychodynamic explanations** — see the origins of depression in repressed childhood conflicts.

Swaffer and Hollin (2001) found that young offenders who repressed anger had increased vulnerability to developing depression, supporting the psychodynamic model.

Harlow et al. (1965) found that baby monkeys that were separated from their mothers at birth exhibited symptoms of depression, supporting the psychodynamic model.

- Psychodynamic explanations have parallels with modern theories of cognitive vulnerability, which also perceive links with experiences of loss.
- Psychodynamic theory is difficult to test scientifically and is therefore difficult to refute or support.

Cognitive

Cognitive explanations see depression as resulting from cognitive vulnerabilities. Beck (1976) saw depression resulting from three types of self-defeating negative thought patterns:

Negative automatic thinking — having negative thoughts about oneself, one's environment and future situations.

Selective attention to the negative — paying attention to negative and not positive aspects of situations.

Negative self-schemas — having a set of negative self-beliefs, influencing perception of future situations.

Abramson et al. (1989) proposed that individuals possessing a negative attributional style (attributing failures to themselves, rather than external factors) as well as hopelessness (believing that negative events will occur) are likely to develop depression.

> **cognitive explanations** — see depression as determined through irrational thought processes.

Examiner's tip

When evaluating biological and psychological explanations of depression, a good way of accessing higher-level marks for evaluation is to refer to associated therapies. If therapies are supported by the findings of research in terms of their effectiveness, then this can be argued to support the theoretical foundations of the explanations they are based on.

Boury et al. (2001) found that depressives misinterpret facts and experiences in negative fashions and feel hopeless about the future, supporting Beck's explanation.

Seligman (1974) reported that students making negative attributions remained depressed for longer after examinations, supporting the cognitive explanation of attributional style.

- Evidence supports the idea of cognitive vulnerability being linked to the onset of depression, with depressives selectively attending to negative stimuli.
- Evidence linking negative thinking to depression is correlational and does not show causality.

Biological therapies for depression

The two common biological treatments for depression are drugs and electro-convulsive therapy (ECT).

Drug therapy

Antidepressant drugs stimulate the production of monoamine neurotransmitters, leading to increased physical arousal. Old-fashioned antidepressants, such as monoamine oxidase inhibitors, stop serotonin, noradrenaline and dopamine being broken down, so their levels are increased, while tricyclics stop serotonin and noradrenaline being reabsorbed, so again their levels increase. Antidepressants are effective in treating depression but side effects such as drowsiness can be experienced.

> **drug therapy for depression** — chemical treatment through tablets and intravenous means.

Modern antidepressants affect the level of one monoamine — for example, Prozac prevents serotonin being reabsorbed or broken down. There is no preferred drug — patients tend to respond differently to different drugs. The symptoms displayed and the side effects exhibited determine drug choice.

Furukawa et al. (2003) found antidepressants to be more effective than placebos, suggesting that antidepressants are an effective treatment.

Kirsch (2008) found that new generation antidepressants work no better than placebos for most patients and accused drug companies of suppressing research evidence casting doubt on these drugs' effectiveness.

- Antidepressant drugs are cost-effective, occur in tablet form (a familiar and trusted form of treatment), and have the added benefit of being self-administered.
- Research indicates that psychological treatments are more effective than antidepressants, but such treatments are not favoured because they are more costly.

Electro-convulsive therapy

Electro-convulsive therapy (ECT) produces a seizure lasting up to a minute. Shocks to both sides of the head (bilateral) are more effective than unilateral shocks to one side, but produce more side effects. Modern ECT uses mild shocks for brief periods, with ECT generally administered two or three times a week for about eight treatments, along with an anaesthetic and a muscle relaxant to prevent bone fractures.

> **electro-convulsive therapy** — the application of electrical voltages across the brain.

ECT is controversial because it seems brutal and has side effects such as temporary memory loss, which get more severe as treatment continues. It is not clear how ECT works, but modern forms are more humane and deemed appropriate when other treatments fail, or when a patient is perceived as a suicide risk.

Paguin et al. (2008) performed a meta-analysis of ECT, comparing studies of ECT, placebos and antidepressant drugs. They found ECT to be superior, suggesting that it is a valid therapeutic tool for treating depression, including severe and resistant forms.

Levy (1968) compared bilateral and unilateral forms of ECT, finding that unilateral treatments incurred less memory loss but bilateral treatments produced better relief of depressive symptoms.

● Side effects of ECT are more severe with children, adolescents, the elderly and pregnant women, and should not be used to treat these categories of people, except as a last resort.

● There is a high relapse rate associated with ECT. Sackheim et al. (2001) found that 84% of patients relapsed within 6 months, implying that the treatment is ineffective in the long term.

Typical mistakes

Many students study and revise biological and psychological therapies of depression as separate from each other. However, a good way of accessing higher levels of marks for evaluation is to compare the therapies, drawing out their appropriateness and effectiveness by contrasting their strengths and weaknesses. It is possible to get a question that asks specifically for such a comparison. For instance, look at Question 5 in the 'Exam practice' section.

Psychological therapies for depression

Revised ☐

Psychodynamic therapy

Psychodynamic therapy explores the patient's childhood, linking this to the current situation, with childhood experiences of loss and rejection crucial to depression. Patients are encouraged to relive experiences and gain insight into their inability to form healthy relationships, especially the transference of anger incurred from early rejection and loss onto others.

Leichsenring et al. (2004) found brief dynamic therapy, a simpler form of psychodynamic treatment, as effective as cognitive-behavioural therapy in addressing depression.

De Clerq et al. (1999) found psychodynamic psychotherapy to be desirable and feasible when delivered by closely supervised, skilled, well-trained nurses, suggesting that the effectiveness of treatment depends on the quality of clinicians administering it.

● Psychotherapy works best when patients attend all scheduled sessions, which requires motivation and effort — not always easy for those exhibiting symptoms of depression.

● Eysenck (1952) found that only 44% of patients improved with psychotherapy, compared to 66% of patients who improved without any form of treatment, suggesting that psychotherapy is less effective than no treatment.

Cognitive-behavioural therapy

The idea behind **cognitive-behavioural therapy** (CBT) is that beliefs, expectations and cognitive assessments of self, the environment and the nature of personal problems affect how individuals perceive themselves and others, how problems are approached and how successful individuals are in coping and attaining goals.

CBT assists patients in identifying irrational and maladaptive thoughts and altering them. Thoughts affect emotions and thus behaviour and it is the patient's thinking that has to be altered to reduce depressive symptoms. Drawings are employed to display links between thoughts, actions and emotions, with comprehension of where symptoms come from being useful in reducing anxiety levels.

psychodynamic therapy for depression — treatment based on psychoanalytic theory that explores unconscious motives to highlight the roots of depression.

cognitive-behavioural therapy for depression — treatment that modifies thought patterns to alter behavioural and emotional states.

Flannaghan et al. (1997) found CBT to be effective in treating depressive stroke victims, suggesting that it is a suitable treatment for specific groups of depressives.

Whitfield and Williams (2003) found that CBT has the strongest research base for effectiveness, but recognised that there is cost problem in delivering weekly face-to-face sessions for patients on the National Health Service.

- CBT is regarded as the most effective psychological treatment for moderate and severe depression and one of the most effective treatments where depression is the main problem.
- An advantage of CBT as a general treatment of depression, compared to other forms of treatment, is that it produces few side effects.

Examiner's tip

When studying and revising biological and psychological explanations of depression, as well as biological and psychological therapies of depression, ensure that you have covered two of each. Sometimes questions will ask specifically for one explanation/ therapy, but if the question asks for explanations/therapies then two will be required.

Anxiety disorders

One in five people experience anxiety levels so high that they are maladaptive, affecting day-to-day functioning in a negative way. Unit 4 deals with **phobias** and **obsessive-compulsive disorder** (OCD), both of which are exaggerated versions of normal behaviour, perceived as mental disorders when they become detrimental to everyday functioning.

anxiety disorders — abnormal conditions characterised by extreme worry, fear and nervousness.

Clinical characteristics: phobias — Revised

Phobias are characterised by extreme, irrational and enduring fears that cannot be controlled, involving anxiety levels out of proportion to any actual risk.

Phobias are twice as common among females. Ten percent of the population suffers from a specific phobia at some point. Most phobias originate in childhood, diminishing in strength during adulthood.

phobias — anxiety disorders characterised by extreme irrational fears.

Symptoms: phobias — Revised

Persistent, excessive fear — high anxiety due to the presence or anticipation of feared situations.

Fear from exposure to phobic stimulus — immediate fear response, even panic attack, due to presentation of phobic situations.

Recognition of exaggerated anxiety — sufferers are aware that their levels of anxiety are overstated.

Avoidant/anxiety response — feared situations are avoided or lead to high anxiety responses.

Disruption of functioning — anxiety/avoidance response is so extreme that it interferes with the sufferer's work and social functioning.

Sub-types of phobia

Phobias divide into:

- *simple phobias* — sufferers fear specific situations (e.g. pediophobia, the fear of dolls)

Examiner's tip

When revising for the Unit 4 examination, ensure you have prepared material for both a short and a longer version of answers requiring an outline. Sometimes an outline may be worth 4 marks, but at other times 8 marks. A very different amount of material would therefore be required for these questions. For instance, look at Questions 1(a) and 6(a) in the 'Exam practice' section.

- *social phobias* — sufferers fear social environments (e.g. talking in public)

Social phobias can be further divided into animal phobias (e.g. arachnophobia, fear of spiders), injury phobias (e.g. haematophobia, fear of blood), situational phobias (e.g. aerophobia, fear of flying), natural environment phobias (e.g. hydrophobia, fear of water).

Clinical characteristics: obsessive-compulsive disorder
Revised

Obsessive-compulsive disorder occurs in 2% of the population. Sufferers endure persistent and intrusive thoughts occurring as obsessions, compulsions or a combination of both.

> **obsessive-compulsive disorder** — anxiety disorder characterised by persistent, recurrent, unpleasant thoughts and repetitive, ritualistic behaviours.

Obsessions consist of forbidden or inappropriate ideas and visual images leading to anxiety, whereas compulsions consist of intense, uncontrollable urges to perform tasks and behaviours repetitively (e.g. constant cleaning). Sufferers realise that their compulsions are inappropriate but cannot exert control over them, resulting in greater anxiety.

Symptoms: obsessive-compulsive disorder
Revised

Obsessions are:

Recurrent and persistent — inappropriate and intrusive thoughts, impulses and images are recurrently experienced, leading to anxiety and distress.

Irrelevant to real life — thoughts, impulses and images experienced are not relevant to real-life situations.

Suppressed — sufferers suppress thoughts, impulses and images with alternative thoughts or actions.

Recognised as self-generated — sufferers recognise that obsessional thoughts, impulses and images are products of their own invention and not introduced externally.

Compulsions are:

Repetitive — sufferers feel compelled to repeat behaviours and mental acts in response to obsessional thoughts, impulses and images.

Aimed at reducing distress — behaviours and mental acts attempt to reduce distress or prevent feared events, although they have little realistic chance of doing so.

Other symptoms:

Recognition as excessive — sufferers realise that obsessions/compulsions are excessive.

Time consumptive — obsessions/compulsions are time consuming, cause distress and interfere with everyday working and social functioning.

Unrelated to substance abuse — OCD is not related to substance abuse or other medical conditions.

Reliability: phobias

Silverman et al. (2001) examined the test–retest reliability of phobias in children aged between 7 and 16 years old. The Anxiety Disorders Interview Schedule (ADIS) for DSM IV was administered twice, results indicating reliability for simple and social phobias.

Alstrom et al. (2009) assessed the inter-rater reliability of phobia diagnosis in Swedish patients, finding inter-rater reliability to be excellent with a 90% concurrence rate.

- Assessment of inter-rater reliability involves one rater interviewing a patient and another observing the interview. Therefore, both diagnoses are based on identical information and, not surprisingly, show high reliability. It is far better for one rater to perform an interview and the second rater to perform a separate independent interview on the same patient.
- Research studies differ in the assessment of reliability even when identical measuring scales are used. Early assessments of ADIS found low reliability for phobias, while later studies found higher levels, suggesting that it is the revision of measuring scales that led to improved reliability of diagnosis.

Typical mistakes

When answering questions on reliability and validity in diagnosing anxiety disorders it is common for candidates to describe what is meant by reliability and validity, and even to outline different types of reliability and validity, believing this to be a good, detailed answer. However unless the descriptions are made fully relevant to the reliability and validity of anxiety disorders such answers will gain little credit.

Reliability: obsessive-compulsive disorder

Di Nardo and Barlow (1987) found that the principal diagnosis of OCD was associated with excellent diagnostic reliability, scoring an 80% concurrence rate, second only to simple phobias among anxiety and mood disorders.

Foa et al. (1987), using Likert scales, obtained large correlations among patients', therapists' and independent observers' ratings of OCD features, including main fear, avoidance and compulsion severity. This suggests good inter-rater reliability.

- The high prevalence of OCD and its secretive nature, leading to under-recognition of the disorder, suggests the need for a simple, quick reliable diagnostic tool to identify cases.
- The fact that OCD has easily observable symptoms assists clear diagnosis, contributing to high levels of reliability.

Validity: phobias

Herbert et al. (1992) assessed the descriptive validity of social phobias, comparing them with avoidant personality disorder (APD). They found social phobias and APD to represent quantitatively, but not qualitatively, distinct disorders, suggesting that social phobias are not a separate disorder.

Vasey and Dadds (2001) tested the predictive validity of anxiety disorder diagnoses, finding few differences in treatment outcomes for different sub-groups, suggesting low predictive validity.

- The predictive validity of diagnostic systems relating to children's anxiety disorders is subject to little research, and studies assessed indicate little evidence of childhood anxiety disorders predicting different outcomes, suggesting low predictive validity.
- Rabung et al. (2009) believe that self-rating instruments are valid measuring tools of phobias because they are sensitive to change, suitable for clinical use and cost-effective since they are downloadable free from the internet.

Validity: obsessive-compulsive disorder

Leckman and Chittenden (1990) assessed the validity of diagnosis of OCD, finding that 50% of patients with Tourette's syndrome also had OCD, indicating that OCD is not a separate disorder.

Deacon and Abramovitz (2004) tested the validity of the Yale–Brown Obsessive Compulsive Scale, regarded as the gold-standard measure of OCD, applying it to patients with a diagnosis of OCD. They found problems with the ability to measure the components of OCD validly, suggesting that the scale needs serious revision.

- Diagnoses of OCD have long-term impact on sufferers' lives, but such diagnoses are made with little evidence of the disorder being a separate condition.
- Although evidence indicates that many measuring scales used to assess OCD are not valid, they are still regarded as the most effective assessment tool in determining diagnostic and treatment outcomes.

Biological explanations of anxiety disorders

Revised

Results from twin and family studies indicate some genetic influence on anxiety disorders, although it is difficult to separate **genetic explanation** from environmental influences.

genetic explanation — sees anxiety disorders as transmitted by hereditary means.

Gene mapping studies involve comparing genetic material from families with high and low incidence of anxiety disorders. Results indicate that particular genes are involved, making some individuals more vulnerable than others.

Genetic explanation: phobias

Kendler et al. (1992) found a 24% concordance rate for social phobia in identical female twins, compared with 15% for non-identical female twins, suggesting a genetic influence.

Reich and Yates (1988) found social phobia rates higher in relatives of social phobics (6%) than in relatives of non-social phobic controls (2%), suggesting some genetic influence.

Gelertner et al. (2004) conducted a gene mapping study on sufferers of social phobias, finding a link to social phobias for various markers of chromosome 16, with additional interest also centred on chromosomes 9, 14 and 18, suggesting evidence of a genetic component.

The onset of phobias may involve the diathesis-stress model, where individuals inherit different degrees of vulnerability but environmental triggers ultimately determine whether individuals develop the disorder.

Although evidence from twin and family studies suggests a genetic influence, related individuals may acquire phobias through similar environmental experiences, or through imitation.

heritability — the degree to which a quality or behaviour is genetically determined.

Genetic explanation: obsessive-compulsive disorder

Grootheest et al. (2005) reviewed 70 years of twin studies into OCD, finding a **heritability** rate of 65% for OCD in children and 47% in adults, suggesting a genetic contribution.

Lenane et al. (1990) studied the prevalence of OCD among related family members, finding evidence for heritability, again supporting the genetic viewpoint.

Samuels et al. (2007) used gene mapping to compare OCD sufferers exhibiting hoarding behaviour with OCD sufferers who did not, finding a link to chromosome 14 marker D14S588. This suggests a genetic influence and may also indicate the existence of separate OCD sub-types.

Weissman (1985) noted that the tendency for OCD to run in families was first observed over a century ago; the idea is therefore not new and has influenced subsequent research.

The fact that family members often display dissimilar OCD symptoms — for example, children arranging dolls and adults constantly washing dishes — weakens support for the genetic viewpoint. If the disorder were inherited, exhibited behaviours would be the same.

Evolutionary explanations of anxiety disorders

Revised

Anxiety disorders continue to be apparent in the population, suggesting an adaptive value.

Biological preparedness is the idea that animals have innate abilities to display certain fears and therefore develop some conditioned fears easily. Such fears are genetic and environmental, since the phobia is learned from environmental experience, with the predisposition to learn the fear being the inherited component.

Phobias serve several adaptive functions, such as the fear element of phobia paralysing an individual, aiding concealment from predators, or the flight response helping to outrun predators. Alternatively, fear bends individuals into submission against dominant aggressors, saving them from harm. The fear response may release hormones that aid the clotting of blood, helping to heal wounds, and stimulate the liver to release glucose for energy, which is important to facilitate 'flight or fight'.

OCD involves repetitive behaviours such as washing, and these were important in the evolutionary past in preventing infection. Similar behaviours increased vigilance and alertness, incurring a survival value. Modern-day versions, such as continually cleaning handles, are an exaggeration of ancient adaptations.

> **evolutionary explanations** — perceive anxiety disorders as having an adaptive purpose.

> **Typical mistakes**
>
> When answering 24-mark questions requiring an outline and an evaluation (e.g. 'outline and evaluate psychological explanations of one anxiety disorder'), many candidates spend too much time on the outline, leaving little time for the evaluation. However, the outline is worth only 8 marks, while the evaluation is worth 16 marks. Therefore one-third of the time should be spent on the outline and two-thirds on the evaluation.

Evolutionary explanation: phobias

> **Cook and Mineka (1989)** demonstrated to laboratory-raised monkeys the fear response of wild monkeys to snakes and rabbits. Subsequently, the laboratory-raised monkeys showed a similar response to a toy snake, but not to a toy rabbit, suggesting an evolutionary readiness to fear snakes, but not rabbits.
>
> **Bennett-Levy and Marteau (1984)** asked participants to rate animals for ugliness, fearfulness and harmfulness. The less human an animal appeared, the bigger the fear response, suggesting an adaptive readiness to fear certain things more than others.

Learned helplessness explains why it is harder to develop fears of dangerous modern-day objects and situations, such as guns, because they were not present in the Environment of Evolutionary Adaptiveness (EEA) and are therefore not coded into genes.

Some phobias are so bizarre and individual that they are better explained as purely conditioned responses, rather than having evolved.

Evolutionary explanation: obsessive-compulsive disorder

> **Marks and Nesse (1984)** state that a lack of concern for others incurs a risk of ostracism from social groups, so the concern of OCD sufferers for the welfare of others reduces the risk, suggesting an adaptive value.
>
> **Chepko-Sade et al. (1989)** found that rhesus monkeys performing the most grooming of others were retained within the group after group in-fighting, suggesting that OCD has an adaptive value.

- Behavioural features of OCD, such as hoarding, were beneficial to hunting and gathering food in our evolutionary past and remain now due to genome lag, where genes take time to evolve and better fit the current environment.
- Evolutionary explanations of OCD do not account for individual and cultural differences.

Psychological explanations of anxiety disorders   Revised

There are several psychological explanations of anxiety disorders, including cognitive and sociocultural ones. Although evidence indicates that biological factors are important, psychological factors are involved too.

Cognitive explanations: phobias

Phobias are seen as originating from maladaptive thinking, occurring as a reaction to anxiety-generating situations.

Another cognitive factor concerns the tendency of people with anxiety disorders to be affected by **attentional bias**, such as phobics concentrating more attention on anxiety-generating stimuli.

> **cognitive explanations** — see anxiety disorders as determined through irrational thought processes.

> **Thorpe and Salkovskis (2000)** assessed conscious beliefs related to exposure to phobic stimuli, finding a major role in specific phobias for thoughts related to harm. This suggests that specific phobias are cognitive in origin.
>
> **Kindt and Brosschot (1997)** found that arachnophobics took longer to name the ink colour of spider-related words on a Stroop test, supporting the cognitive explanation.

- The cognitive explanation is deterministic, perceiving phobias as caused by psychological factors over which sufferers have no control.
- The cognitive viewpoint explains how phobias are maintained but not why they originate. Phobias could be caused by conditioning or genetics and are then perpetuated by faulty thinking.

Cognitive explanations: obsessive-compulsive disorder

OCD is seen as originating from sufferers having impaired, persistent thought processes, leading to self-blame, depression and heightened anxiety. Behaviours that lessen impaired, obsessive thoughts become compulsive because of their anxiety-reducing qualities, and become difficult to control.

> **Davison and Neale (1994)** found that OCD patients cannot distinguish between imagination and reality, supporting the idea of faulty thinking processes being linked to OCD.
>
> **Clark (1992)** reported that intrusive thinking is more common in OCD sufferers than the normal population, supporting the cognitive argument.

- Cognitive treatments of OCD work by correcting cognitive bias, helping sufferers to become less vigilant, providing support for the cognitive explanation.
- The cognitive explanation does not explain emotional aspects of irrational beliefs, weakening support for the viewpoint.

Sociocultural explanations: phobias

Some phobias occur more in certain cultures while others are culture-specific, implying a cultural influence.

Social factors concern the role that family dynamics play in developing anxiety disorders, such as fearful and socially anxious parents unknowingly transferring information to children about the dangers of social situations and the children developing the same anxiety themselves.

> **Kleinknecht et al. (1997)** reported on Taijin Kyofusho, a Japanese social phobia where sufferers fear offending others with inappropriate behaviour, suggesting that some phobias are culturally determined.
>
> **Bruch and Heimberg (1994)** found that children of socially isolated parents are more socially isolated themselves and therefore more at risk of developing social phobias.

- The fact that children of parents with an anxiety disorder are at risk of developing the disorder themselves is as easily explained in genetic terms as by social factors.
- Media emphasis on demonstrating 'normal' and 'attractive' personal characteristics may contribute to individuals feeling inferior and insecure, and thus developing social phobias.

Sociocultural explanations: obsessive-compulsive disorder

OCD occurs in a remarkably similar fashion and prevalence across cultures, suggesting that cultural factors do not play a large role. However, culture can affect the actual symptoms displayed, which tend to reflect the characteristics of a given culture.

> **Fontenelle et al. (2004)** found that obsessions centred on aggression and religious observations were common in Brazilian and middle-eastern populations, implying that OCD symptoms take on the characteristics of a given culture.
>
> **Jaisoorya et al. (2008)** found that male OCD sufferers had earlier onset of the disorder and more religious obsessions, while females had more cleaning and hair-pulling compulsions, suggesting that social factors are involved.

- The fact that prevalence rates of OCD are similar cross-culturally suggests that biological factors are involved.
- The prevalence rate of OCD is similar for males and females, suggesting that biological factors are involved.

> **sociocultural explanations** — see anxiety disorders as determined through family and social environments.

Examiner's tip

When evaluating biological and psychological explanations of anxiety disorders, a good way of accessing higher-level marks for evaluation is to refer to the associated therapies. If therapies have research support in terms of their effectiveness, then this can be argued to support the theoretical foundations of the explanations they are based on.

Biological therapies for anxiety disorders — Revised

Drugs

Anxiolytics, such as the benzodiazepines (BZs), increase the effect of the neurotransmitter GABA and reduce anxiety in phobics and OCD sufferers. There are side effects though, such as drowsiness.

Phobics and OCD sufferers are also treated with antidepressants. Serotonin-specific reuptake inhibitors (SSRIs) elevate serotonin levels, while monoamine oxidase inhibitors (MAOIs) increase serotonin and noradrenaline levels.

Antipsychotic drugs with a dopamine-lowering effect are also useful in treating OCD.

Beta-blockers reduce the physical symptoms of anxiety disorders by countering the rises in blood pressure and heart rate associated with anxiety, by lowering adrenaline and noradrenaline production.

Drug therapy: phobias

Slaap et al. (1996) treated social phobics with antidepressant serotonin-specific reuptake inhibitors (SSRIs), finding that 72% had reductions in heart rate and blood pressure, suggesting that drug treatments are effective in addressing the physical symptoms of the disorder.

Den Boer et al. (1994) found that monoamine oxidase inhibitors (MAOIs) such as moclobemide are effective in reducing social anxiety and social avoidance, although there is an increased risk of hypertension.

> **drug therapy for anxiety disorders** — chemical treatment through tablets and intravenous means.

- Drug treatments are effective in reducing physical symptoms of phobias so that psychological treatments can be applied.

- As well as their addictive qualities, another problem with BZs is that once patients stop treatment they can again experience a sharp rise in anxiety levels.

Drug therapy: obsessive-compulsive disorder

Beroqvist et al. (1999) investigated the effect of low doses of the antipsychotic drug risperidone in treating OCD, finding treatment to be effective due to the drug's dopamine-lowering effect.

Flament et al. (1985) tested the antidepressant clomipramine's ability to address symptoms of childhood OCD, finding it superior to placebo treatment, supporting the use of drug treatments.

- Drug treatments for OCD are cost-effective and user-friendly.
- Drugs do not 'cure' OCD behaviours; once treatment stops, symptoms reappear.

Psychosurgery for anxiety disorders

Psychosurgery is occasionally used for severe cases of anxiety disorders that are unresponsive to other treatments. It is a last resort, entailing the usual risks of surgery, involves irreversible destruction of tissue without guarantee of success and can incur serious side effects, such as reduced intellect.

> **psychosurgery** — treatment of anxiety disorders by irreversible destruction of brain tissue.

Psychosurgery involves drilling holes in the skull so that heated probes can be inserted to burn away specific, small areas of brain tissue.

Certain criteria must be met before psychosurgery is considered. There must be clinical diagnosis of an anxiety disorder, symptoms must be severe, obstructing purposeful everyday living, other treatments must have failed, and patients must give fully informed consent, with total knowledge of the procedures and risks involved.

Psychosurgery: phobias

Ruck et al. (2003) reported that patients who had capsulotomies performed for severe social phobias generally had large reductions in anxiety levels, demonstrating the technique's effectiveness, although some patients suffered severe side effects.

Balon (2003) reported thermocapsulotomy to be an effective treatment for acute phobias, but is an extreme option, carrying risks of severe side effects.

- Modern forms of psychosurgery are targeted on localised, specific brain areas, therefore avoiding large-scale destruction and reducing the risk of irreversible side effects.

- It is improbable that different mental symptoms are relieved by one single form of brain operation, and therefore only operations suitable for precise psychiatric diagnoses should be used.

Psychosurgery: obsessive-compulsive disorder

Kelly and Cobb (1985) reported that 78% of OCD patients displayed improved symptoms 20 months after limbic leucotomies were performed, giving support to the treatment.

Hindus et al. (1985) followed up gamma capsulotomy patients 3 and 7 years after treatment, finding that only a few showed improvements. This suggests that different forms of psychosurgery have different success rates.

- It is debatable whether patients with severe OCD can give fully informed consent, suggesting that there are ethical problems in administering the treatment.

- Psychosurgery is not a cure for OCD; patients undergoing neurosurgery continue to need psychiatric care.

Typical mistakes

Many students study and revise biological, surgical and psychological therapies of anxiety disorders as separate from each other. However, a good way of accessing higher levels of marks for evaluation is to compare the therapies, drawing out their appropriateness and effectiveness by contrasting their strengths and weaknesses. Questions may ask for such a comparison. For instance, look at Question 5 in the 'Exam practice' section.

Psychological therapies for anxiety disorders
Revised ☐

Behavioural therapies

Systematic desensitisation (SD) is based on classical conditioning. Patients learn in stages to associate phobic situations with feelings of calm rather than fear. The idea is that it is not possible for the two opposing emotions of anxiety and relaxation to exist together (**reciprocal inhibition**).

A hierarchy is drawn up before treatment commences, from least to most feared type of contact with the phobic situation, the patient being taught relaxation strategies to use at each stage. With implosion (flooding), patients go to the top of the hierarchy and imagine, or have direct contact with, the most feared scenario. Patients are not allowed to make avoidance responses, anxiety peaking at such levels that it cannot be maintained.

SD is used against OCD, sufferers being introduced to obsession-causing situations and then, through relaxation strategies, having their anxiety levels lowered.

Another treatment for OCD is exposure and response prevention (ERP). Sufferers are introduced to situations causing their obsessions, but are not allowed to make obsessive responses. If OCD has occurred through reinforcement, avoiding anxiety-creating scenarios means that reinforcement is prevented and relearning can occur.

behavioural therapies for anxiety disorders — treatments that modify maladaptive behaviour by substituting new responses.

systematic desensitisation — behavioural treatment based on classical conditioning where patients learn in stages to associate fear/obsessive-causing responses with feelings of calm.

Behavioural therapies: phobias

Rothbaum et al. (1998) reported on virtual reality exposure therapy where patients are active participants in a computer-generated three-dimensional world that changes naturally with head movements. SD-like treatment occurs without leaving the therapist's office, more control is gained over phobic stimuli and there is less exposure of patients to harm and embarrassment.

Wolpe (1960) used implosion to remove a girl's phobia of driving in cars. The girl was forced into a car and driven around for hours until her hysteria subsided, demonstrating the effectiveness of the treatment.

- SD is suitable only for patients who are able to use relaxation strategies and can imagine feared situations.

- Although patients may be able to gradually confront phobias in an imaginary sense, there is no guarantee that this works with actual situations, which is why in vivo treatment is thought superior to covert desensitisation.

Behavioural therapies: obsessive-compulsive disorder

Gertz (1966) reported that in vivo SD worked well with OCD patients. 66% of sufferers responded to treatment, suggesting that the treatment is effective.

Baer (1991) found that a self-directed, step-by-step form of exposure and response prevention (ERP) was as effective for mild forms of OCD as seeing a therapist, so it is considered cost-effective.

- ERP incurs large dropout rates due to high levels of anxiety; therefore it is usually combined with drug treatment so that anxiety levels can be controlled.
- ERP is considered more effective than drug treatments because relapse rates are lower, suggesting it brings long-term, lasting benefits.

Cognitive-behavioural therapy

Cognitive-behavioural therapy (CBT) helps patients identify irrational and maladaptive thinking patterns and change them to rational, adaptive ones. By changing modes of thinking, feelings and behaviour also change.

For snake phobia, for example, therapists encourage phobics to express beliefs about snakes and then challenge these with rational arguments. Patients are encouraged to interact with snakes and record details, which are referred to if sufferers return to irrational beliefs.

In dealing with OCD, CBT is orientated at changing obsessional thinking, for instance habituation training, where sufferers re-live obsessional thoughts repeatedly to reduce the anxiety created by them.

> **cognitive-behavioural therapy for anxiety disorder** — treatment that modifies thought patterns to alter behavioural and emotional states.

Cognitive-behavioural therapy: phobias

Spence et al. (2000) assessed the value of CBT in children with social phobias, finding child-focused CBT and CBT plus parental involvement effective in reducing social and general anxiety levels, with these improvements apparent at a 1-year follow-up. This suggests that CBT has long-term effectiveness with phobic children.

Kvale et al. (2004) conducted a meta-analysis of treatment studies for people with dental phobias, finding that CBT resulted in 77% of patients regularly visiting a dentist 4 years after treatment.

- There are long-term benefits to CBT. The techniques used to combat phobias can be used continually to stop symptoms returning.
- An advantage of CBT compared with other treatments is that it produces few side effects.

Cognitive-behavioural therapy: obsessive-compulsive disorder

O'Kearney et al. (2006) assessed the ability of CBT to treat children and adolescents with OCD, finding it effective but more so when combined with drug treatments.

Sousa et al. (2007) compared group CBT with the seratonin-specific reuptake inhibitor (SSRI) antidepressant drug sertraline, finding that group CBT increased complete remission of OCD symptoms more successfully, demonstrating CBT's superiority.

- Trained nurses are as effective as psychiatrists and psychologists in treating clients with OCD, demonstrating the simplicity of the treatment and its cost-effectiveness.
- CBT is not suitable for patients who have difficulty talking about their inner feelings, or for those who lack the verbal skills to do so.

> **Examiner's tip**
>
> When studying and revising biological, evolutionary and psychological explanations of anxiety disorders, and the associated therapies of anxiety disorders, ensure that you have covered two of each. Sometimes questions will ask specifically for one explanation/therapy, but if the question asks for explanations/therapies then two will be required.

Now test yourself

For your chosen disorder:

1   Outline the clinical characteristics.
2   Explain whether diagnoses are (i) reliable (ii) valid.
3   Outline biological explanations.
4   To what extent can biological explanations be supported?
5   Outline psychological explanations.
6   To what extent can psychological explanations be supported?
7   Outline biological therapies.
8   Evaluate biological therapies in terms of their strengths and weaknesses.
9   Outline psychological therapies.
10 Evaluate psychological therapies in terms of their strengths and weaknesses.

Answers on pp. 125–126

Exam practice

1	(a) Outline clinical characteristics.	[4]
	(b) Outline and evaluate issues of reliability and/or validity.	[20]
2	Discuss biological explanations.	[24]
3	(a) Outline and evaluate one psychological explanation.	[12]
	(b) Outline and evaluate one biological therapy.	[12]
4	Outline and evaluate psychological therapies.	[24]
5	Critically compare biological and psychological therapies.	[24]
6	(a) Describe clinical characteristics.	[8]
	(b) Evaluate either biological or psychological explanations.	[16]

Answers and quick quiz 9 online

Online

Examiner's summary

✔ The clinical characteristics of mental disorders focus on the descriptive qualities, symptoms and sub-types of mental disorders.

✔ The reliability and validity of classification and diagnosis of mental disorders centres on the use of classification systems.

✔ Biological explanations see mental disorders as having genetic and biochemical origins and as possessing an adaptive advantage.

✔ Psychological explanations see mental disorders as determined through psychodynamic, cognitive and sociocultural factors.

✔ Biological therapies see mental disorders as being treatable via physiological means, such as through drugs, electro-convulsive therapy and psychosurgery.

✔ Psychological therapies see mental disorders as treatable via non-physiological means, such as through behavioural therapies, cognitive-behavioural therapy and psychodynamic therapy.

10 Media psychology

Media influences on social behaviour

Social learning theory

Learning via the media can occur by indirect reinforcement, where observed behaviours are reinforced and imitated (vicarious learning), enabling us to learn how and when to imitate specific acts.

Bandura (1965) outlined four steps of modelling:

1 **attention** — concentration on attractive, high-status, similar models

2 **retention** — where observed behaviours are memorised

3 **reproduction** — where imitation occurs if individuals have skills to reproduce observed behaviours

4 **motivation** — where direct and indirect reinforcements and punishments influence motivation to imitate

Good levels of **self-efficacy** (situation-specific confidence) are also required.

If observers identify with perpetrators of aggression and/or the more realistic aggression is, the more likely it is that they will be imitated. However if perpetrators of aggression are punished, the chances of imitation are decreased.

> **media influences** — the effects of public communication formats on pro-social and antisocial behaviour.
>
> **social learning theory** — the acquisition of pro- and antisocial behaviours through observation and imitation of role models.

> **Bandura et al. (1961, 1963)** found that children were more likely to imitate aggressive acts against a Bobo doll if aggressive models were reinforced, but less likely if models were punished. Aggression was also more likely if children identified with the model, supporting social learning theory (SLT).
>
> **Lovelace and Huston (1983)** found that learning from pro-social programmes is situation-specific and that discussion with children after watching such programmes, plus related play, enhances pro-social effects.

● Bobo dolls are not real, cannot retaliate and are designed to be hit. As the situation was unfamiliar, children may have acted as they thought they were supposed to.

● Many studies measure only the short-term effects of pro- and antisocial media and do not differentiate between real aggression and play fighting.

Cognitive priming

The presentation of cues in programmes affects **antisocial** and **pro-social behaviour**, people storing violent and pro-social acts that they have seen in their memory as scripts for later behaviour. Being in a similar scenario 'triggers' the script into action.

> **pro-social behaviour** — actions intended to benefit others.
>
> **antisocial behaviour** — actions that go against the basic principles of society.
>
> **cognitive priming** — the presentation of media cues that affect pro and antisocial behaviour.

Murray et al. (2007) took fMRI brain scans of children watching violent and non-violent films, finding that the active brain areas of those watching violence were associated with emotion and arousal and also linked to episodic memory. This suggests the storing of aggressive scripts for later use.

Josephson (1987) found that boys who watched a violent programme involving communicating via walkie-talkies and who subsequently received walkie-talkie instructions while playing ice-hockey were more aggressive than boys who watched a non-violent film, which implies that the walkie-talkies acted as cognitive cues that primed aggression.

- Cognitive priming suggests a practical application in developing pro-social behaviours via media sources.
- Cognitive priming may have more effect on individuals with dispositions for aggression and pro-social behaviour.

Effects of computers and video games on behaviour — Revised

Video games

Children exposed to video games are retarded in development of their emotion regulation skills, leading to desensitisation to cues that normally trigger an empathetic response and increasing the likelihood of violent behaviour. Cognitive desensitisation occurs when the belief that violence is rare is replaced with one that violence is usual. Desensitisation disrupts moral evaluation, causing actions without considering ethical implications. There is also a tendency to promote addictive behaviour. Some research however, shows game playing to have positive aspects related to learning and levels of self-esteem.

> **Typical mistakes**
>
> Possibly due to the common perception that video games and computers have a destructive influence on behaviour, many candidates concentrate too much, or even solely, on their negative influences. Better answers provide a more balanced view by focusing additionally on positive effects, for which there is ample research support.

Sanger (1996) found that game playing develops mastery and control in individuals with low self-esteem.

Kestanbaum and Weinstein (1985) found that game playing helped adolescent males manage developmental conflicts and safely discharge aggression, suggesting that negativity is a parental concern.

Strasburger and Wilson (2002) found that video games desensitise users to the consequences of violence, bringing increased pro-violence attitudes.

Sopes and Millar (1983) found that video game users exhibit addictive tendencies, turning to crime to fund their habit. This suggests that video games have negative consequences.

- Evidence suggests that video games contribute to how individuals construct reality, with an acceptance of violence merged with desensitisation to its consequences.
- Studies have not focused on the long-term effects of game playing.

Computers

Interest focuses on relationships lacking face-to-face communication and learning effects. Computers are a positive tool for communicating, learning and developing social relationships in those lacking social skills and confidence and those living in remote communities. There is a possibility of deindividuation leading to disinhibition, causing individuals to act in non-typical ways.

Durkin and Barber (2002) found that computer users had superior measures of healthy adolescence than non-users.

Valkenburg and Peter (2009) reported that social network sites encourage and permit communication and relationship building in shy adolescents, demonstrating the positive usage of computers.

Pearce (2007) found that information presented via printed paper had superior recall than when presented via computers.

Daft (1987) found that computer-mediated communications (CMCs) negatively affect factors important in communication and negotiation, demonstrating negative aspects of computers.

- Behrmann (2000) argued that computers are beneficial if children are encouraged to engage in social interactions and stimulated to acquire knowledge.

- Zhou et al. (2001) believes that deception cues in CMCs (indicating the use of deception) could be incorporated into an automated tool to detect deception, protecting young people from those with negative intentions.

> **Examiner's tip**
>
> If a question requires material on the positive and negative effects on behaviour of both computers and video games then it would be good practice to ensure that their individual effects are fully differentiated from each other (i.e. by saying what their different effects are), rather than just lumped together. In this way you will create a coherent answer.

Now test yourself

Tested ☐

1 Outline (i) social learning theory (SLT) (ii) cognitive priming, in terms of how the media affects pro- and antisocial behaviour.

2 What evaluative points, including research evidence, can be made concerning (i) social learning theory (ii) cognitive priming?

3 Outline the positive and negative effects of (i) video games and (ii) computers on behaviour.

4 (a) What has research told us about the effects of video games and computers?

(b) What other evaluative points can be made?

Answers on pp. 126–127

Media and persuasion

Models explaining the persuasive effects of media

Revised ☐

Hovland-Yale model

Hovland's work centred on the role of persuasion, perceiving **attitude** change as a response to communication.

Target characteristics relate to receiving and processing communications, less intelligent individuals being more persuadable. Individuals with moderate self-esteem are more easily persuaded than those of high or low levels. Mood is also a characteristic.

Source characteristics focus on the credibility of communicators, more credible communicators being more persuasive. Credibility focuses on the expertise, trustworthiness and attractiveness of communicators.

Message characteristics concentrate on the nature of communications, presentation of both sides of an argument being more persuasive towards attitude change.

Overall attitude change is perceived as a sequential process, comprising stages of:

- **attention** — target attends to the message
- **comprehension** — target understands the message

> **Hovland-Yale model** — an explanation of attitude change as a sequence of stages in response to communication.
>
> **attitude** — a predisposition towards an object or situation.

- **reactance** — target reacts to the message either positively or negatively
- **acceptance** — message is accepted if perceived as credible

> **Meveritz and Chaiken (1987)** discovered that scary messages were more persuasive towards attitude change, suggesting that fear plays a role. However, extremely scary messages were ignored.
>
> **Allyn and Festinger (1961)** found that distracting people made them more persuadable than capturing their full attention, suggesting a strategy to achieve attitude change.

- The model describes the process of attitude change rather than explaining it.
- Research exploring the role of fear in persuasive messages is harmful and therefore unethical.

Elaboration likelihood model

The model explains how persuasive messages are processed, perceiving two forms of cognitive routes by which persuasive attitude change occurs through cognitive evaluation:

1 The **central route** concerns motivation to analyse and reach attitude-changing conclusions. This route is used for messages requiring elaborated cognitive effort. If favourable thoughts are produced, attitude change is likely.

2 The **peripheral route** concerns motivation to consider sources of communications to change attitudes, rather than messages themselves. This route considers superficial cues, such as the perceived credibility of communicators and the quality of presentations; the logic behind messages is seen as irrelevant with no elaboration required.

> **elaboration likelihood model** — an explanation of how persuasive messages are processed through cognitive evaluation.

As motivation and ability to process messages increases, it becomes more likely that the central route will be used. Motivational factors include personal relevance of messages, accountability and an individual's innate desire to indulge in thinking. Ability factors include the availability of cognitive resources, such as distractions, and the knowledge necessary for analysis.

> **Miller (2005)** found that peripheral route processing relies on environmental conditions, such as the perceived credibility of sources, the quality of presentation, the attractiveness of sources and catchy slogans. This supports the model.
>
> **Petty et al. (1981)** found that students were influenced by persuasive messages when personally motivated and by peripheral cues when not personally motivated.

- The model has explanatory power but lacks predictive ability in different contexts.
- Research focuses on unfamiliar topics where participants have no pre-existing attitudes, therefore measuring attitude change, not attitude formation.

Explanations for the persuasiveness of television advertising   Revised

Hovland-Yale model

Three factors explain the persuasiveness of television advertising:

1 **Communicators** — television advertisers use skilled communicators who possess attractive qualities and excellent communicative abilities. Constant exposure increases persuasiveness as we identify with and admire them.

2 **Message** — the means by which messages are communicated is important, television being influential due to its immediacy, availability and numerous formats. The persuasiveness of television works best for simple messages, with alternative means, such as written media, better for complex ones.

3 **Audience** — males are more persuadable by female-based topics and females more persuadable by male-based topics. Research also indicates age-related differences.

Sistrunk and McDavid (1971) found female-orientated topics more persuasive on male attitudes than female ones, suggesting a gender difference in the persuasiveness of television advertisements.

Gorn (1982) found that participants preferred a pen presented in an advertisement with a likeable song to one presented with a dislikeable song, showing how associating emotions with advertisements is persuasive.

● Producing attitude change by using communicators with positive qualities and similarities to the audience is explicable in terms of social learning theory, where the audience observes and imitates the communicator as a form of vicarious reinforcement.

Elaboration likelihood model

Effective persuasion comes from the central route, where individuals are motivated to analyse material carefully. Messages must be robust and personally important, requiring elaborated cognitive effort. Strong arguments encourage analysis and removing distractions helps achieve this.

The peripheral route, where sources of communications rather than messages themselves are considered, is important in the persuasiveness of television advertisements, with contented people more likely to use this route, because they want to maintain positive emotive states.

Audience attention is captured through heightened emotions, such as fear, although too much heightened emotion makes people defensive and unwilling to elaborate cognitive processing.

Typical mistakes

Many students will study and revise the Hovland-Yale and elaboration likelihood models as separate from each other. However a good means of gaining higher-level evaluative marks is to compare the theories with each other, drawing out similarities/differences and strengths/weaknesses. You may even get an exam question that specifically asks you to compare them, so be prepared for this.

Witte and Allen (2000) found that messages containing strong fear and high efficacy content produce the greatest change in attitudes in anti-smoking campaigns.

Berscheid and Walster (1974) found that physically attractive sources, such as sports stars, make advertisements more persuasive, especially with less involving products, showing the importance of likeability in peripherally processed messages.

● Advertisers are aware that persuasion via the central route is problematic, because people do not engage with messages due to conflicting demands for attention. Therefore peripheral routes are used to sell products.

Now test yourself

Tested ☐

5 Describe how (i) the Hovland-Yale model and (ii) the elaboration likelihood model explain the persuasive effects of media.

6 (a) To what extent are these models supported by research?
   (b) What other evaluative points can be made about the models?

7 Describe how (i) the Hovland-Yale model and (ii) the elaboration likelihood model can explain the persuasiveness of television advertising.

8 (a) To what extent are both explanations supported by research?
   (b) What other evaluative points can be made?

Answers on p. 127

The psychology of 'celebrity'

The attraction of 'celebrity' Revised

Social psychological explanations

- **Social learning theory** — media celebrities have qualities that cause us to identify with them as role models and imitate them through vicarious reinforcement.

- **Social construction theory** — celebrity is perceived as a self-serving, social invention of the media, providing continual interest and focus, which generates income.

- **Absorption–addiction model** — individuals develop interest in celebrities through a lack of meaningful relationships and to escape mundane reality. In stronger forms, interest in celebrity becomes addictive; individuals need more involvement with celebrities, correlating strongly with diminished psychological health.

> **Escalis and Bettman (2008)** found that celebrity endorsement enhances products when consumers aspire to be like the celebrity, supporting social psychological explanations, especially social learning theory.
>
> **Belch and Belch (2007)** found that celebrities are well liked, leading to identification in an attempt to seek a relationship with the celebrity, supporting the absorption–addiction model.

- The fact that 20% of advertisements in the USA feature celebrities suggests a social learning effect.

- Most research into the attraction of celebrity has been done in Western cultures and so findings may be culturally specific.

Evolutionary explanations

The attractiveness of celebrity serves an adaptive function.

- **Gossip** — Dunbar (1997) believes that groups grew so large that gossip became a means of communicating information about social relationships and hierarchies, explaining the appeal of celebrity journalism as communicating observations about alpha males and females.

- **Gender** — celebrity interest is more female orientated because females compare males as a means of selection. Interest in female celebrities occurs as females compete in levels of attractiveness and learn attractiveness skills from alpha females.

- **Prestige hypothesis** — individuals benefit from imitating prestigious people, such imitation bringing more resources, protection and reproductive opportunities.

> **Dunbar (1997)** reports that two-thirds of conversation is spent on social topics, supporting the idea that language evolved for social purposes.
>
> **Fieldman (2008)** found that females find male celebrities attractive because of qualities advertising toughness, stamina and high levels of testosterone, all indicators of good genetic quality and resource provision.

- Celebrity journalism focuses on attractiveness, romantic liaisons and reproductive success, supporting the idea that celebrity attraction has an evolutionary basis.

---

celebrity — a person of public fame.

social psychological explanations for celebrity attraction — perceiving it as being transmitted by social means.

Examiner's tip

When answering questions concerning the attraction of celebrity, it is important to provide full explanations (e.g. social learning in terms of its theoretical basis that learning requires observation and imitation of role models etc.) and to tie this to the attraction of celebrity (i.e. that celebrities have desirable qualities that cause us to identify with and imitate them).

---

evolutionary explanation — perceives celebrity attraction as serving an adaptive function.

- Reynolds (2009) believes that evolution programmes us to find certain individuals attractive because we share similar genes and have identical perceptions of beauty, suggesting a reason for celebrity popularity.

Research into intense fandom Revised

Celebrity worship

McCutcheon et al. (2002) developed the Celebrity Attitude Scale, measuring items on three categories of celebrity worship:

1 **Entertainment sub-scale** — social aspects of celebrity worship, such as discussions with friends.
2 **Intense personal sub-scale** — strength of feelings and levels of obsession.
3 **Borderline pathological sub-scale** — levels of uncontrollable feelings and behaviour.

Celebrity worship has a single dimension, with lower-scoring individuals showing an avid interest in celebrities, such as reading about them, while high-scoring individuals over-identify with and become obsessive about celebrities.

Maltby et al. (2003) found three dimensions of fandom:

1 **Entertainment social** — people attracted to celebrities for entertainment value.
2 **Intense personal** — people developing obsessive tendencies towards celebrities.
3 **Borderline pathological** — people developing uncontrollable fantasies and behaviour patterns.

> **Examiner's tip**
>
> Due to the wording of the specification questions on this topic will focus on research, so a good means of building evaluative credit would be to comment on the methodology and ethical concerns of such research, as long as this is orientated to specific research studies rather than general methodological/ethical points.

> **fandom** — the collective supporters of a particular celebrity interest.
>
> **celebrity worship** — the idolisation of celebrities.

Maltby et al. (2004) found that those in the entertainment-social category were mentally healthy, but those in higher categories were prone to poor mental and physical health.

- Mild forms of celebrity worship are beneficial. Larsen (1995) found that intense attachments to celebrities provided young people with attitudinal and behavioural exemplars.
- West and Sweeting (2002) recommend media training in schools, illustrating the dangers of celebrity worship and eating disorders, especially in adolescent girls.

> **celebrity stalking** — the obsessive pursuit and observation of celebrities.

Celebrity stalking

Mullen (2008) scrutinised 20,000 incidents of stalking the royal family, finding that 80% were by people with psychotic disorders, such as schizophrenia. This is very different from people who stalk non-famous people, suggesting that celebrity stalking is a separate phenomenon.

Meloy (1998) reported that celebrity stalkers often have a history of failed sexual relationships and are not in a sexual relationship when stalking, suggesting that celebrity stalking is a reaction to social incompetence and loneliness.

McCutcheon et al. (2006) measured attraction to celebrities, finding that adults with insecure attachment types had positive attitudes towards obsessive behaviours and stalking and that pathological attachment types have a tendency to stalk, suggesting that celebrity stalking is related to childhood attachment types.

- Research into celebrity stalking may aid understanding of the behaviour, leading to the formation of effective therapies.

- Legal intervention, such as trespassing orders, is the most effective means of dealing with celebrity stalkers, but this can lead to increased obsessiveness and persecution towards their targets.
- Psychopathic stalkers who prey on celebrities are resistant to treatments such as psychotherapy, illustrating the difficulty in changing their behaviour

Typical mistakes

When outlining research in intense fandom, many candidates simply describe research studies in terms of aims/procedures/findings. This is fine to gain marks for description, but it will not gain evaluative credit. You must state what the findings tell us about intense fandom (e.g. suggesting that celebrity stalking is related to childhood attachment patterns) to gain evaluative credit.

Now test yourself

Tested

9 Explain (i) social psychological (ii) evolutionary explanations of the attraction of celebrity.

10 (a) To what extent are these explanations supported by research?

(b) What other evaluative points can be made concerning these explanations?

11 (a) What has research taught us about (i) celebrity worship (ii) celebrity stalking?

(b) What evaluative points can be made about such research?

Answers on p. 127

Exam practice

1 (a) Outline the positive and negative effects of computers on behaviour. [4]

(b) Outline and evaluate explanations of media influences on pro- and antisocial behaviour. [20]

2 Discuss explanations for the persuasiveness of television advertising. [24]

3 Outline and evaluate the application of (i) the Hovland-Yale model and (ii) the elaboration likelihood model to explaining the persuasive effects of media. [12 + 12]

4 Discuss explanations for the attraction of celebrity. [24]

5 (a) Outline research into intense fandom. [8]

(b) Consider the negative and positive effects of video games on computers. [16]

Answers and quick quiz 10 online

Online

Examiner's summary

✔ The media influences pro-social and antisocial behaviour through social learning theory and cognitive priming, while computers and video games incur both positive and negative effects.

✔ The Hovland-Yale model of persuasion perceives attitude change as a response to communication, while the 'elaboration likelihood' model sees persuasive messages as processed through central and peripheral routes.

✔ Both the Hovland-Yale and the elaboration likelihood models can be used to explain the persuasiveness of television advertising.

✔ Social psychological explanations for the attraction of celebrity include social learning theory, social construction theory and the absorption–addiction model, while evolutionary explanations see adaptive advantages to being attracted to celebrity.

✔ Research has identified categories of celebrity worship and dimensions of fandom and suggested motivations behind celebrity stalking.

11 The psychology of addictive behaviour

Models of addictive behaviour

Biological, cognitive and learning approaches Revised

Biological model

The model perceives **addiction** as a physiologically controlled pattern of behaviour. Initiation of addiction occurs through genetic vulnerability, while maintenance of addiction occurs through activation of dopamine, which drugs such as cocaine affect directly. Relapse occurs through physiological cravings.

Drugs affect the frequency of nerve impulses and block neurotransmitter receptor sites. They also attach to receptors, preventing neurotransmitters from recycling, so that they remain in the synapse and reattach to receptor sites.

> **biological model** — sees addiction occurring as a physiologically controlled pattern of behaviour.
>
> **addiction** — dependence on something physically or psychologically habit forming.
>
> **cognitive model** — sees addiction occurring as distorted thinking relating to dysfunctional beliefs.

Nielsen et al. (2008) compared DNA from former heroin addicts and non-addicts, finding a relationship between addiction and certain gene variants. Some genes also act against becoming addicted, indicating a genetic basis to addiction.

- Addiction to one drug can produce cross-tolerance of other related drugs, such as opiates. In addition, withdrawal symptoms after abstaining from one drug can be addressed by taking similar drugs, such as methadone for heroin. This suggests that similar drugs act on the nervous system in the same way, supporting the biological model.

Cognitive model

Addiction is seen as due to distorted thinking relating to dysfunctional beliefs, like intellectual functioning being dependent on drug use. These maladaptive cognitive processes may relate to mood, causing addicts to believe that happiness is impossible without drugs. Dysfunctional beliefs are self-fulfilling, leading to a perception of personal incapability in controlling usage, and an inability to direct attention away from addictive behaviour.

Faulty thinking leads addicts to focus on the positive features of usage and to minimise the negative ones, strengthening dependency. Another cognitive feature is impaired decision-making, with addicts focusing on strategies of immediate pleasure in spite of knowing that such choices are harmful in the long term.

The model therefore sees initiation, maintenance and relapse as due to maladaptive thought processes.

> **Typical mistakes**
>
> Many students study and revise models of addiction as being separate from each other, but a good means of accessing higher-level evaluation marks is to compare the theories, drawing out their similarities/differences and their strengths/weaknesses.

Ratelle et al. (2004) found that gambling addicts had persistent thoughts about gambling and poorer concentration on daily tasks, indicating a cognitive element to addiction.

- The relative success of cognitive-behavioural treatments implies that addiction has a cognitive component.

Learning model

Dependency is explained by classical conditioning, operant conditioning and social learning theory (SLT). With classical conditioning, usage becomes associated with environmental factors until those factors alone produce 'highs'. Operant conditioning sees addiction arising from positive reinforcements, such as euphoric 'highs', and negative reinforcements, such as anxiety reduction, which strengthens addiction by increasing the chances of recurrence, with increased usage perceived as attempting to increase reinforcements. The neurotransmitter dopamine acts as a reinforcer within the brain reward system, many drugs acting on dopamine synapses to produce euphoria.

Social learning theory sees addiction as resulting from vicarious learning, dependent behaviour being observed and imitated if the model incurs a reinforcement.

> **Meyer et al. (1995)** found that the sight of hypodermic needles created positive feelings in addicts, demonstrating the role of classical conditioning in addictive behaviour.

Many addictions respond to behavioural treatments, indicating a learning component. However, such treatments often produce short-term benefits, suggesting that symptoms are being addressed but not causes, implying that others factors are involved.

> **learning models** — addiction by environmental interactions that produce euphoric outcomes.

Explanations for smoking

Biological — nicotine affects the production of dopamine and acetylcholine, leading to reinforcement. Genetic variations indicate that some are more vulnerable to dependency.

Cognitive — smokers possess irrational thoughts, such dysfunctional ideas being self-fulfilling, creating belief that they cannot quit, leading to a 'vicious circle' of continually surrendering to cravings.

Learning — smoking occurs via observation and imitation of role models, due to vicarious reinforcement. Maintenance is due to positive reinforcements of nicotine inhalation. As nicotine is removed from the body, frequent reinforcements via smoking are required.

> **Pergadia et al. (2006)** found a heritability factor in the experience of nicotine withdrawal symptoms, suggesting a genetic link and supporting biological explanations.
>
> **National Institute on Drug Abuse (2005)** found that 90% of smokers started as adolescents by observation and imitation of peers, suggesting that initiation of smoking is due to social learning.

● Many smokers quit without using nicotine replacement or suffering cravings, suggesting a role for social and cognitive factors.

Explanations for gambling

Biological — gambling increases dopamine production, creating pleasurable sensations in the brain reward system. Genetic factors are involved, with some at risk of multiple addictions. Genetics also bestows different levels of vulnerability.

Cognitive — irrational thought patterns distort beliefs, successes being perceived as due to skill and losing due to luck. Superstitions for winning and losing develop, leading to increased risk taking and persistence.

Learning — gambling occurs through observation and imitation of successful models, with maintenance due to the positive reinforcements of winning.

> **Griffiths (1994)** found that habitual users of fruit machines hold irrational beliefs about losing, such as not concentrating, and attributed successes to skill, suggesting a cognitive explanation.
>
> **Grosset et al. (2009)** found that dopamine agonists used to treat Parkinson's disease turned 10% of patients into pathological gamblers, suggesting that dopamine is linked to gambling dependency, supporting the biological explanation.

● 20% of teenage gambling addicts contemplate suicide, demonstrating the need for explanations of the condition in order to develop effective treatments.

Now test yourself

1 (a) Outline the (i) biological (ii) cognitive (iii) learning approaches to explaining initiation, maintenance and relapse.
   (b) Explain their applications to (i) smoking (ii) gambling.
   (c) What evaluative points, including research support, can be made about these models?

Answers on p. 127

Tested ☐

Vulnerability to addiction

Risk factors — Revised ☐

Stress

Increased **stress** levels correlate positively with increased **vulnerability** to dependency, often as a maladaptive way of dealing with stress; some individuals seem to be more vulnerable to developing stress-related dependencies.

The added stress of trying to quit addictive behaviours (and maintaining abstinence) is often responsible for relapses and there is some evidence of cellular and molecular changes in response to stress-related addiction, showing a biological link.

Being dependent can also heighten stress levels (e.g. through financial dependency, leading to greater dependency).

> **vulnerability** — degree of susceptibility to addiction.
> **stress** — the effects of emotional strain.
> **peers** — people of equal status.

> **Cleck and Blendy (2008)** reported a link between stress-related psychiatric disorders and the use of addictive substances. Stress exposure was also linked to increases in usage and relapses back into dependency, demonstrating the relationship between stress and addiction.

● Stress research suggests a practical application in devising a stress index to predict risk levels of developing dependency, to permit interventions before addiction levels become difficult to treat.

Peers

If **peers** have positive attitudes towards addictive behaviours, individuals will have increased vulnerability to dependency.

Adherence to peer pressure is a form of normative social influence, where individuals conform to be accepted. When peer groups adopt addictive behaviours as a 'norm', such behaviours soon become part of an individual's 'in-group' behaviour to show identity with the group.

Peer pressure is also a form of operant conditioning where the group reinforces participation in addictive behaviours. Peers can also influence recovering addicts to relapse.

> **Typical mistakes**
>
> The specification lists four risk factors in the development of addiction (stress, peers, age and personality) but take care when answering questions on addiction that the correct number of factors are addressed. Read the question carefully before starting to write. For example, if a question asks for two factors, offering more will not gain extra credit but will waste valuable time better spent on another question.

Sussman and Ames (2001) found that peer use of drugs is a strong predictor of drug use among adolescents, with deviant peer groups role-modelling and offering drugs, demonstrating the power of social networks in realising degrees of individual vulnerability.

- Peers are just one social context influence, along with economic and social deprivation etc., and all of these should be considered when assessing levels of vulnerability because dependency rarely relates to just one factor.

Age

Initiation of dependency behaviours mainly starts in adolescence. The earlier the onset, the less likelihood there is of later abstention and those who start early are more likely to relapse after quitting. Early onset of dependency behaviour also acts as a 'gateway' behaviour to other dependencies.

There is also increased vulnerability in old age to addiction, with a third of alcoholics developing dependency after retirement due to changes in lifestyle and the increased stresses of old age, such as the death of loved ones.

Health Canada Youth Smoking Survey (2006) found that early onset smokers were more likely to binge drink and smoke cannabis than non-smokers, illustrating how early onset dependencies act as 'gateway' behaviours to other dependencies.

- Dependency in old age is a taboo area, with individuals reluctant to discuss their addictions. Such dependencies are less apparent, which makes research in this area difficult and interventions by friends and family less likely.

Personality

Research indicates that maladaptive personality traits influence the formation of dependencies, with neurotic and psychopathic personalities more vulnerable as substance abuse helps such individuals to escape everyday stressors that do not bother psychologically fit people. Neurotic personalities are characterised by moodiness, irritability and anxiety, while psychotism is characterised by aggressiveness, emotional coldness and impulsiveness.

Other common traits include not valuing achievement, a desire for immediate gratification and high levels of perceived stress.

Chein et al. (1964) found that low self-esteem, negative outlook, learned incompetence and dependent relationships characterised ghetto adolescent addicts, which suggests that personalities with a negative view of life are more vulnerable to addiction.

- The idea of dependency being linked to personality is supported by the fact that many recovered addicts develop less harmful addictions, such as religious fervour or sporting participation.
- Although evidence suggests that personality characteristics predispose some individuals to vulnerability, the existence of an 'addictive personality' is not supported.

Media influence on addictive behaviour — Revised

The many forms of media have varying influences on the addictive behaviour of different age groups, many of which present enhanced opportunities for the promotion of dependency behaviours due to social learning effects.

Media is addictive itself, creating physiological dependence on social media and user-generated content. Research indicates that it is a growing problem due to the increasing provision of media formats designed for use in all areas of people's lives, such as the internet and social networking. The media also affects perceptions of addiction risks, often in an invalid manner.

> **Kimberley (2006)** found social media to be addictive in themselves, leading to increased usage to sustain 'highs' and increased anxiety without periodic access. Even minor exposure creates physical and psychological dependence, suggesting social media addiction (SMA) to be a real and troublesome condition.

- There is a danger that addicts can be demonised through media-created moral panics, seriously affecting the chances of addicts receiving adequate social support to help them abstain, or even to seek treatment in the first place.

Examiner's tip

A good way to signal which parts of an answer are the descriptive parts and which the evaluative parts is to 'signpost' the evaluative material. For example, when detailing relevant research studies, use phrases such as 'this suggests...' or 'this supports...' to indicate to the examiner that this is evaluation.

Now test yourself

2 (a) Outline the following risk factors in the development of addiction: (i) stress (ii) peers (iii) age (iv) personality.

(b) To what extent can these factors be supported by research?

(c) What other evaluative points can be made about these factors?

3 (a) Explain how media can influence addictive behaviour.

(b) What evaluative points can be made concerning media influences?

Answers on p. 127

Tested

Reducing addictive behaviour

Theory of planned behaviour

Revised

The **theory of planned behaviour** (TPB) model has several components:

- **Behavioural beliefs** link behaviour to expected outcomes and comprise the subjective probability that behaviour produces a given response. Behavioural beliefs determine the prevailing attitude towards behaviour.

- **Normative beliefs** refer to perceived behavioural expectations of a relevant social group, combining with motivational levels to determine prevailing subjective norms, the perceived social pressure to be involved, or not involved, in behaviour.

- **Control beliefs** involve the perceived presence of factors that help or hinder performance of behaviour, and they determine perceived behavioural control, beliefs about the ability to perform given behaviours. Perceived behavioural control can, along with intention, predict behaviour, intention being a measure of an individual's willingness to perform a behaviour.

TPB considers an individual's reasons for continuing with dependency behaviours and their personal belief in their resolve to abstain, these being important in resolving to abstain and in resisting withdrawal effects and cravings. To succeed, a person's perceived behavioural control must lead them to believe they can overcome dependency. The more an individual believes they have behavioural control, the more the model predicts success in abstaining, and the harder abstention is perceived to be, the more persistent they will be in attempting to quit.

> **theory of planned behaviour** — an explanation of factors influencing dependent behaviour.

Examiner's tip

As questions can be worth varying amounts of marks, it is good practice to be able to produce explanations with short and longer versions. For example, a question asking you to outline the theory of planned behaviour could be worth 4 marks for the description, therefore requiring the shorter version, or 8 marks for the description, therefore requiring the longer answer with more content and depth.

- The model assumes that behaviours are conscious, reasoned and planned, which may not always be the case with addicts.

Interventions and their effectiveness

Revised

Biological interventions

Drug maintenance therapy involves the use of replacement drugs, for instance methadone for heroin addicts. Methadone produces less of a high, is taken orally and does not involve contextual cues, such as needles.

Antagonistic drugs lessen or eliminate the effects of neurotransmitters by blocking cellular activity, altering the effects of addictive drugs.

Agonistic drugs are site-specific drugs that trigger cellular activity. Since many drugs act on dopamine levels to produce a 'high', dopamine agonists are used, also lessening withdrawal symptoms by producing more dopamine in the brain.

Nicotine replacement therapy — although nicotine is addictive, it is the other components of cigarettes, such as tar, which are directly dangerous to health. In nicotine replacement therapy, nicotine is imbibed by a means other than smoking, for example patches or gum.

biological interventions in dependency — therapeutic methods of abstention from dependency based on physiological means.

psychological interventions in dependency — therapeutic methods of abstention from dependency based on non-physiological means.

- Drugs can have side effects. Varenicline is used to treat smoking dependency but can incur depression and suicide, although withdrawal symptoms may contribute too.

Psychological interventions

Cognitive-behavioural therapy (CBT) affects thoughts about dependency. Behavioural self-control training, enabling addicts to realise when they are at risk, is combined with coping skills, such as relaxation techniques, to resist temptation.

Cognitive therapies take an active, focused approach to identify and deconstruct false beliefs, reduce cravings and establish control over addictive behaviours. Triggers are identified and strategies developed that increase willpower. Increased control is developed by creating situations producing cravings and developing methods of resistance.

Aversion therapy is a behaviourist treatment based on classical conditioning, where a negative effect is paired with the addictive substance so that the two become associated.

- CBT can be tailored to many individuals' circumstances and situations. Its effects are long lasting and can address the dependencies of the severely addicted.

Public health interventions

Legislation and policing — making drugs illegal prevents some usage but increases criminality. Bans on smoking indoors lead to increased smoking outdoors and attempts to ban gambling and drinking can drive them from public view, again heightening criminal activity.

Health promotions occur in many ways with varying degrees of success: *fear arousal* is used to strengthen the persuasiveness of arguments against addictive practices and *targeting risk groups* is based on the idea that health promotion campaigns succeed if they are specifically orientated at those at risk.

Conrod et al. (2004) found that targeting resources at adolescents at risk of developing substance abuse incurred successful outcomes.

- It is difficult to evaluate legislative attempts to curb addictive practices, because criminalisation makes it difficult to assess how many users there are.

public health interventions in dependency — communal campaigns to reduce and protect against dependency behaviours.

Now test yourself

4 (a) Describe the components of TPB.
 (b) Describe how TPB explains abstention from dependency.
 (c) What evaluative points can be made concerning TPB?
5 (a) Outline the following types of intervention: (i) biological (ii) psychological (iii) public health.
 (b) What degree of support do these intervention types have?

Answers on p. 127

Tested ☐

Exam practice

1 (a) Outline and evaluate stress and peers as risk factors in the development of addiction. [12]
 (b) Outline and evaluate the biological and cognitive approaches to explaining initiation, maintenance and relapse of dependency. [12]
2 Discuss the theory of planned behaviour as an explanation for addiction prevention. [24]
3 (a) Discuss the effectiveness of biological and psychological interventions in reducing addictive behaviour. [12]
 (b) Outline and evaluate age and personality as risk factors in the development of addiction. [12]
4 (a) Outline and evaluate applications to smoking and gambling of one or more models of addictive behaviour. [12]
 (b) Discuss public health interventions as a means of reducing addictive behaviour. [12]

Answers and quick quiz 11 online

Online ☐

Examiner's summary

✔ The biological approach perceives addiction as a physiologically controlled pattern of behaviour, while the cognitive approach sees it as involving distorted thinking relating to dysfunctional beliefs and the learning approach sees it as involving environmental interactions.

✔ The biological, cognitive and learning approaches all help explain smoking behaviour and gambling.

✔ Risk factors increasing vulnerability to addiction include stress, peers, age and personality.

✔ The media influences addictive behaviour through social learning theory and misrepresentations of addiction risk, while being addictive itself.

✔ TPB is an explanation of the factors influencing dependent behaviour, consisting of behavioural, normative and control beliefs.

✔ Biological interventions consist of physiological means of abstention, such as drugs, which are effective but incur side effects.

✔ Psychological interventions involve non-physiological therapeutic methods of abstention, such as cognitive-behavioural therapy and aversion therapy, both showing high levels of effectiveness.

✔ Public health interventions include legislation, which can be ineffective, and health promotions, which are successful if targeted at the vulnerable.

11 The psychology of addictive behaviour

12 Anomalistic psychology

The study of exceptional experience

Pseudoscience Revised

Pseudoscience refers to the body of supposed scientific disciplines that have little or no scientific basis. Practical applications based on pseudoscience are doomed to failure, having no basis in reality. Pseudoscientific eugenic beliefs saw thousands of low-IQ Americans, mostly blacks, forcibly sterilised, an example of racism dressed up as 'science'.

There is an on-going debate in China about traditional practices and beliefs, such as those relating to Chinese medicines, which are denounced as pseudoscientific by the scientific community. The traditional beliefs are popular due to widespread superstition and the scientific community is accused of obstructing 'innovative' practices. Scientists counter-argue that all theories/practices must abide by accepted scientific principles and offer persuasive, scientifically testable evidence.

> **anomalistic psychology** — the study of extraordinary phenomena in behaviour and experience.
>
> **pseudoscience** — a body of supposedly scientific knowledge, which fails to comply with scientific methods.

Sagan (2010) reported that pseudoscience obstructs proper science by providing easy answers, dodging scrutiny and championing desirable but impossible ideas. Pseudoscience is popular because it fulfils emotional needs, such as satisfaction of spiritual hunger, promises cures for disease and reassures about the existence of an afterlife etc.

- It is important to be able to distinguish between science and pseudoscience because acceptance of pseudoscientific beliefs leads to inefficient and dangerous practices in healthcare, education, law etc.

The scientific status of parapsychology Revised

Parapsychology is the scientific study of phenomena that seemingly exceed the physical capacities of the senses. Rhines founded modern parapsychology in the 1930s, seeking to dissociate the discipline from the discredited pseudoscience of spiritualism and establish a truly scientific discipline rooted in the unbiased setting of the laboratory.

> **parapsychology** — the scientific study of extraordinary, or paranormal, phenomena.

Parapsychology is ever-shrinking, because scientists gradually develop our understanding of phenomena such as hypnosis and hallucinations. Once phenomena are scientifically explicable they are no longer paranormal.

Sceptics argue that paranormal phenomena are impossible, thus rejecting any scientific legitimacy of their study. However pre-judgements about the impossibility of paranormal phenomena are scientifically inappropriate. Parapsychologists argue that the case for paranormal phenomena is already scientifically proven and great care is taken to develop and use rigorous scientific methods of study.

- An enduring problem with parapsychology is that significant results are produced by a small number of researchers who believe in psychic phenomena. Replications by sceptics rarely back up such claims.

- Examples of fraud in parapsychology are fewer than they were as modern investigative procedures are so rigorous (e.g. automated result recording with no human input) and thus opportunities for fraud and unconscious bias are greatly reduced.

Methodological issues in paranormal cognition

Revised ☐

Extrasensory perception

Honorton (1974) developed the **Ganzfeld technique**, to assess **extrasensory perception** (ESP). *Receivers* relax in a room for half an hour with halved table-tennis balls on their eyes, receiving white noise through headphones, creating a mild sense of sensory deprivation. *Senders* communicate mentally with receivers, using randomly chosen objects, with receivers describing any mental communications received. Receivers choose which of four possible targets best fits the images experienced and therefore should get 25% correct. Some claim results beyond this figure, but sceptics claim that evidence is inconclusive and does not prove the existence of ESP.

> **Hyman and Honorton (1985)** produced independent meta-analyses of Ganzfeld data. Honorton claimed support for ESP, but Hyman did not, stating that procedures were not rigorous enough. Honorton claimed that Hyman assessed too little data to perform proper factor analysis.
>
> **Honorton (1986)** conducted autoganzfeld experiments with computer control tests and receivers isolated in a soundproof, steel-walled, electromagnetically shielded room, reporting a statistically significant 34% accuracy rate.

- There is a danger of demand characteristics with the Ganzfeld technique. Results from Ganzfeld studies tend to match the beliefs of the researcher, believers in paranormal experiences producing seemingly correct answers.

Psychokinesis

Psychokinesis (PK) is the process of moving or affecting physical objects by the mind, with no physical contact. *Macro-PK* shows significant physical effects, for example bending spoons; *micro-PK* shows small effects on systems of probability, such as throwing dice. Psychics also make claims for the phenomena of levitation, moving objects and controlling weather patterns.

> **Benson et al. (2006)** asked Christians to pray for heart bypass patients, with a control group of similar patients not prayed for. They found no significant differences in recovery rates; indeed, the prayed-for group had more complications. This suggests that prayer has no effect, although the control group may have been prayed for by friends and family.

- There is a misconception that, if researchers are testing paranormal ability, they must be measuring it. However, they may be merely measuring the difference between chance predictions and actual outcomes, with a bias towards the existence of psychokinesis emerging, because studies not finding significant results are not published.

Typical mistakes

The specification focuses on methodological issues, so it is perfectly acceptable (and indeed good practice) to make explicit points about methodology (e.g. the role of rigorous investigative procedures in Ganzfeld experiments and the role of researcher bias in determining results).

Ganzfeld technique — research methodology of forced-choice pre-recognition target identification.

extrasensory perception — the ability to gain environmental information without reference to normal sensory channels.

psychokinesis — a technique of mind over matter through invisible means.

- Magicians such as James Randi have demonstrated the skills required for psychic processes, implying that other more natural processes are operating. They argue that if psychokinesis exists, why isn't it used for human good rather than bending spoons etc?

Now test yourself

Tested

1 Explain what is meant by pseudoscience?
2 What is the scientific status of parapsychology?
3 Outline the Ganzfeld procedure.
4 Does research support the idea of extrasensory perception (ESP)?
5 What is psychokinesis?
6 What evaluative points, including research evidence, can be made concerning psychokinesis?

Answers on pp. 127–128

Explanations for exceptional experience

Role of coincidence

Revised

Coincidences occur when two unrelated events correspond. Although no obvious relationship exists, a belief forms, creating a cognitive bias that one causes the other. The perception of coincidences leads to occult or paranormal claims, supporting the belief system of fatalism, where events are seen as predestined. Coincidences also happen due to shortcuts in information processing, occurring as an attempt to simplify understanding.

> coincidence — a sequence of accidental events perceived as planned.

Falk (1982) found that when extraordinary coincidences occur, people commit the error of singling that event out and according it significant status, suggesting a bias in cognitive processing.

Blakemore and Troscianko (1985) found, using coin tossing, that believers in the paranormal underestimate the probability of chance events. This suggests that believers are more likely to perceive events as beyond coincidence and thus as examples of paranormal phenomena.

Examiner's tip

Always make good use of research studies, because they provide both descriptive and evaluative comment. Outlining aims, procedures and findings will earn credit as descriptive material, while commenting on what research findings reveal in terms of support for explanations/theories will gain credit as evaluative material. Research studies often suggest practical applications, regarded as an additional source of evaluative material.

- The calculation of coincidences depends on accurate memory (detailing how often, when etc. apparently related events have previously occurred). As memories are reconstructive and subject to error, wishful thinking and suggestion, this is not consistently achievable.

Probability judgements

Revised

Some misjudge the probability of unrelated events, believing instead that such events are paranormal. Several cognitive factors explain incorrect **probability judgements**:

- **Intuitive thinking styles** involve a lack of reasoning and critical thinking so that evidence is not analytically evaluated.

> probability judgements — the reasoning associated with the calculation of possibility of events.

- **Cognitive illusions** involve a perceptual style where probability is misperceived, coupled with a poor understanding of randomness, significance being read into random patterns.
- **Confirmatory bias** — paranormal believers tend to ignore evidence that refutes their beliefs and over emphasise confirmatory evidence.
- **Illusion of control** — paranormal believers perceive random processes as under personal control, especially when perceived as involving skill.

> **Aarnio and Lindeman (1975)** found that superstitious people assign physical attributes to mental phenomena, and believe that inanimate objects have psychological properties. This suggests that paranormal believers are characterised by cognitive errors and intuitive thinking.
>
> **Langer and Roth (1975)** found that early success in picking lottery numbers increased the illusion of control, making participants believe that skill is involved, supported by a bias in recalling a higher numbers of successes than actually occurred. This suggests that believers are subject to an illusion of control that biases probability judgements.

- Research does not identify whether cognitive factors, such as cognitive illusions, are innate or learned. However, Banziger (1983) found that participants on a parapsychology course emphasising scepticism developed more sceptical thinking, implying that cognitive styles can be altered by learning.

Explanations for superstitious behaviour — Revised ☐

Superstitions are often linked to magical thinking and ritual behaviours, if these are seen as magically affecting an outcome.

The motivation behind the belief in superstitions is a desire for control and certainty, with individuals searching for explanations of why things happen. The creation of false certainties is regarded as better than having no certainty at all.

Behaviourism explains superstitions through operant conditioning, either by positive reinforcement (where certain behaviours or objects become associated with pleasurable outcomes) or by negative reinforcement (where behaviours or objects become associated with reducing the anxiety levels associated with uncertainty).

> **Skinner (1948)** found that pigeons adopted body movement superstitions, learning to associate them with rewards of food pellets.
>
> **Lustberg (2004)** found superstitions among sportspeople beneficial, because they increase confidence, motivation and persistence, enhancing chances of winning.

- Foxman (2009) believes that superstitions create expectations that can be powerful and suggestive, leading to biases to see them as true, but that they can have negative influences, by reinforcing maladaptive behaviours such as gambling.

Typical mistakes

The specification focuses on 'explanations for superstitious behaviour and magical thinking', so when creating evaluations take care not to focus on other areas, such as methodological issues, because this approach won't gain much credit. Instead, evaluations should focus explicitly on explanations, for instance their degree of research support.

superstition — irrational belief that an object, action or circumstance not logically related to a course of events influences its outcome.

Magical thinking — Revised ☐

Magical thinking (MT) involves the idea that the reality of irrational beliefs can be demonstrated by wishing for them and that all things are connected by paranormal phenomena, such as energy forces. MT is also

magical thinking — the belief that the mind has a direct effect on the physical world.

related to cognitive factors, often acting as coping mechanisms for those suffering trauma.

MT serves to represent both culturally specific and culturally universal symbolism, with paranormal beliefs existing as shared belief systems to bind people together within cultural groupings.

The **law of similarity** proposes that similar events and objects are connected in causal ways that defy scientific explanation, while the **law of contagion** argues that things which have been associated with each other retain paranormal connections, such as the bones of dead saints retaining spiritual powers.

> **Lawrence (1994)** found a correlation between childhood trauma and magical thinking, supporting the idea of MT acting as a coping mechanism.
>
> **Bonser (1963)** reported that Mapuche Indians in Chile favoured taking red pills, because red was associated with exorcism and was perceived therefore as purging illness. This suggests a cultural basis to MT.

● Magical thinking can produce real effects, since if people believe something, it increases the chances that, through elevated confidence, motivation and persistence, the 'magical' event will in fact occur.

Examiner's tip

Questions can be worth varying amounts of marks, so it is good practice to be able to produce explanations with short and longer versions. For example, a question asking you to outline explanations for magical thinking could be worth 4 marks for the description, therefore requiring a short answer, or worth 8 marks for the description, therefore requiring a longer answer with more content and depth.

Personality factors

Revised ☐

Research has tried to identify the particular personality traits associated with exceptional experience.

Neuroticism is characterised by anxiety, moodiness and emotional instability. Neurotics find the paranormal world comforting, because it allows them to interpret and predict events and thus quells their tendency to be over-emotional. However, their paranormal beliefs could also be a product of their over-emotionality

Extroversion is associated with extrasensory perception (ESP) abilities, because extroverts have lower natural levels of arousal, which makes them amenable to displaying such abilities.

Defensiveness is a personality trait linked to exceptional experience and involves cognitive resistance to perceiving situations as threatening. Individuals with defensive reactions have lower ESP scores than non-defensive individuals.

personality factors — individual dispositional traits affecting behaviour/experiences (e.g. traits associated with or affecting exceptional experience).

> **Honorton (1998)** found extroversion correlated with extrasensory perception ability, which suggests a link between personality and psychic ability. However, there was an element of flawed methodology, with participants completing personality questionnaires after they had had feedback on their ESP ability.
>
> **Wiseman and Watt (2004)** found a positive correlation between neuroticism and beliefs in the paranormal, suggesting a link to personality.

● Extroverts may perform better on ESP tests, because they are aroused, motivated and comfortable with being tested, while introverts don't perform so well, owing to a dislike of being tested.

Answers on p. 128

Now test yourself

Tested

7 How are (i) coincidence and (ii) probability judgements associated with exceptional experience?

8 What evaluative points, including research evidence, can be made concerning (i) coincidence (ii) probability judgements?

9 What explanations are there for (i) superstitions (ii) magical thinking?

10 What evaluative points, including research evidence, can be made concerning (i) superstitions (ii) magical thinking?

11 In what way do personality factors underlie exceptional experience?

12 What evaluative points can be made, including research evidence, concerning personality factors?

Research into exceptional experience

Psychic healing

Revised

Claims are made for **psychic healing** powers, often by therapeutic touch known as the 'laying on of hands'. Other claims are made for distance healing, where people are treated without physical contact, often over large distances. Charismatic religious figures are seen as possessing such a 'gift' and thus attain elevated status.

> **psychic healing** — the restoration of health through spiritual practices.

Psychic healers sometimes use mediums such as crystals to tap into bodily energy fields. Much of the theory surrounding such ideas is subjective and not backed up by empirical evidence.

Braud and Schlitz (1988) investigated distance healing, getting healers to focus on photographs of patients. Patients were unaware of this, ruling out the possibility of placebo or suggestive effects. Galvanic skin responses, associated with activity in the sympathetic nervous system, altered, suggesting a biological influence.

● Mollica (2005) suggests that psychic healers are beneficial in dealing with traumas occurring during catastrophes. After the Asian tsunami, patients treated by culturally familiar methods, such as psychic healing, benefited more than those receiving medical treatments because they were offering 'psychological first aid' that was not intrusive or anxiety creating.

● Many studies were not rigorously controlled; experimenter effects and demand characteristics therefore occurred. More stringent studies are required, especially replications of earlier studies.

Near death and out-of-body experiences

Revised

Out-of-body experiences (OBEs) involve floating outside one's body, or being able to see one's body from an exterior place. People having **near-death experiences** (NDEs) may have OBEs.

> **out-of-body/near-death experiences** — vivid sensations of being outside one's physical being.

Parasomatic OBEs are where individuals feel that they have a body other than their usual one. *Asomatic* OBEs are where individuals feel that they have no body. A rare type involves individuals perceiving a connecting cord between bodies. Most OBEs occur in bed, suggesting a link to sleep and dream states. They can also be seen as due to drugs, such as ketamine.

Some of those who have experienced an OBE believe that they willed it themselves, while others report being pulled involuntarily from their bodies usually after a feeling of general paralysis. This suggests that OBEs occur during the borderline stage between REM sleep and arousal when sleep paralysis occurs and dream images mix with usual sensory input.

Blanke et al. (2005) found that OBEs could be simulated in participants with no history of them by electrically stimulating the right temporal-parietal brain area, suggesting a biological explanation.

- Entering a tunnel is a common experience associated with OBEs, and tunnel-like experiences also occur with epilepsy, falling asleep, meditation and some drugs, suggesting that the experience is understandable by reference to brain structures.

Typical mistakes

The section of the specification that deals with research into exceptional experience focuses on explanations as well as research, and so answers need to focus on the explicit requirements of the question. If a question concerns explanations and only research evidence is offered, few marks, if any, will be gained.

Psychic mediumship

Revised

Mediums are people who claim special powers allowing them to communicate with the afterlife, and they also help people come to terms with the death of loved ones. There are two sub-types:

psychic mediumship — the claimed ability to experience contact with spirits.

Physical mediums — spirit people communicate to the living by raps, audible figures and materialised figures.

Mental mediums — mental phenomena are demonstrated through the mind of a medium, occurring in four ways: *clairvoyance* (where a medium sees a spirit), *clairaudience* (where a medium hears a spirit), *clairsentience* (where a medium senses the presence and thoughts of a spirit) and *trance mediumship* (where a medium is overshadowed by a spirit communicator speaking directly through the medium).

Schwartz et al. (2001) arranged for five mediums to interview a woman who had experienced six significant losses in the past decade. The woman only answered 'yes' or 'no' to questions, cutting down on the chances of the medium using intuitive reasoning. The mediums performed at an accuracy level of 83%, compared to 36% for control interviewers, suggesting a real psychic effect.

- Keen (1976), a well-known medium, confessed to fraud and detailed techniques used by mediums to fool people. Professional magicians have used such techniques to produce the same effects, suggesting psychic mediumship to be a mental trick.

Now test yourself

Tested

13 Explain the following: (i) psychic healing (ii) near death/out-of-body experiences (iii) psychic mediumship.

14 For each of the above, what evaluative points, including research evidence, can be made?

Answers on p. 128

Exam practice

1 (a) Outline research and/or explanations for psychic healing. [4]
   (b) Outline and evaluate personality factors underlying exceptional experience. [20]

2 Discuss methodological issues relating to the study of paranormal cognition. [24]

3 (a) Outline and evaluate research and explanations for near-death and out-of-body experiences. [12]
   (b) Outline and evaluate research and explanations for psychic mediumship. [12]

4 Discuss explanations for superstitious behaviour and magical thinking. [24]

5 Outline and evaluate pseudoscience and the scientific status of parapsychology. [24]

6 Outline and evaluate the role of coincidence and probability judgements in exceptional experience. [24]

Answers and quick quiz 12 online

Online

Examiner's summary

✔ Pseudoscience is a body of supposedly scientific knowledge, which fails to comply with scientific methods.

✔ The scientific status of parapsychology revolves around the legitimacy of studying paranormal phenomena and the refusal of sceptics to contemplate their existence.

✔ The Ganzfeld technique tests for ESP, believers claiming significant results but sceptics reporting methodological failings.

✔ Psychokinesis sees the mind affecting matter by invisible means, again with results contested between believers and sceptics.

✔ Coincidences and errors in probability judgements lead to paranormal claims through cognitive processing factors.

✔ Superstitious behaviour involves a need for control and certainty and is explicable through operant conditioning.

✔ Magical thinking is explicable through cognitive factors acting as coping mechanisms.

✔ Personality factors underlying anomalous experience include neuroticism and defensiveness, with extroversion associated with ESP abilities.

✔ Research into psychic healing suggests a biological explanation, out-of-body experiences and near-death experiences link to sleep and dream states, while psychic mediumship arouses arguments over its authenticity.

13 Psychological research and scientific method

Application of scientific method in psychology

Replicability

Replicability involves repeating research under identical conditions. Research must be fully written up so that it can be replicated properly and reliability and validity established. Fleischmann and Pons (1989) claimed to have created cold fusion, a form of low-energy nuclear reaction, in the laboratory, raising hopes of abundant, cheap energy. However, enthusiasm dropped when **replications** did not yield similar results. They either witnessed a separate phenomenon, or made procedural errors. Only by replication were scientists able to realise this.

Objectivity

Scientific research should be objective, outcomes being perceived without distortion of personal feelings or bias in interpretation. **Objectivity** is an integral part of **empiricism**, where observations are made through sensory experience and not from researchers' biased viewpoints. Such bias is often unintentional (e.g. the results from Ganzfeld studies, testing for the existence of extrasensory perception, match the beliefs of individual researchers).

Cyril Burt was famous for research on the heredity of intelligence, leading to the formation of school entry examinations affecting people's educational opportunities. However, Burt's research was faked to match his biased, subjective views about intelligence. His lack of objectivity led to false findings, further leading to flawed practical applications.

Theory construction

Science acquires knowledge through the scientific method of theory construction and testing, defined as the observation, identification, description, experimental investigation and theoretical explanation of phenomena. The process has three parts:

- **observation and description** of phenomena
- **formulation of a hypothesis to explain phenomena** — use of the hypothesis to predict the existence of other phenomena, or predict quantitatively the results of new observations
- **performance of tests of the predictions** by independent experimenters in rigorously performed experiments

> **scientific method** — a means of acquiring knowledge based on observable, measureable evidence.
>
> **replication** — repetition of research to authenticate results.
>
> **objectivity** — observations made without bias or expectation.
>
> **empiricism** — the belief that knowledge is gained only from sensory data.

> **Examiner's tip**
>
> It is good practice when explaining features such as objectivity to include relevant examples, in order to create detail and show understanding in answers (e.g. that results from Ganzfeld studies, which search for evidence of extrasensory perception abilities, are affected by whether researchers believe in or are sceptical of ESP).

Hypothesis testing

Part of the scientific process is the idea of **falsifiability**, where hypotheses are found to be false. Exact replication of research procedures is the accepted way of achieving this. To be scientific, a theory must therefore be capable of being assessed and being found to be false by hypothesis testing. The Chinese pseudoscience debate centres on the question of whether or not traditional Chinese philosophies and practices are actually scientific, since the majority are **irrefutable** (incapable of being validated via hypothesis testing). Indeed some critics have called for the banning of traditional Chinese medicines on the grounds that they have not been scientifically validated.

Empirical methods

Empirical methods involve observations based on sensory information, rather than on thoughts and beliefs. Scientific ideas are subjected to empirical testing by the use of rigorous observation of events/phenomena. For science to make sense there has to be an explanation of empirically observed phenomena, achieved by developing theories that can be tested empirically.

Science therefore involves making predictions tested by scientific observations made without bias or expectation by the researcher and performed under controlled conditions. In this way hypotheses are either validated (found to be true) or falsified (found to be untrue).

Validating new knowledge

Revised

Part of the scientific verification process is **peer review**, which is considered fundamental to scholarly communication. Peer review opens research to independent expert scrutiny before being made public. This procedure serves as a security system that reduces the chances of flawed or unscientific research being accepted as fact.

> **peer review** — scrutiny of research papers by experts in the same field to determine scientific validity.

Many organisations promote scientific research, for example drug companies. Therefore it is difficult to decide which research is worthy and which is spurious, especially when scientists argue completely different viewpoints.

Journal editors send copies of research studies to expert reviewers. There are four options that reviewers can recommend: (i) accept the work unconditionally, (ii) accept it if it is improved in certain ways, (iii) reject it, but suggest revisions and a resubmission, (iv) reject it outright.

Peer review is not an unbiased procedure. Research occurs in a narrow social world that inevitably affects impartiality. The ability to remain unbiased is further compromised by scientists' jobs being funded by organisations that are interested in their research being deemed acceptable. Reviewers should therefore be anonymous and independent.

Peer review can take years, and there may be resistance to revolutionary ideas.

The consequences of false or unscientific research being accepted as true are serious, because other research may be built on the original research. Cyril Burt falsified research into the heritability of intelligence, but his research, accepted as valid, greatly influenced subsequent researchers, who took his work as a starting point for their own.

Now test yourself

1 Outline the following major features of science: (i) replicability (ii) objectivity (iii) theory construction (iv) hypothesis testing (v) empirical methods.

2 (a) Describe peer review and its purpose.

   (b) Is peer review truly unbiased?

Answers on p. 128

Designing psychological investigations

Selection and application of research methods

Experiments establish causality. The laboratory experiment is preferred, allowing strict control over variables. Field and natural experiments occur in natural circumstances, but with reduced control. Field experiments use artificially induced independent variables, whereas natural experiments use naturally occurring ones.

Correlations show direction and intensity of relationships, but not causality. Correlations are used when experiments would be unethical and identify areas worthy of further investigation.

Self-reports, such as questionnaires, interviews and surveys, gain information from participants about themselves. A lot of data are gained relatively quickly, although causality cannot be established and there is a risk of idealised and socially desirable answers. Areas worthy of further research are identified.

Observations are conducted to study natural behaviour in natural environments (though they can be conducted under laboratory conditions too). Causality cannot be established and replication is difficult, but ecological validity is high.

Case studies are conducted on one person, or a small group, to assess unique circumstances or find the source of a problem. They provide rich, detailed data, but their findings cannot be generalised, nor can they establish causality.

> **research methods** — experimental and non-experimental means of conducting practical investigations.

Implications of sampling strategies

Random sampling occurs when members of a target population are selected without bias. Truly random samples are difficult to obtain because all members of target populations are not available for selection. Random samples are not necessarily representative: random selection could theoretically produce biased samples, making generalisation difficult.

Opportunity sampling is popular, use being made of people's availability. Opportunity samples are biased because those available may be unrepresentative, making generalisation difficult.

Self-selected (volunteer) sampling — generally obtained through respondents to advertisements, so require little effort. Volunteers tend

> **sampling** — selection of part of a target population for research purposes.

to be certain personality types, however, and therefore unrepresentative. They are often keen to help and therefore more at risk of demand characteristics.

Systematic sampling is achieved by selecting every *n*th person. It is unbiased and produces fairly representative samples.

Stratified sampling involves selecting participants in proportion to frequency in the target population. Stratums (groups) are randomly selected, producing representative samples. If random sampling is not used for the stratums, it is known as quota sampling.

Issues of reliability
Revised

Reliability refers to consistency. **Internal reliability** concerns the extent to which something is consistent within itself. **External reliability** concerns the extent to which a measure of something is consistent with other measures of the same thing.

There are several ways to assess reliability.

Inter-observer (rater) reliability concerns the extent to which there is agreement between different observers on what they are observing. Observers should agree **operational definitions** of the key categories being observed.

Split-half method assesses the extent to which individual test items are consistent with each other. The test is split into halves after data are obtained. If findings from the halves correlate highly, they are reliable; if not, the test needs revising.

Test–retest measures the stability of a test, interview etc. over time. It involves giving the same test to the same participants twice. If identical results are obtained, reliability is established.

Validity cannot be established without reliability being established first. However, reliability does not guarantee validity.

reliability — a measure of consistency within a set of scores and over time.

validity — the extent to which findings are generalisable beyond research settings.

Assessing and improving validity
Revised

Validity concerns the degree to which something measures what it claims to measure. Validity also refers to the legitimacy of studies and the extent to which findings are generalisable beyond research settings (as a consequence of a study's internal and external validity, see below).

Internal validity concerns the extent to which observed effects are attributable to the influence of the independent variable (IV) on the dependent variable (DV). Milgram's study of obedience was internally valid because participants believed it was real.

External validity concerns the extent to which experimental effects are generalisable to other settings (**ecological validity**), other people (**population validity**) and over time (**historical validity**). Milgram's study of obedience lacked external validity because it is not usual to shock people for getting questions wrong, it only used males and was a product of its time.

Face (content) validity involves the extent to which items look like what the test claims to measure.

Concurrent validity assesses validity by correlating scores on a test with another test known to be valid.

Ethical considerations in psychological research — Revised

Informed consent — participants receive all details of the research so that they can make a considered decision about whether to participate. Informed consent comes from the parents/legal guardians of those below 16 years of age.

Right to withdraw — participants can withdraw at anytime. No attempts can be made to persuade people to continue.

No deceit — participants should not be deceived. Informed consent is not possible where deceit occurs.

Protection from harm — participants should leave experiments in the same state in which they entered it. Research should not subject participants to levels of risk outside those normally encountered. Debriefings reduce the risk of harm. If unexpected harm occurs, it is the responsibility of investigators to deal with it (e.g. by providing counselling).

Confidentiality and **anonymity** are related considerations. Details of participants' identities and performances should not be made public. Participants must consent to the uses to which research findings are put before research commences.

> **ethical considerations** — measures to protect participants from harm and retain their dignity.

> **Typical mistakes**
> Many students refer to debriefing as an ethical issue, when really it is more of a way of dealing with an ethical issue (debriefing being used, for example, to reduce psychological harm that may have occurred in the research). For instance, Milgram used debriefing to reduce the psychological impact of his electric shock study on his participants.

Now test yourself — Tested

3 Describe experimental and non-experimental research methods.
4 Describe sampling strategies and their implications.
5 Describe issues of (i) reliability (ii) validity.
6 Describe ethical considerations in the design and conduct of research.

Answers on p. 128

Data analysis and reporting on investigations

Selection of graphical representations — Revised

Bar charts — the height of the bar represents frequency. Bar charts differ from histograms in that empty categories are excluded. There is no true zero and data on the horizontal axis are not continuous.

Histograms are similar to bar charts but the area within the bars is proportional to the frequencies represented, the horizontal axis is continuous and there are no gaps between the bars.

Frequency polygon — an alternative to the histogram, used when two or more frequency distributions are compared on the same **graph**. A line is drawn linking the midpoints from the top of each bar in a histogram.

Scattergrams allows representation of the degree of correlation between two co-variables. Scattergrams can display negative and positive correlations.

> **graph** — pictorial means of data presentation.

Examiner's tip

Ensure that you can describe graphs and their use and that you can create suitable examples of them; this may be a requirement of an exam question. All graphs should have a title that identifies the type of graph and what is being represented. The horizontal (x) axis and the vertical (y) axis should be labelled clearly, with units of measurement identified.

Probability and signficance

Revised

Probability concerns the degree of certainty that observed differences or relationships between sets of data are real differences or relationships rather than chance occurrences. There is never 100% certainty that differences and relationships shown in sets of data are beyond the boundaries of chance, so an accepted cut-off point (probability level) of $p \leq 0.05$ is used. This means that there is a 5% possibility that an observed difference and/or relationship between two sets of data is not a real difference but simply occurred by chance.

> **probability** — the degree of certainty that results beyond the boundaries of chance have occurred.

Type 1 and 2 errors

Type 1 errors occur when differences or relationships are wrongly accepted as real because the significance level was too high. This means that the null hypothesis was wrongly rejected.

Type 2 errors occur when differences or relationships are wrongly accepted as insignificant because the significance level was too low. This means that the null hypothesis was wrongly accepted.

A 5% significance level is the accepted level, striking a balance between making type 1 and type 2 errors.

Factors affecting choice of statistical test

Revised

Appropriate statistical tests are needed to analyse data. Four statistical tests are referred to in the specification (see 'Inferential analysis' below) and criteria exist to determine which to use:

- For *correlations* Spearman's rho is used.
- For *differences* a Wilcoxon signed-matched ranks test, a Mann–Whitney test, or a chi-squared test is used.

Levels of data measurement

Nominal — data occur as frequencies/categories (e.g. how many people prefer Pepsi or Coke).

Ordinal — data occur as ranks (e.g. finishing places 1st, 2nd, 3rd in a running race).

Ratio — data occur as units of equal size, with a true zero point (e.g. inches on a ruler).

Interval — data occur as units of equal size, using both positive and negative numbers.

Experimental design

For repeated measures and matched-pairs designs, Wilcoxon tests are performed. If data are at least ordinal and samples are independent, Mann–Whitney tests are used. If data are at least nominal and samples are independent, chi-squared tests are used.

Inferential analysis   Revised

Inferential tests are used to show how likely it is that patterns observed in sets of data occur by chance.

A **chi-squared test** is used when differences are predicted between sets of data of at least nominal level and an independent measures design was used. Chi-squared is also used as a test of association.

A **Mann–Whitney test** is used when differences are predicted between sets of data of at least ordinal level and an independent groups design was used.

A **Wilcoxon signed-matched ranks test** is used when differences are predicted between sets of data of at least ordinal level and a repeated or matched pairs design was used.

A **Spearman's rho test** is used when relationships are predicted between sets of data of at least ordinal level and the data are pairs of scores.

> **inferential tests** — statistical tests that determine how likely it is that patterns in sets of data occur by chance.

> **Examiner's tip**
>
> You will not be asked to carry out statistical tests in an exam but you may be asked to identify the correct test to use in given circumstances. It is essential that you are aware of the different requirements governing the selection of tests.

Analysis and interpretation of qualitative data   Revised

Qualitative data are non-numerical (e.g. the narrative of an interview). Such data provide insight about feelings and thoughts that quantitative data cannot. When analysing qualitative data, researchers look for underlying meanings. This can be subjective, based on the researcher's own interpretation. Qualitative data can be converted into quantitative data by being changed into categories or themes, to allow objective analysis by statistical means.

Content analysis involves counting frequencies of occurrences: for example, children's drawings of a Christmas tree and presents could allow counting of the number of presents and their sizes, worth etc.

> **qualitative data** — data occurring in a non-numerical form.

Reporting on psychological investigations   Revised

Research is published in academic journals after peer review. There is a conventional way of presenting research, in six set sections.

1   The **abstract** summarises details of the research's aim(s), hypotheses, participants, methods, findings and conclusions.

2 The **introduction** reviews previous research, progressing into aims and hypotheses.

3 The **method** section presents details of methodology and ethical considerations necessary to permit replication. The tests and questionnaires used are placed in the appendices, but referred to here.

4 The **results** section summarises raw data and measures of central tendency and dispersion in words, graphs and tables. Details of inferential statistical analysis indicate whether results are significant. Raw data and statistical calculations are referred to, but placed in the appendices.

5 The **discussion** assesses findings in terms of previous research, outlines limitations, while suggesting possible modifications, proposes ideas for future research and outlines implications of the research.

6 The **appendices** include raw data, questionnaires, calculations, references, materials used etc.

Now test yourself

7 What types of graph are used in psychological research? Give details of each.

8 Outline the concept of probability.

9 What are type 1 and 2 errors?

10 Outline the criteria for use of the following statistical tests: (i) Mann–Whitney (ii) Wilcoxon signed-matched ranks (iii) chi-squared (iv) Spearman's rho.

11 What are qualitative data and how are they interpreted?

12 Outline the conventional way of presenting psychological investigations.

Answers on p. 128

Tested ☐

Exam practice

1 A psychologist presented information to participants either via printed-paper (group A) or displayed on a computer screen (group B). Group A recalled 85% of the information and group B 4%.

(a) Write a suitable non-directional hypothesis for this investigation. [2]

(b) The investigation generated quantitative data. Give one advantage of this type of data. [1]

(c) A Mann–Whitney statistical test was used to analyse the data from this investigation. Give two reasons for using this statistical test. [2 + 2]

(d) Describe one conclusion that can be drawn from this investigation. [2]

(e) An opportunity sample was used in this investigation. Give one strength and one weakness of this sampling method. [2 + 2]

(f) The research was subjected to peer review before being published. Explain the role of peer review. [10]

(g) The psychologist noticed that older participants seemed to have more difficulty operating computers than younger participants. Design a study to investigate possible age differences in operating computers. You should include sufficient details to permit replication: for example, a hypothesis, variables, details of design and procedure, and sampling. [12]

Answers and quick quiz 13 online

Online ☐

Examiner's summary

✔ The major features of science include replicability, objectivity, theory construction, hypothesis testing and the use of empirical methods.

✔ New knowledge is authenticated through peer review, which assesses scientific validity of research before publication.

✔ Designing scientific investigations involves the selection and application of appropriate methods, the implications of selection strategies, issues of reliability and validity, and ethical considerations.

✔ Data analysis and reporting of psychological investigations involves appropriate selection of graphs, probability and significance, factors affecting choice of statistical test, the use of inferential analysis and conventions of reporting on scientific investigations.

Now test yourself answers

Chapter 1

1 Explanations are required that define the rhythms in terms of their differing cyclical natures (how often they occur).

2 Use could be made of the following studies: circadian — Siffre (1972); infradian — Russell et al. (1980); ultradian — Gerkema & Dann (1985).

3 Focus could be on: endogenous pacemakers — the main pacemaker being the SCN; exogenous zeitgebers — their role in resetting circadian rhythms.

4 Focus for both factors could be on desynchronisation, as well as phase delay/phase advance.

5 Points could focus on: shift work — Czeisler (1982), Sharkey (2001); jet lag — Klein et al. (1972), Schwartz (1995). The answer could also focus on accidents, (e.g. Chernobyl) as well as practical applications.

6 IDA points could be drawn from the gender bias of shift-work studies and practical applications of research findings.

7 Brief bullet-point descriptions are required of stages 1–4 and REM sleep.

8 Reference is required to the biological features of sleep (e.g. the role of hormones).

9 This outline could be presented as a table, relating the different features of sleep patterns to the different ages.

10 Relevant points could be made with reference to Van Cauter (2000), Floyd (2007), Dement & Kleitman (1957), including relevant methodological and ethical considerations, theoretical support and practical applications.

11 Focus should be on (i) evolutionary explanations — their adaptive nature (ii) restoration explanations — rejuvenation of body and mind.

12 Research support could be demonstrated from (i) evolution — Meddis (1979), Stear (2005), Siegel (2008); (ii) restoration — Oswald (1980), Horne (1988), Stern & Morgane (1974).

13 Evaluative points that support or weaken the explanations should be made.

14 IDA points could be drawn from the practical applications of explanations, as well ethical considerations of the associated animal research.

15 (a) Outlines need to focus on factors that influence sleep disorders, such as (i) insomnia — apnoea and personality (ii) sleepwalking — age, genetics and anxiety-related personality disorders (iii) narcolepsy — genetics.

(b) Research support could be demonstrated from
(i) insomnia — Chest (2001), Kales (1976);
(ii) sleepwalking — Hublin (1997), Broughton (1968);
(iii) narcolepsy — Mignot (1999), Hufford (1982).

(c) Reference could be made to evaluative points that support or weaken explanations, including relevant methodological and ethical considerations and practical applications.

16 IDA points could be drawn from practical applications, such as effective treatments for sleep disorders, as well as the holistic nature of research into insomnia.

Chapter 2

1 Gregory's theory should be outlined, in terms of the factors listed, in a way that emphasises how perception is built from sensory information in an indirect fashion.

2 Reference could be made to Aarts and Dijksterhuis (2002), Solley & Haigh (1948), McGinnies (1949), Segall (1963).

3 Points could include relevant methodological considerations, the degree of support for the theory's explanatory power and comparisons with Gibson's theory.

4 Gibson's theory should be outlined in terms of the factors listed, in a way that emphasises the way in which perception occurs directly from sensory information.

5 Research support could include Johansson (1973), Frichtel (2006), Creem-Regehr (2003), Warren (1984).

6 Evaluative points could include relevant methodological considerations, the degree of support for the theory's explanatory power and comparisons with Gibson's theory.

7 IDA points could be drawn from the practical applications of Gibson's theory and the nature (Gibson) versus nurture (Gregory) debate.

8 Focus should be on explaining what these perceptual skills consist of and how they develop.

9 Evaluative points should concentrate on how these perceptual skills develop in terms of innate and learned factors. Research points could be taken from Gibson & Walk (1960), Bower (1970), Campos (1970), Imura (2008), Bower (1966), Dannemiller & Hanko (1987).

10 Focus should be on explaining what studies have revealed about how perceptual skills develop.

11 A list of evaluative points can be made relating to Sann & Steri (2007), Chien (2003), Dannemiller and Hanko (1987), Allport & Pettigrew (1957), Turnbull (1967), Montello (2006).

12 Two possible IDA points are cultural bias in research and the nature versus nurture debate.

13 The theory should be explained in terms of its components, with focus on how familiar and unfamiliar faces are processed.

14 Reference could be made to the research of Bruce & Valentine (1988), Ellis (1979), as well as case studies of prosopagnosia.

15 Evaluation could centre on the degree of research support, methodological considerations and practical applications.

16 Explanations should centre on identification of brain-damaged areas linked to prosopagnosia.

17 Reference could be made to research by Bauer (1984), Brunsdon (2006), Kurucz (1979), Bruyer (1983), Campbell (1986), Kanwisher (1997).

18 The list of evaluative points should focus on the methodological limitations of case studies, whether face recognition is separate from object recognition, the ethics of studying brain-damaged individuals and the degree of support for Bruce & Young's theory.

19 The two IDA points could refer to practical applications, such as face-recognition systems and the holistic nature of Bruce & Young's theory.

Chapter 3

1 (i) *Sociobiological* theory — should be outlined in terms of its adaptive nature with a highlighting of gender differences (ii) the *reinforcement and need satisfaction* theory — in terms of conditioning processes (iii) *social exchange* theory — in terms of maximising benefits and minimising costs and the mutual exchange of rewards between partners (iv) *equity* theory — in terms of the motivation to achieve fairness (v) *Duck* and (vi) *Lee* — in terms of their stages of dissolution.

2 References to positive and negative criticisms could be drawn from (i) *sociobiological* theory — Dunbar (1995), Davis (1990); (ii) *reinforcement and need satisfaction* theory — Cunningham (1988), May & Hamilton (1980); (iii) *social exchange* theory —

Rusbult (1983), Hatfield (1979); (iv) *Equity* theory — Yum (2009), Canary & Stafford (1992); (v) *Duck* — Kassin (1996), Akert (1992); (vi) *Lee* — Lee (1984), Argyle & Henderson (1984). Comparison of theories should be done in a way that emphasises similarities/differences and strengths/weaknesses. Focus could also be made, where relevant, on methodological and ethical considerations, as well as practical applications, such as relationship counselling.

3 Differences need to be explained in terms of the different evolutionary pressures on males and females.

4 Male and female reproduction strategies need to be outlined in terms of the evolutionary advantages they bring to both sexes.

5 Reference to research support could be made from Birkhead (1990), Dewsbury (1984), Buss (1993), Zahavi (1975), Partridge (1980), Moller (1992).

6 Differences should be outlined in terms of evolutionary pressures on both sexes.

7 A list of evaluative points/research support could be drawn from Pollett (2007), Gross & Shine (1981), Dawkins & Carlisle (1976), Krebs & Davies (1981).

8 (a) The continuity hypothesis needs to be explained in terms of early attachment types forming an internal working model to act as a template for future adult relationships.

   (b) The temperament hypothesis needs to be explained in terms of adult relationships being determined by innate personality.

9 Focus should be on the degree of research support, with reference to Hazan & Shavers (1987), McCarthy (1999), Hamilton (1994), as well as methodological and ethical considerations, where relevant, theoretical considerations and practical applications.

10 Differences could be outlined in terms of Western/non-Western cultures and/or voluntary/arranged marriages.

11 Evaluative points could be drawn from the degree of research support, with reference to Mwamwenda and Monyooe (1997), McKenry and Price (1995), relevant methodological and ethical considerations, such as the use of an imposed etic, theoretical considerations and issues such as culture bias.

Chapter 4

1 The acquisition of aggression should be outlined by (i) SLT — in terms of observation and imitation of role models (ii) deindividuation — in terms of loss of identity and the lessening of social restraints.

2 Reference could be made to: SLT via Bandura (1961) (1963), Williams (1981) (ii) deindividuation via Watson (1973), Silke (2003), as well as relevant methodological and ethical considerations, theoretical considerations and practical applications, such as closed-circuit television systems.

3 The terms should be identified in ways that highlight their purposes and show the differences between them.

4 (i) Warfare should be explained in terms of its origins and the role of situational factors (ii) terrorism should be explained as a form of minority influence.

5 Evaluative points could be focused on the degree of research support, with reference to: warfare — Kruuk (1972), Goodall (1986); terrorism — Ministry of Defence (2005), Barak (2004), as well as theoretical considerations, methodological and ethical considerations, where relevant, and practical applications, such as strategies to negate the negative effects of war and terror.

6 Serotonin and testosterone should be outlined in terms of their roles in heightening/reducing aggression levels.

7 (a) Reference could be made to: serotonin — Delville (1997), Popova (1991); testosterone — Higley (1996), Edwards (1968).

   (b) Evaluative points should focus on theoretical considerations, methodological and ethical considerations, where relevant, and practical applications. IDA material could comment on the determinist nature of hormonal and neural mechanisms.

8 Genetic factors should be explained in terms of their direct and indirect influences on aggression.

9 Focus should be on the adaptive nature of human aggression.

10 Focus should be on the adaptive gender differences of jealousy and infidelity that can motivate aggressive behaviour.

11 Reference could be made to Daly & Wilson (1988), Buss & Dedden (1990), as well as theoretical considerations, relevant methodological and ethical considerations and practical applications, such as in relationship counselling. IDA material could also refer to the lack of gender bias, as explanations for both male and female jealousy and infidelity are given.

12 Focus should be on the ritualised and territorial nature of group displays in sport.

13 Reference and evaluation should be made to research support: jealousy — Schwartz & Barkey (1977), Morris (1980), as well as theoretical considerations, relevant methodological and ethical considerations and practical applications, such as decreasing the negative effects of sports hooliganism.

14 Focus should be on the adaptive nature of lynch mob behaviour.

15 Reference could be made to Blalock (1967), Tolnay & Beck (1995), as well as theoretical considerations, relevant methodological and ethical considerations and practical applications, such as addressing the tensions that lead to lynch mob behaviour. Further IDA material could focus on the lack of consideration of other non-evolutionary explanations.

Chapter 5

1 Outlines should focus on (i) mood — small and large effects on eating; (ii) cultural influences — transmission of eating practices via reinforcement and SLT and indirect and direct influences; (iii) health concerns — effects on attitudes and behaviour. Evaluations could make reference to (i) mood — Wansink (2008), Wolff (2000) (ii) cultural influences — Stefansson (1960), McFarlane & Pliner (1987) (iii) health concerns — Monneuse (1991), Tuorila & Pangborn (1988), as well focus on relevant methodological and ethical considerations, practical applications towards healthy eating and relevant issues, such as the nature versus nurture debate.

2 Definitions should be phrased in terms of restriction of eating and the maintenance of weight loss.

3 (a) Explanations should focus on factors that contribute to successful dieting.

   (b) Reference could be made to the research of Miller-Kovach (2001) and Bartlett (2003).

4 (a) Explanations should focus on factors that contribute to unsuccessful dieting

   (b) Reference could be made to the research of Cummings (2002), Williams (2002).

   (c) Evaluative points should focus on practical applications towards effective dieting, relevant issues, such as individual differences, methodological and ethical considerations when relevant and theoretical considerations, such as explanations of obesity.

5 (a) (i) Dual-control theory should be explained in terms of homeostasis, while (ii) set-point theory should be explained in terms of how body weight is maintained and set.

   (b) Reference should be made to the following research support (i) dual-control theory — Hetherington & Ranson (1940), Stellar (1954); (ii) set-point theory — Powley & Keesey (1970), Proc & Frohman (1970).

(c) Evaluative points should focus on theoretical considerations, such as support for the biological approach, practical applications in controlling food intake, methodological and ethical considerations, where relevant, and relevant issues, such as biological determinism.

6   Food preferences should be explained in terms of their survival value.

7   (a) The following food preferences should be explained in terms of (i) sweet tastes — non-toxicity and high energy content (ii) bitter tastes — toxicity (iii) salty tastes — body maintenance (iv) meat eating — energy/protein content, intelligence and toxicity.

   (b) Reference could be made to research evidence and evaluative points in (i) sweet tastes — De Araujo et al. (2008); (ii) bitter tastes — Mennella (2008); (iii) salty tastes — Dudley (2008); (iv) meat — Foley & Lee (1991), as well as theoretical considerations, methodological and ethical considerations, where relevant, and practical applications, such as in flavouring medicines.

8   The explanations should be detailed in terms of (i) psychodynamic — unresolved childhood conflicts; (ii) cognitive — maladaptive thinking; (iii) neural — the hypothalamus, neural circuits and hormones and neurotransmitters; (iv) evolutionary — adaptive advantages.

9   Reference could be made to evaluative points, research evidence and IDA points as follows: (i) psychodynamic — Felliti (2001); (ii) cognitive — Braet and Crombez (2001), Cserjesi et al. (2007); (iii) neural — Stice (2008), Reeves & Plum (1969); (iv) evolutionary — Di Meglio & Yates (2000), Rowe (2007). Theoretical considerations, practical applications in addressing the negative effects of obesity and methodological and ethical considerations, should be commented on where relevant.

Chapter 6

1   Kohlberg's theory can be summarised in terms of its developmental nature in set stages. Gender schema theory can be summarised in terms of the cognitive processing of information from social interactions.

2   Similarities between the two theories can be expressed in terms of cognitive development, differences in terms of what developments are seen as necessary for gender-consistent behaviours to occur.

3   Reference could be made to: Kohlberg — Frey & Ruble (1992), Thompson (1975); gender-schema theory — Masters (1979), Aubry (1999), as well as theoretical considerations, relevant issues, such as the exclusion of biological factors, methodological and ethical considerations, where relevant, and practical applications in childrearing.

4   Hormones and genes should be outlined in terms of their biological influences on gender development.

5   Reference could be made to Deady (2006), Koopman (1991) and other relevant evaluative material.

6   Evolved differences in gender role behaviour should be detailed in terms of their adaptive advantages to both sexes.

7   Reference could be made to the degree of support found in Holloway (2002), Buss (1989).

8   Explanation should be focused on how gender is seen as being socially and biologically influenced.

9   Reference could be made to the degree of research support found in Wetherell & Edley (1999), Smith & Lloyd (1978).

10 Evaluative points should focus on theoretical considerations, such as strengths and weaknesses, relevant methodological and ethical considerations and practical applications towards childrearing.

11 Gender dysphoria should be described in terms of its features.

12 (a) Gender dysphoria should be explained in terms of both psychological and biological influences.

   (b) Research suggests both explanations are valid, with a role for biology through genetic factors and for psychology through conditioning and social learning theory.

13 Reference could be made to Rekers (1995), Hare (2009), as well as theoretical considerations, relevant methodological and ethical considerations and practical applications in treating the condition.

14 Explanations for both (i) and (ii) should be focused on reinforcements and SLT.

15 (a) Reference could be made to the research evidence of Eccles (1990), Fagot and Leinbach (1995), Renzetti and Curran (1992), Colley (1994).

   (b) Evaluative points should focus on theoretical considerations, methodological and ethical considerations, where relevant, and practical applications towards effective childrearing.

16 The answer should be focused on the determination of innate and learned features.

17 Reference could be made to the cross-cultural studies of Barry (1957), Mead (1935), Williams & Best (1990).

18 Evaluative points should focus on theoretical considerations, such as the degree of support for biological and learning theories, methodological and ethical considerations, where relevant, practical applications and relevant issues, such as the nature versus nurture debate and cultural bias.

Chapter 7

1   Outlines for (i) and (ii) should focus on the identification of basic factors of intelligence and the use of factor analysis.

2   Reference could be made to evaluative points drawn from Johnson & Bouchard (2005), Kitcher (1985), Guildford (1985), including theoretical considerations in terms of strengths and weaknesses, relevant methodological and ethical considerations and practical applications, such as intelligence testing.

3   Outlines should focus on (i) Sternberg — three facets of intelligence; (ii) Case — factors influencing the development of information processing ability.

4   Reference could be made to evaluative points drawn from Merrick (1992), Chi (1978), including theoretical considerations in terms of strengths and weaknesses, relevant methodological and ethical considerations and practical applications, such as teaching methods.

5   Outlines should be focused on (i) classical conditioning — the association of neutral stimuli with unconditioned stimuli; (ii) operant conditioning — the use of reinforcements.

6   Focus should be on the role of classical and operant conditioning in animal behaviour.

7   Reference could be made to evaluative points drawn from Baker (1984), Fisher & Hinde (1949), Garcia & Koelling (1966), Breland & Breland (1961), including theoretical considerations in terms of strengths and weaknesses, relevant methodological and ethical considerations and practical applications in animal training.

8   (a) Explanations should focus on (i) imitation — observation and direct imitation; (ii) enhancement — focusing of attention on particular environmental features; (iii) emulation — reproduction of the consequences of behaviour; (iv) tutoring — encouragement, punishment and provision of behavioural examples.

   (b) Reference could be made to (i) imitation — Whiten (1999); (ii) enhancement — Nagell (1993); (iii) emulation — Tomasello (1987); (iv) tutoring — Rendell & Whitehead (2001).

9   (a) Explanation of Machiavellian intelligence should focus on the use of deception and alliance formation that does not hinder social cohesion.

(b) Reference could be made to Nishida (1992), Whiten & Byrne (1988), as well as other relevant evaluative points.

10 Outlines should focus on the adaptive advantages of the development of human intelligence.

11 (a) Reference could be made to research evidence in Dunbar (1982), Boesche (1992), Holekamp & Enghe (2003), Ehmer (2001).

(b) Focus should be on theoretical considerations, relevant methodological and ethical considerations, such as those associated with performing research on wild animals and relevant issues, such as the deterministic nature of evolutionary theory.

12 Outlines should focus on the relative contributions of genetic and environmental factors to intelligence levels.

13 (a) Reference could be made to Bouchard and McGue (1981), Petrill & Deater-Deckard (2004), Lahn (2004), Zajonc & Marcus (1975), Atkinson (1990).

(b) Evaluative points should focus on theoretical considerations, relevant methodological and ethical considerations, such as the difficulties in separating out genetic and environmental influences in twin studies, practical applications, and relevant issues, such as the nature versus nurture debate.

14 (a) Outlines should focus on the cultural nature of intelligence and attempts to create culture-free tests.

(b) Evaluative points could be made with reference to Williams (1972), including theoretical considerations, relevant methodological and ethical considerations, practical applications in intelligence testing, and relevant issues, such as cultural bias and the use of an imposed etic.

Chapter 8

1 Outlines should focus on (i) Piaget — invariant processes and variant structures, as well as stages of cognitive development; (ii) Vygotsky — the socio-cultural construction of knowledge and thinking.

2 Lists of evaluative points could be made with reference to (i) Piaget — Piaget (1954), Piaget & Inhelder (1956); (ii) Vygotsky — Berk (1994), Wertsch et al. (1980), including theoretical considerations, relevant methodological and ethical issues and practical applications in childrearing.

3 Descriptions should focus on how the theories can be used to facilitate better teaching.

4 Reference could be made to evaluative points drawn from Modgil (1983), Danner & Day (1987), Cloward (1967), Gokhale (1995), including theoretical considerations, relevant methodological and ethical issues, such as researcher bias, and practical applications in education.

5 Descriptions should focus on morality developing in innate set stages related to biological maturation.

6 Focus should be on how ethical decisions in moral dilemmas are used to assess Kohlberg's levels of morality.

7 The outline should focus on describing the features of Kohlberg's three levels of morality.

8 In compiling the list, reference could be made to research support via Kohlberg (1969), Kohlberg (1975), Fodor (1972), as well as theoretical considerations, relevant methodological and ethical issues, practical applications and relevant issues, such as the gender bias of Kohlberg's theory.

9 Descriptions should focus on self-recognition, self-referential emotions, self-esteem and the theory of mind.

10 Reference could be made to the degree of research support in Mans (1978), Lewis (1989), Vershueren et al. (2001), Avis & Harris (1981).

11 Perspective taking should be explained in terms of the ability to understand another person's thoughts, intentions and feelings by assuming their viewpoint.

12 The outline should focus on describing the dominant features of each of Selman's stages.

13 Evaluative points could be made with reference to Schultz & Selman (1990), Underwood & Moore (1982), including theoretical considerations, relevant methodological and ethical considerations and practical applications, such as in reducing violence levels by developing empathy.

14 Explanation should focus on the interaction of biological and environmental factors in establishing social cognition.

15 Explanation should focus on the role of mirror neurons in perceptions of others' feelings and thoughts through empathy and imitation.

16 Evaluative points could be made with reference to Rizzolato & Craighero (2004), Gallese (2001), Stuss (2001), including theoretical considerations, relevant methodological and ethical considerations, such as the reliance on animal research, practical applications, such as with autism, and relevant issues, such as the reductionist and determinist nature of biological explanations.

Chapter 9

Schizophrenia

1 Schizophrenia should be outlined in terms of its symptoms, including positive and negative ones, as well as its sub-types.

2 Explanations could be given with reference to (i) reliability — Beck (1962), Read (2004); (ii) validity — Hollis (2000), Heather (1976), Jansson & Parnas (2007), as well as related evaluative points.

3 Biological explanations should be outlined in terms of hereditary influences through genetics, evolutionary adaptive advantages and biochemical factors.

4 Reference should be made to: genetics — Torrey (1994), Kety & Ingraham (1992) (ii) evolution — Peters (1999), Storr (1997); biochemistry — Iversen (1979), Javitt (2000), as well as theoretical considerations, relevant methodological and ethical considerations and practical applications, such as therapies based on the approaches.

5 Psychological explanations should be outlined in terms of psychodynamic factors, such as unresolved childhood conflicts and cognitive explanations linked to maladaptive thinking and sociocultural factors.

6 Reference could be made to: psychodynamic — Read (2005); cognitive — Bentall (1991); sociocultural — Leff (1976), as well as theoretical considerations, relevant methodological and ethical considerations and practical applications, such as therapies based on the approaches.

7 Biological therapies should be outlined in terms of electrical voltages to the head through ECT and the use of antipsychotic drugs, both typical and atypical.

8 Evaluations could be made with reference to: ECT — Tharyan & Adams (2005), Tang (2002); drugs — Kahn (2008), Davis (1989), as well as theoretical consideration, such as the degree of support therapies give to the theories they are based on, relevant methodological and ethical considerations and the effectiveness of therapies in terms of cost, side effects etc.

9 Psychological therapies should be outlined in terms of conditioning through behavioural therapies and the reduction of psychotic thinking through CBT.

10 Reference could be made to the following therapies: behavioural — McMonagle & Sultana (2000), Upper & Newton (1971); CBT — Turkington (2006), Tarrier (2005), as well as theoretical consideration, such as the degree of support therapies give to the theories they are based on, relevant methodological and ethical considerations and the effectiveness of therapies in terms of cost, side effects etc.

Depression

1 Depression should be outlined in terms of its symptoms, as well as its sub-types, such as unipolar and bipolar.

2 Reference could be made to (i) reliability — Einfeld (2002), Sato (1996); (ii) validity — Zigler & Phillips (1971), Sanchez-Villegas (2008), as well as related evaluative points.

3 Biological explanations should be outlined in terms of hereditary influences through genetics and biochemical factors, such as abnormal levels of hormones and neurotransmitters.

4 Reference should be made to: genetics — Sevey (2000), Wender (1986), Caspi (2005); biochemistry —Mann (1996), Zhou (2005), Chen (2006), as well as theoretical considerations, relevant methodological and ethical considerations and practical applications, such as therapies based on the approaches.

5 Psychological explanations should be outlined in terms of psychodynamic factors, such as unresolved childhood conflicts and cognitive explanations linked to maladaptive thinking.

6 Reference could be made to: psychodynamic — Swaffer & Hollin (2001), Harlow (1965); cognitive — Boury (2001), Seligman (1974) as well as theoretical considerations, relevant methodological and ethical considerations and practical applications, such as therapies based on the approaches.

7 Biological therapies should be outlined in terms of antidepressant drugs and the application of electrical voltages to the head through ECT.

8 Evaluations could be made with reference to: drugs — Furukawa (2003), Kirsch (2008); ECT — Paguin (2008), Levy (1968), as well as theoretical consideration, such as the degree of support therapies give to the theories they are based on, relevant methodological and ethical considerations and the effectiveness of therapies in terms of cost, side effects etc.

9 Psychological therapies should be outlined in terms of gaining insight into unresolved childhood traumas through psychodynamic means therapies and the reduction of maladaptive thinking through CBT.

10 Reference could be made to the following therapies: psychodynamic — Leichsenring (2004), De Clerq (1999); CBT — Flannaghan (1997), Whitfield & Williams (2003), as well as theoretical consideration, such as the degree of support therapies give to the theories they are based on, relevant methodological and ethical considerations and the effectiveness of therapies in terms of cost, side effects etc.

Phobias

1 Phobias should be outlined in terms of characteristics, symptoms and sub-types.

2 Reference could be made to: reliability — Silverman (2001), Alstrom (2009); validity — Herbert (1992), Vasey & Dadds (2001), as well as related evaluative points.

3 Biological explanations should be outlined in terms of hereditary influences through genetics and evolutionary adaptive advantages of phobias.

4 Reference should be made to: genetics — Kendler (1992), Reich & Yates (1988); evolution — Cook & Mineka (1989), Bennett-Levy & Marteau (1084), as well as theoretical considerations, relevant methodological and ethical considerations and practical applications, such as therapies based on the approaches.

5 Psychological explanations should be outlined in terms cognitive explanations linked to maladaptive thinking and sociocultural factors.

6 Reference could be made to: cognitive — Thorpe and Salkovskis (2000), Kindt and Brosschot (1997); sociocultural — Kleinknecht (1997), Bruch & Heimberg (1994), as well as theoretical considerations, relevant methodological and ethical considerations and practical applications, such as therapies based on the approaches.

7 Biological therapies should be outlined in terms of the use of drugs, such as BZs, and irreversible destruction of brain tissue through psychosurgery.

8 Evaluation could be made with reference to: drugs — Slaap (1996), Deb Boer (1994); psychosurgery — Ruck (2003), Balon (2003), as well as theoretical consideration, such as the degree of support therapies give to the theories they are based on, relevant methodological and ethical considerations and the effectiveness of therapies in terms of cost, side effects etc.

9 Psychological therapies should be outlined in terms of conditioning through systematic desensitisation and the reduction of maladaptive thinking through CBT.

10 Evaluation could be made with reference to: systematic desensitisation — Rothbaum (1998), Wolpe (1960); CBT — Spence (2000), Kvale (2004), as well as theoretical consideration, such as the degree of support therapies give to the theories they are based on, relevant methodological and ethical considerations and the effectiveness of therapies in terms of cost, side effects etc.

Obsessive-compulsive disorder

1 OCD should be outlined in terms of characteristics and symptoms.

2 Reference could be made to: reliability — Di Nardo & Barlow (1987), Foa (1987); validity — Leckman and Chittenden (1990), Deacon & Abramovitz (2004), as well as related evaluative points.

3 Biological explanations should be outlined in terms of hereditary influences through genetics and evolutionary adaptive advantages of OCD.

4 Reference should be made to: genetics — Grootheest (2005), Lenane (1990), Samuels (2007); evolution — Marks & Nesse (1984), Chepko-Sade (1989), as well as theoretical considerations, relevant methodological and ethical considerations and practical applications, such as therapies based on the approaches.

5 Psychological explanations should be outlined in terms cognitive explanations linked to maladaptive thinking and sociocultural factors.

6 Reference could be made to: cognitive — Davison & Neale (1994), Clark (1992); sociocultural — Fontenelle (2004), Jaisoorya (2008), as well as theoretical considerations, relevant methodological and ethical considerations and practical applications, such as therapies based on the approaches.

7 Biological therapies should be outlined in terms of the use of drugs, such as BZs, and irreversible destruction of brain tissue through psychosurgery.

8 Evaluation could be made with reference to: drugs — Beroqvist et al. (1999), Flament (1985); psychosurgery — Kelly & Cobb (1985), Hindus (1985), as well as theoretical consideration, such as the degree of support therapies give to the theories they are based on, relevant methodological and ethical considerations and the effectiveness of therapies in terms of cost, side effects etc.

9 Psychological therapies should be outlined in terms of conditioning through behavioural therapies and the reduction of maladaptive thinking through CBT.

10 Evaluation could be made with reference to: behavioural — Gertz (1966), Baer (1991); CBT — O'Kearney (2006), Sousa (2007), as well as theoretical consideration, such as the degree of support therapies give to the theories they are based on, relevant methodological and ethical considerations and the effectiveness of therapies in terms of cost, side effects etc.

Chapter 10

1 Outlines should focus on (i) SLT — in terms of observation and imitation of models; (ii) cognitive priming — through the use of media cues as 'scripts' for later behaviour.

2   Evaluative points could be made with reference to (i) SLT —
    Bandura (1961) (1963), Lovelace & Huston (1983); (ii) cognitive
    priming — Murray (2007), Josephson (1987), as well as theoretical
    considerations, relevant methodological and ethical considerations
    and practical applications, such as the development of pro-social
    behaviours.

3   Outlines for (i) and (ii) should focus on factors associated with
    positive and negative effects, such as desensitisation, addictive
    tendencies and disinhibition.

4   (a) Reference could be made to: video games — Sanger (1996),
        Kestanbaum and Weinstein (1985), Strasburger & Wilson (2002),
        Sopes & Millar (1983); computers — Durkin & Barber (2002),
        Valkenburg & Peter (2009), Pearce (2007), Daft (1987).

    (b) The focus of evaluative points should be on theoretical
        considerations, relevant methodological and ethical
        considerations and practical applications, such as the
        development of communication skills in adolescents.

5   Focus should be on (i) Hovland-Yale — explaining attitude change as
    a sequence of stages in response to communication (ii) elaboration
    likelihood — explaining how persuasive messages are processed
    through cognitive evaluation.

6   (a) Reference could be made to: Hovland-Yale — Meveritz and
        Chaiken (1987), Allyn & Festinger (1961); elaboration likelihood
        — Millar (2005), Petty (1981).

    (b) Evaluative points should focus on theoretical considerations,
        relevant methodological and ethical considerations and practical
        applications, such as in the world of advertising.

7   The focus of description should be on (i) Hovland-Yale — in terms
    of the factors of communicators, messages and audiences;
    (ii) elaboration likelihood — in terms of the roles of the central and
    peripheral routes.

8   (a) Reference could be made to (i) Hovland-Yale — Sistrunk &
        McDavid (1971), Gorn (1982); (ii) elaboration likelihood — Witte
        & Allen (2000), Berscheid and Walster (1974).

    (b) Evaluative points should focus on theoretical considerations,
        for instance attitude change as a result of SLT, relevant
        methodological and ethical considerations, such as the ethics
        of using psychology to persuade people to buy products, and
        practical applications.

9   Explanations should focus on (i) social psychological — in terms of
    SLT, social construction theory and the absorption-addiction model;
    (ii) evolutionary — in terms of adaptive advantages.

10 (a) Reference could be made to: social psychological — Escalis &
        Bettman (2008), Belch & Belch (2007); evolutionary — Dunbar
        (1997), Fieldman (2008).

    (b) Evaluative points should focus on theoretical considerations,
        relevant methodological and ethical considerations and practical
        applications, such as the use of celebrities in advertising.

11 (a) Reference could be made to (i) celebrity worship —
        McCutcheon (2002), Maltby (2003), Maltby (2004); (ii) celebrity
        stalking — Mullen (2008), Meloy (2008), McCutcheon (2004).

    (b) Evaluative points should focus on theoretical considerations,
        relevant methodological and ethical points, such as the non-
        experimental nature of research, and practical applications, such
        as strategies to counteract the negative effects of stalking.

Chapter 11

1   (a) Outlines should focus on (i) biological — how addiction
        occurs as a physiologically controlled pattern of behaviour; (ii)
        cognitive — how addiction occurs as distorted thinking related to
        dysfunctional beliefs; (iii) learning — how addiction forms through
        environmental interactions that produce euphoric outcomes.

(b) Focus for (i) and (ii) should be on the biological, cognitive and
    learning factors that contribute to initiation, maintenance and
    relapse of smoking and gambling.

(c) Reference could be made to (i) biological — Nielsen (2005),
    Pergadia (2006), Grosset (2009) (ii) cognitive — Ratelle
    (2004), Griffiths (1994) (iii) learning — Meyer (1995), National
    Institute on Drug Abuse (2005), as well as theoretical
    considerations, methodological and ethical considerations
    and practical applications, such as effective means of
    addressing addiction.

2   (a) Outlines should focus on (i) stress — in terms of how
        stress contributes to addiction and the stressful effects of
        addiction; (ii) peers — as a form of normative influence
        and behavioural reinforcements; (iii) age — in terms
        of increased vulnerability in adolescence and old age;
        (iv) personality — in terms of identifying traits associated
        with addiction.

    (b) Reference could be made to: stress — Cleck & Bendy (2008);
        peers — Sussman & Ames (2001); age — Health Canada Youth
        Smoking Survey (2006); personality — Chein (1964).

    (c) The focus of evaluative points should be on theoretical
        considerations, relevant methodological and ethical
        considerations, such as the sensitivity of researching on people
        with dependencies and practical applications, such as effective
        therapies for dependencies.

3   (a) Explanation should focus on social learning effects, as well as the
        addictive qualities of media itself.

    (b) Evaluative points could be made with reference to Kimberley
        (2006), as well as to theoretical considerations, relevant
        methodological and ethical considerations and practical
        applications.

4   (a) The description should focus on the components of the
        theory of planned behaviour (TPB) that influence dependent
        behaviour.

    (b) The description should focus on the role of behavioural control
        in overcoming dependency.

    (c) Reference could be made to evaluative points from Oh &
        Hsu (2001), as well as theoretical considerations, relevant
        methodological and ethical considerations and practical
        applications, such as the reduction of dependency
        behaviours.

5   (a) Outlines should focus on (i) biological — therapeutic methods
        of abstention based on physiological means; (ii) psychological —
        therapeutic methods of abstention based on non-physiological
        means; (iii) public health — communal campaigns to reduce and
        protect against dependency behaviours.

    (b) Reference could be made to: biological — Moore (2009);
        psychological — Carroll (2008); public health — Conrod (2004),
        as well as other relevant evaluative material.

Chapter 12

1   Explanations should focus on alleged scientific practices and theories
    that actually lack scientific content.

2   The answer should focus on the development of parapsychology
    as a scientific discipline and whether the study of exceptional
    experience can ever have scientific legitimacy.

3   Outlines should focus on the procedural techniques that occur
    between receivers and senders in the Ganzfeld procedure.

4   Reference could be made to Hyman & Honorton (1985), Honorton
    (1986).

5   Focus on an explanation of the movement of objects without
    physical contact through macro and micro effects.

6 Reference could be made to evaluative points drawn from Benson (2006), as well as theoretical considerations, relevant methodological and ethical considerations and issues such as possible fraud.

7 Focus should be on (i) coincidence — how sequences of accidental events are perceived as planned; (ii) probability judgements — how several cognitive factors explain incorrect probability judgements.

8 Evaluative points could be made drawn from (i) coincidence — Falk (1982), Blakemore and Troscianko (1985); (ii) probability judgements — Aarnio & Lindeman (1975), Langer & Roth (1975), as well as theoretical considerations, relevant methodological and ethical considerations and issues such as the nature versus nurture debate in determining whether cognitive factors are innate or learned.

9 Explanations should focus on (i) superstitions — as irrational beliefs that objects, actions or circumstances not logically related to a course of events influences outcomes, as well as the desire for control and certainty; (ii) magical thinking — as perceiving the mind to have a direct effect on the physical world.

10 Evaluative points could be made drawn from (i) superstitions — Skinner (1948), Lustberg (2004); (ii) magical thinking — Lawrence (1994), Bonser (1963), as well as theoretical considerations, relevant methodological and ethical considerations and practical applications, such as addressing the superstition element of dependency behaviours such as gambling.

11 The focus of the answer should be on identification of traits associated with paranormal beliefs and abilities.

12 Reference could be made to evaluative points in Honorton (1998), Wiseman & Watt (2004), as well as theoretical considerations, relevant methodological and ethical considerations, such as extroverts being more motivated at being tested, and practical applications.

13 Focus should be on evaluative points related to (i) psychic healing — on claims made for the restoration of health through spiritual practices; (ii) near-death and out-of-body experiences — on the parasomatic and asomatic experiences of being exterior to one's body; (iii) psychic mediumship — the claimed ability to experience contact the spirit world.

14 Evaluative points should focus on: psychic healing — Braud and Schlitz (1988); (ii) near-death and out-of-body experiences — Blanke (2005); (iii) psychic mediumship — Schwartz (2001), as well as theoretical considerations, such as the linking of NDEs/OBEs to biological explanations, relevant methodological and ethical considerations, and practical applications, such as the therapeutic value of psychic healing.

Chapter 13

1 Outlines should focus on (i) replicability — the repetition of research to authenticate results; (ii) objectivity — the desirability of making observations made without bias or expectation; (iii) theory construction — the acquisition of knowledge through hypothesis generation and testing; (iv) hypothesis testing — the need for experimental predictions to be falsifiable; (v) empirical methods — where knowledge is gained only from direct experience of sensory data.

2 (a) Description should focus on detailing the procedures involved in peer review and the functional ideas underpinning the process.

  (b) Focus should be on factors that may impede the unbiased use of peer review.

3 Description should focus on detailing the defining characteristics of laboratory, field and natural experiments and correlations, self-reports, observations and case studies.

4 Description should focus on detailing the defining characteristics of random, opportunity, volunteer, systematic and stratified sampling techniques, including their strengths and weaknesses in terms of producing generalisable findings.

5 Description should focus on (i) reliability — different forms of reliability and methods of assessing reliability; (ii) validity — different forms of validity and methods of assessing validity.

6 Description should focus on detailing ethical issues that need to be considered when designing and carrying out research.

7 Detail the distinctive characteristics of bar charts, histograms, frequency polygons and scattergrams.

8 Outline should focus on the degree of certainty that observed differences/relationships between sets of data are in fact real differences/relationships as opposed to chance occurrences.

9 Detail the distinctive characteristics of type 1 and 2 errors in a way that differentiates between the two.

10 Outline the criteria for selection based on level of data measurement, type of experimental design and whether a difference or relationship is being tested for.

11 Explanation should focus on the non-numerical nature and forms of qualitative data, as well as on the conversion of such data into numerical forms.

12 Outlines should focus on detailing the presentation of research via abstract, introduction, including aims and hypotheses, methodology, results, discussion and appendices, as well detailing the purpose of this in aiding replication to assess the validity of findings.